UPPING the Downside

64 Strategies for Creating Professional Resilience by Design

Mike R. Jay

With Resilient Essays by:

Tim Condon
Phil Faris
Richard Freis
Sandy McMullen
William Murray
Lesley Parrott
John H. Richards
Mo Riddiford
Harrison Sheppard
Mari Smith
Steven Wilke

Publisher

City

2008

Printed in the United States by 48 Hr. Books, 540 S. Main St., Akron, Ohio, 44311

Book layout by: Stimulus Design, Victoria British Columbia, Canada
Phone: (250) 516-5056   Email: stimulusdesign@shaw.ca

2   3   4   5   6   7   8   9

Preface

Creating professional resilience by design is the second in a series of resilience formats that are created to give domain-specific instruction to aspiring professionals. Over time, I've discovered four essential domains: personal, professional, business, and network.

These four domains encompass large amounts of territory and create very specific challenges in designing resilience. In personal resilience, though the domain is personal, it extends into family and relationship webs that also encompass professional services and business, given that everything is also connected to everything else in a network of intended and unintended effects. Yet, there is some reason to draw these artificial boundaries and work within domains. By bounding the territory, we can create workable practices that then can be tested in the whole.

In large part, the domains signify boundaries that are phase transitions. Just like water becomes ice or vapor at specific points on the temperature scale, our focus moves from personal to professional and into business at times, while still being a single person. I believe this is what makes it difficult to teach resilience across a system.

I've therefore created four different but interconnected, and certainly intersubjective, modes of working in resilience. Each is designed to improve the other, but stand alone, if necessary. So it was with that charter that I embarked on putting together the team for this book. My coauthors each took it upon themselves to share unique and distinct areas of concern. I wanted to open the door to people who were in various stages of practicing resilience to write about their experiences, while also sharing with you their thoughts about the experience.

For those who may not have read my first book in this series, CPR *for the Soul: Coaching Personal Resilience By Design*, I wrote the first book on personal resilience because I believe that most people are suffering from the *design* of their lives. In my opinion, people don't really understand themselves at a deep soul level. For the most part they do not know what to do, even when their own soul work *appears* in their lives.

CPR is an acronym both for *coaching personal resilience* and *creating professional resilience*, as it's difficult if not impossible to separate these two domains.

One of my daughters said, "I believe that most people are suffering because their lives are being designed without their knowledge. When we don't understand ourselves at a deep soul level or know what to do when we encounter that knowledge, we are not consciously participating in the design of our lives." Kids are amazing, aren't they!

The personal resilience book was about knowing your own soul—*your soul mate is you!*

Over the years, I've been fortunate to live a charmed life. It's not because everything I've done has been great, lucky, or easy, but in large part because I've been blessed with an ambitious soul. In recent years, I've come to realize that not everyone has been so blessed. Unfortunately, you can't necessarily be like me. Fortunately, you wouldn't want to be.

I define resilience as *the integrated power to persist when things don't work out at first, to navigate ambiguity and uncertainty, to transcend common problems and barriers, and to collaboratively anticipate the future.*

Why would people want more resilience? Essentially, we have a simple equilibrium to deal with: *to live our lives and to be lived by our lives.* The soul's art is the construction of a life fully lived. Each of us has the opportunity to find equilibrium of life and living that is resilient and true for us.

Our soulful expression of who we are and how we approach life is to be honored in whatever forms the authentic dance of soul emerges. There is no right or best way for your soul to emerge as life. It just is.

Life will present us with opportunities for resilience, and these are challenges to the soul in our families, our relationships, our activities, our faith, and our work. In those moments, we may choose to engage, account, author, and respond through design—*or not.* The methodology I present in this book will give you tools with which to become more resilient by design . . . *if you choose.*

What is soul?

First off, I don't pretend to know the truth about soul, but I will share with you my insights on the subject and why I've chosen to use *soul* in this manner.

I believe soul is an emergent set of properties that arises from our authentic nature via nurture, as Matt Ridley noted. Religion and spirituality aside, these properties seek fitness in a world that is constantly changing, growing, and renewing itself—a world that is expanding like a spider web, regenerative like a starfish.

I do not consider resilience to be good or bad, right or wrong. I'll leave that judgment to you and your maker. Yet, I will state emphatically that you have choices—that your life is not just a clock or machine, but a canvas on which you have the opportunity to paint your own picture, albeit in some cases limited by nature's lottery.

Because of the myth of life and living, resilience is often relegated to a place beyond our choice. I'm here to express another viewpoint about resilience, its effect and affect in our lives, and the amazing journey possible.

Essentially, the path of resilience emerges out of our motivational sensitivity to sixteen basic desires. These desires are the product of research by Dr. Steven Reiss, who over the years found what I think are the secrets to resilience. What's more, these secrets are at our disposal and are the subject of a resilient life.

Fortunately for all of us, whether we understand the secrets or not, our soul emerges. It is not just the so-called self-aware, or the cultural creative, or the spiritual sage that takes communion of the soul, but each and every sentient being in the universe. Out of our primal nature emerges the soulful life and in so doing, a resilience in life. So, if you choose to do nothing, your soul will find its way. If you choose, as I do, to participate with the soul in designing a life, the soul will find its path.

What is design?

Design works whether we do it or not. It's simply the form, process, matter, and meaning of life that creates aliveness. Consciously or unconsciously, we are alive. There is some argument as to what being alive means, and that is where design comes in. I'm not here to argue for or against intelligent, natural, or creative design. I'll leave that to the scientists, philosophers, and sages. What I am here to show you is how you may reenergize who you are by giving CPR to your soul.

When I use the term *design*, I'm talking about both unconscious natural design and the "cynthetic" design that I use in the methodology. *Cynthetic* is a term I coined to represent "creative synthesis" (see *www.cynthetics. com*). By working with the creative processes in our lives, each of us emerges by design, either consciously or unconsciously. I'm here to show you the ideas I have about focusing on conscious cynthesis to promote the opportunities we all have to live together on one planet—or in *one* universe with those we have yet to meet.

I believe that design, whether it be natural or cynthetic, can be used to produce powerful opportunities for resilience, in part because there will be fits and starts in our universe as we jump from one paradigm to the next. At this time, we're in the middle of one of those leaps, and CPR may be required for those who consciously decide to support the uncertainty of the jump we're now making in finding a way to bridge the challenge of the times.

What is the pressing need?

I suppose I could offer what is a long list of pressing needs that can be found in every corner of the planet. Instead I'll choose to focus on only one: *adaptability*.

I can't say with any certainty what the next problem, crisis, or calamity will be. I *can* say with certainty that it will require adaptability. I don't know what specifically to prepare you for in the future. Life is uncertain, *at best*. What I can do is show you how to become adaptable, and I can show you how to resuscitate your soul in the process.

As I reviewed the constructs on which the personal and professional resilience models are founded, I felt reinforced that of the two, professional resilience is more concrete, more earthy, and more grounded in specific actions that you can take to increase—dramatically—your professional resilience.

As the future unwinds, complexity is increasing exponentially. Information is doubling in shorter and shorter time spans, and knowledge is increasing faster than our wisdom can take into account.

In forming the professional resilience model, I wanted to be more prescriptive and certain about how professional resilience is created. I devised it out of the natural emergence of professional success based on more than ten thousand hours of coaching professional people and more than twenty years of experience. It's a model that anyone can follow as a single professional or a professional group to ascertain resilience in an unpredictable future.

Of course there are always unseen forces at work, and my goal was to create a system that gives you as a professional the highest probability of success. In the following pages, I have recorded my lectures on professional resilience, as well as transcribed the specific criteria of concern, which will increase the probability of success in any given future. They have been amazingly formed into coherent paragraphs by our editor, Cynthia Sampson.

While this approach to professional resilience is not a guarantee that everything will be okay, it is, I believe, the most probable way to insure success in an uncertain world.

Mike R. Jay
Mitchell, Nebraska
November 2007

Contents

Part One:
Essays on Resilience

Chapter 1

Knowing Yourself: The Key to Resilience

by Steven Wilke

You never change things by fighting the existing reality.
To change something, build a new model that makes the existing model obsolete.

— Buckminster Fuller

How often do you look back on your life and marvel (or despair) at how you got to where you are today? And then, if you have not become everything you had once envisioned, do you wonder what book, program, conference, or seminar will help you achieve what you are lacking?

In 2005, in the United States alone, over $9.6 billion was spent on self-help literature and programs.[1] Is it possible we really need this much help? And more important, is all this self-help and personal-development activity leading us to a happier life?

Adrian White, a social psychologist at the University of Leicester's School of Psychology, analyzed various sets of data published by UNESCO, the CIA, the New Economics Foundation, World Health Organization, Veenhoven Database, Latinbarometer, Afrobarometer, and the United Nations Human Development Report to create a global projection of subjective well-being. He found that the United States ranks twenty-third among the 178 countries studied in its level of happiness.[2] Additional research has shown that the level of happiness in the United States has been dropping steadily since World War II. The average American, though certainly richer, is not a bit happier. In 1957, when the happiness data was first recorded, some 35 per cent said they were "very happy," as did slightly fewer—30 percent—in 2002.[3]

3

Does money buy happiness? It surely helps us to avoid certain types of pain. Yet, though buying power has more than doubled since the 1950s, the average American's reported happiness has remained almost unchanged. Indeed, if we can judge from the statistics—a doubled divorce rate, more-than-doubled teen suicide rate, and mushrooming rates of depression—contemporary Americans seem more often than not to be miserable.

Maybe the key to happiness lies in education? Certainly, as people become more educated and more opportunities are available to them, one would think happiness should increase. Unfortunately, the exact opposite is true. In research done by Andrew Oswald and Andrew Clark, two European economists, it was shown that there is actually an inverse relationship between education and measures of satisfaction.[4] The authors theorized that as education increases, aspirations increase even more so, and therefore a greater disparity between expectations and reality is created. In my life this has certainly proven true. A return to graduate school at age thirty did nothing to increase my long-term happiness; although it has certainly created many opportunities, it has also created greater frustrations, as it heightened my expectations for even greater personal and financial success.

Then, maybe the answer is in overcoming your weaknesses. For more than twenty years, I was on the self-help bandwagon, believing that the next book, tape set, or seminar would finally give me the answer to what I needed to do to improve my professional life and bring me happiness. Certainly I could "Awaken the Giant Within" to unleash my "Personal Power" with my "Master Strategies for Higher Achievement" to "Think and Grow Rich" while I "Lead the Field." But first I must learn "How to Master Your Time" and "The Secrets to Manifesting Your Destiny" so that I can have "Unlimited Power" to use "The Success Principles" to complete "Mastery University."

But with every program or seminar, no matter how logical or helpful I found the material, within the next six days to six months I would be pretty much back to living the life I had before I discovered the next thing "Guaranteed to Change My Life!" So what is wrong with me that all of these wonderful programs that have "obviously" worked wonders for the person selling it and for the individuals who wrote the testimonials (but were most likely written shortly after the seminar was over), haven't been able to create lasting change in my life? And what is wrong with the rest of my fellow Americans that we need to shell out almost $10 billion every year trying to fix ourselves, while all the while becoming more affluent and less happy?

One important factor in this process is that humans are inclined to perceive that they have received the benefits they expected from a program, even when there is no objective proof.[5] This allows us to be utterly convinced that the seminar or book we just completed has made a significant difference in our lives, when in fact, to an outside observer we have not changed one iota. If we have just invested hundreds of dollars in a new tape program or spent thousands of dollars for a weekend seminar, we have a vested interest in believing that we are different, no matter the evidence to the contrary.

Most important, however, there is a fundamental flaw in the self-help industry. That flaw is the belief that we are all a blank slate—a theory that views all behavior, thought, and cognition as learned and assumes that differences in human capability are due to environmental factors. Therefore, it is possible to become or have anything we want if we just work hard enough or believe without doubt.

I know that I will never play golf like Tiger Woods or basketball like Michael Jordan. I will never run a marathon in under 2:20 or ski in the Olympics, and I'm guessing that you won't either. Why is it that everyone reading this understands the limits of our physical bodies, but many still buy into the belief that our potential in other areas is unlimited?

Who hasn't heard that the great thing about the United States is that anyone can become President? Is there anyone who still believes it? As we approach the 2008 nominating process with a prediction that it will take more than $100 million just to win the nomination, much less the presidency, I doubt there are many who do. But I believe this belief that we can be anything we want and its corollary, it is only our weaknesses and lack of will power that keep us from greatness, is a key contributing factor to our steadily dropping level of happiness.

The event that began my awakening was a lecture I attended at which the speaker said that the goal of life is to be happy, and the first step in that process is to learn who you are. At first glance this seemed ridiculous. Of course I already knew who I was. I have an entire life of experiences, an awareness of what I want, an understanding of what I think is important, and a career through which I make a significant difference for the people I work with. But as I began to explore the concept, I realized that continually working to strengthen my weaknesses had not been productive and that possibly identifying my strengths and using them more effectively would be useful. I also saw that learning what motivates me would help me to make better decisions in the future.

At that point, I proceeded to complete a package of personality assessments and can say without a doubt, nine months later, that it was the best investment I've ever made. The results gave me a new lens through which I could clearly see why I made the choices I have and why I have often felt frustrated with some aspects of my life. As I have continued to work with my results, I'm creating a new direction for my life from which I am already seeing many positive results.

I also realize that I'm not alone in making poor career choices. A British insurance company, in an informal survey they recently performed, found that 75 percent of people have chosen a career that does not fit with their personality. Examples given were people-oriented individuals working in banking, secretaries who display strong leadership skills, or assertive individuals who have jobs in the creative arts.[6] So, it seems we are not actually a nation of people who need to be fixed, but a nation of people who need to simply learn who we are, so we can do those things that we are best at and which we will find most fulfilling.

An example of how this mismatch can occur is in evidence as I look back on my life. What I now see is all of my career choices have involved being highly involved with the public, either in sales or as an entrepreneur working with people individually. One thing I have learned from my assessments, however, is that I am highly motivated to avoid social contact. It doesn't take much, then, to see that this creates a tremendous conflict. So no matter what training or self-help program I would go through, I will always unconsciously sabotage any attempt that does not align with this motivation.

Why is it that like the people in the British insurance company's study and maybe someone you know, so many people are not doing what is in alignment with what motivates them? Do most people even have an awareness of what truly motivates them? Another surprising result this study revealed was that 50 percent of the respondents misjudged their personality type. So, if we do not know how we function in the world, there is little chance that we can choose effectively what will be in alignment with who we are.

This lack of self-awareness is then reinforced by how we see the events in our lives, which is demonstrated by the adaptation of Chris Argyris' Ladder of Inference shown below.[7]

Ladder of Inference
How We Short-Circuit Reality

Actions
↑
Beliefs
↑
Conclusions
↑
Assumptions
↑
Affixed
Meaning
↑
Selected Data
& Experience
↑
Real Data &
Experience

What the diagram implies is that we begin with **Real Data & Experience,** the kind that would be captured by a video camera that didn't lie. We then choose a set of **Selected Data & Experience** that we pay attention to. To this **Selected Data & Experience** we **Affix Meaning,** develop **Assumptions**, come to **Conclusions**, and finally develop **Beliefs**. These Beliefs then form the basis of our **Actions,** which create additional **Real Data & Experience.**

The circular nature of this description becomes evident when the diagram is redrawn with an added influence.

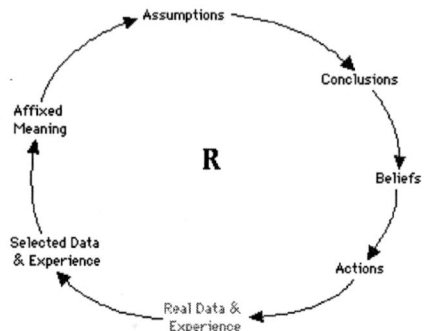

This diagram indicates the reinforcing nature (R) of this structure, as each action builds on the one before it. Yet there is an apparent difficulty with this structure. It is our **Beliefs** that influence the **Selected Data & Experience** we pay attention to.

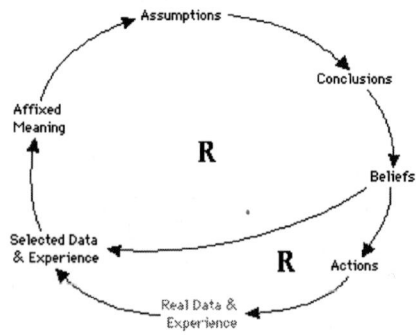

This fuller diagram indicates that as our **Beliefs** influence the **Selected Data and Experience** we pay attention to, they essentially establish an internal reinforcing loop that short circuits reality. *The tendency is to select data to pay attention to that supports our beliefs.* And, I would expect, as our **Beliefs** become more and more rigid, the **Selected Data & Experience** we are willing to pay attention to will become a smaller and smaller portion of reality.[8]

Many years ago, I heard the story of a frustrated, middle-aged dentist who woke up one morning and realized he was living a life that was the choice of an eighteen-year-old kid. By using the Ladder of Inference, I now see how the choices I made as a teenager and a college student have shaped my life. By creating the belief at a very young age, that I would be best served by working for myself, I have had more than twenty years of bypassing my Real Data & Experience showing that I was not well suited to the path I had chosen. Instead, I accumulated Selected Data & Experience that showed me my path was correct but that I just needed to strengthen my weaknesses. This is where the self-help industry lives, reinforcing the belief that there is something wrong with you that is keeping you from accomplishing what you want.

Although it is beyond the scope of this chapter to go in depth into the numerous assessments I completed, it is critical to look at the Reiss Profile of Motivational Sensitivity, created by Dr. Steven Reiss, author of *Who Am I?*[9] In his book, Reiss makes a distinction between feel-good happiness and value-based happiness. The former is powerfully documented by the BBC documentary "Century of the Self,"[10] in which we find that a vast majority of what we believe we want has actually been created for us by Madison Avenue, whether it be a new car, boat, perfume, or kitchen cleaner. What Reiss makes clear is that feel-good happiness will never last and will most often be an elusive target that is never reachable. Indeed, if we take a closer look at the research comparing income to happiness, it is not hard to see that any income spent above what is necessary for survival, any money spent in pursuit of feel-good happiness without clarity that that is what is occurring, is money wasted. Literally, money cannot buy happiness!

Value-based happiness, on the other hand, is what can be achieved when we act in alignment with our motivations. Based on my Reiss profile, I am strongly motivated by curiosity and less so by interdependence. It should surprise no one, then, when I say the eight most satisfying years of my life were the ones I spent in college and in graduate school.

Now, I love my wife and I love my kids, and it takes a great leap of faith to admit to everyone who is reading this book how much I enjoyed functioning in an academic setting. I do it, however, to make completely clear the power of knowing your motivations. I could feel guilty, as I did for years, that I did not gain greater satisfaction out of taking care of my kids. With my Reiss Profile, however, I now understand that I'm actually motivated *against* nurturing children and so no longer need to feel guilty, but can accept that is who I am. I can say with complete confidence it is a much healthier way to live your life! Even better, I know that as my kids get older, our relationship will continue to improve as I can understand and relate to them in what will be for me a more meaningful way.

With this information, then, I began to design a life that is more in alignment with my motivations. I now reserve time to fulfill my curiosity, and I work in online communities to fulfill my need for interdependence without overwhelming me with too much social contact. I'm freed by understanding that I am highly motivated to eat and to not be physically active, instead of feeling guilty that I just don't have enough willpower to choose a "healthier" lifestyle. It is freeing to know who you are and accept it so you can create a life that works. In my experience, it is the difference between swimming upstream or down. You're going to get a lot farther in life moving with the current.

To conclude, I want to leave you with a concept I jokingly call "Wilke's Law," and that is, 87 percent of the time I use the word "should," I am either trying to create feel-good happiness, or I'm working in an area of weakness rather than strength. By using the information I gained from my assessments, however, I once again have Real Data to restore integrity to the Ladder of Inference. And I can now use that data to begin to design a life that will take advantage of my strengths, while at the same time designing around my weaknesses. I now have clarity around feel-good happiness and value-based happiness, which allows me to make much better choices as an informed consumer. Together, these processes allow me to more effectively *up the downside.*

To learn more about this process, please visit my website at *www. drstevenwilke.com* or visit *www.uppingthedownside.com.*

The Author

Dr. Steven Wilke has spent a life in pursuit of the answer to the question, why do we choose what we choose and do what we do? On that path, he has worked in manufacturing, both the retail and wholesale grocery industries, insurance, and for the past thirteen years, as a chiropractor. He has a BA from Luther College in Decorah, Iowa, and his DC is from Palmer College in Davenport, Iowa. He currently practices and resides in Madison, Wisconsin, with his wife, Julie, and children, Michael and Sophia.

Notes

1. Marketdata Enterprises, Inc., *The U.S. Market for Self-Improvement Products and Services* (http://www.marketresearch.com/map/prod/1338280.html, 2006).

2. *Science Daily,* "Psychologist Produces The First-ever 'World Map Of Happiness'" (http://www.sciencedaily.com/releases/2006/11/061113093726.htm).

3. David G. Myers, *Psychology, 8th Edition* (New York: Worth Publishers, 2004).

4. Andrew E. Clark and Andrew J. Oswald, "Satisfaction and Comparison Income," *Journal of Public Economics* 61 (1996): 359–381.

5. David G. Myers, *Intuition: Its Powers and Perils* (New Haven, CT: Yale University Press, 2002).

6. Andy McSmith, "Britain is a nation of professional misfits, personality study finds," *The Independent* (March 29, 2007).

7. Peter Senge, Art Kleiner, Charlotte Roberts, Rick Ross, and Bryan Smith, *The Fifth Discipline Fieldbook* (New York: Doubleday, 1994), as adapted from Chris Argyris, *Overcoming Organizational Defenses: Facilitating Organizational Learning* (Englewood Cliffs, NJ: Prentice Hall, 1990).

8. Mike R. Jay, "Ladder of Inference: How We Short Circuit Reality" (www.coachingedge.com).

9. Steven Reiss, *Who am I? The 16 Basic Desires That Motivate Our Actions and Define Our Personalities* (New York: Tarcher/Putnam, 2000).

10. British Broadcasting Corporation, "Century of the Self" (http://www.moviesfoundonline.com/century_of_the_self.htm, 2002).

Chapter 2

Clarity of Purpose: The Ultimate Resilience
by Mo Riddiford

Clarity of purpose is the one resilience principle that is always available. It never fails. Its importance as our authentic internal anchor will only grow as the pace of external change continues to accelerate.

Purpose is the thread, the theme, the thrust, the full-throated roar that provides the grand foundation for all other resilient requirements. Clear purpose can be our first call and final relief. In the face of the greatest confusion and the deepest depression, it is purpose that stands ever accessible. Purpose is that "still small voice within," different from the navigating light of a distant star. Purpose remains when all hope is gone.

> *Everything can be taken away from man but one thing—to choose one's attitude in a given set of circumstances, to choose one's own way.*
>
> —Viktor Frankl, Auschwitz survivor and author of *Man's Search for Meaning*

This essay explores this essential requirement for resilience. It will include the never-ending inner process that is necessary to discover, and maintain, the deepest clarity of intention. We will use the example of five entrepreneurial professionals who are working within a global context. They are ordinary people choosing to live within the large and often chaotic context of the global marketplace. Inevitably, because of the internal nature of intention, we must use personal anecdote. But as will be discussed, we find that the facts of modern science provide a powerful empirical foundation that supports our inner journey of discovery.

While this book focuses on resilience, this chapter also offers a practical pathway to enduring happiness, or "value-based happiness."[1] While there is nothing inherently wrong in feeling happy based on "feel-good" pleasure, its effects tend to decline over time. In contrast, the general feeling of well-being that people experience when their lives are meaningful — value-based happiness — offers a variety of advantages: It can be present even when we feel bad; it can endure over many years; it can arise based on a fond memory; and finally, it is potentially available to anyone anywhere. While many forms of feel-good happiness need time, wealth, and/or relationships not available to all, there are frequent examples of people who may be suffering greatly, but still find great strength and, yes, a form of happiness based on the meaningful purpose of their situation. In short, discovering and following our own self-recognized purpose will make us happy over the long term. Now that sounds like something worth pursuing, doesn't it?

While preparing this essay I, too, have once again had my own resilience deeply challenged. This story illustrates the necessity of resilience designed before the crisis strikes, before the tough times. In my own case, it's a recent story of loss and of unexpected renewal. Indeed, it very much exemplifies Richard Freiss' essay (in this book) on paradoxical grace.

My story began five months ago (at the time of writing) when my lovely wife of five years unexpectedly informed me she wanted to separate. In so many words, she told me we had grown too far apart, with our diverging interests now outweighing the mutual warmth, love, and respect we shared together.

My wife's announcement began with a phone call in the middle of the night. I received the news over the phone because we had recently chosen to live in two cities. A few months prior, we had both agreed that my wife should move to London to accept a full scholarship for original research at a top British university, while I should continue my growing professional life in Berlin. Our great joy, as we saw our careers blossoming, was mixed with sadness as we approached our newly separated life. We knew it would not be easy, and so it has proven.

Her news left me devastated. It was truly a bolt out of the blue. My shock revealed just how much I had not recognized her dissatisfactions, or at least how much I had not seen their real "deal-breaking" or marriage-breaking significance. Here, too, Mari Smith's advice (in this book) on the "hardy couple" is entirely appropriate and would have been very helpful! So, as I tossed and turned, I was overwhelmed by a wild storm of thoughts and emotions.

The following morning I got up, made a cup of tea, and placed my cushion on the floor in the living room, consciously preparing myself for my daily meditation practice. Internally, as always, I turned my attention towards the next step, which would be to sit upright, cross-legged, in total stillness, fully attentive, and yet remaining as relaxed as humanly possible. Just before I sat down, I was engulfed by an almost indescribable but enormously powerful "silent wind" that seemed to enter the room. This intangible "wind" completely destroyed my profound despair. It was as though the deep black hole into which I had fallen had never ever existed. Nothing had changed and everything had changed. I remained completely aware of my shocking news, but I simply could not relate to my feelings of the previous night. The darkness had been destroyed by an unshakeable conviction: This nightmare scenario had its own mysterious positive purpose.

The experience itself lasted only half an hour. I would love to say this is the clichéd happy ending. I would love to say I have never again felt moments and hours of aching loss. I would dearly love to say I've never, at times, found myself raging within myself at this turn of events, so utterly out of my control. Dreams die hard, but this is one fake fairy tale. The fact is we have little control over the inner experience of our own emotions. The truth is that since that day five months ago, I have ridden a wild emotional roller coaster. Indeed, studies show that such a process often takes over two years to resolve.[2] But, and here's the very big but, that initial experience of overwhelming positivity has continued to repeat itself every day in some way. It has given me great confidence to allow the full range of thoughts and emotions to play itself out as it must. The message remains: There is greater purpose.

So how did this happen? How did I experience purpose in the middle of apparent chaos? Was this simply an unexplainable gift of grace bestowed from "above"? One could always make such a claim, impossible to prove as it is, but here I'm suggesting something different: I believe this glimpse of purpose came out of consciously designed resilience built up over decades.

In my own case and with few exceptions, meditation has been my daily practice for over twenty years. It remains an ever-fresh encounter with a source of creativity, insight, meaning, purpose, and unspeakable awe. By now I simply cannot imagine a life without it. This daily "event," with its powerful yet indefinable impact, builds a foundation and a momentum that mysteriously infuses my day with an extra dimension. It clarifies and energizes whatever I'm doing.

I am also well aware that, at the very least, meditation doesn't seem to work for everyone. While a longstanding commitment to meditation delivered internal resilience for me, the appropriate resilience practice for someone else might be something quite different. The overriding message here is that resilience is enhanced by longstanding commitment that is independent of prevailing circumstances.

This daily commitment, practiced in good times and bad, does build resilience. In this case, such resilience generated the right response at a time of crisis, and thus it allowed recognition of purpose.

What Is Meant by "Purpose"?

Before we examine purpose within a wider context, we need to look more closely at what is meant by the word itself. The *Times English Dictionary and Thesaurus* gives twenty synonyms for *purpose* in the meaning here intended. We have aim, design, function, idea, intention, object, point, principle, ambition, aspiration, design, desire, end, goal, Holy Grail, hope, objective, target, view, and wish.

Purpose includes everything from our own initiation of the first internal step to the final culmination of a long-term project, while *intention* refers only to the initial personal step in the process of taking goal-directed action. When recognized at the deepest level, however, intention is the one decision that is potentially independent of any life circumstance.

> *The foundation of spiritual life is clarity of intention. Do I want to be Free, here and now? You have to decide, do I really want to be Free? Once the intention is clear, the mind becomes focussed. When the mind is focussed there is one-pointedness. When there is one-pointedness, the heart will guide you. It will indicate what needs to be left behind and what needs to be avoided.*
>
> *Clarity of intention reveals the Heart. When the Heart is revealed, trust is found and intuition flowers. Then one starts to understand what it means to live in the unknown. Then you can know what it is to be blind, and see everywhere.*
>
> —Andrew Cohen, *Enlightenment Is a Secret*

A deepening clarity of purpose happens in myriad ways. For one person it is forged from repeated hard times, for another it is based on the response to a person in need, for another it is founded on deep exploration of the obvious truth of the brevity of life and the certainty of death,[3] for another it is a powerful burst of deep clarity about the underlying nature of things, and for another it can come from inspiring contact with powerful role models. For many it is a combination of various experiences that finally cause them to pursue their deepest intention.

It is also striking to note, however, how two people can undergo an identical experience and one immediately forgets it, while the other changes their life forever. One cannot force someone to consider clarity of intention—the interest must be there. So for this essay, I can only speak honestly about what I myself have found helpful.

If one has decided to pursue deep clarity of purpose then one needs to ask two questions: "Who am I?" and "How shall I live?" Almost anyone can recall those moments of deep quietude, perhaps while looking at a sunset, when they ask themselves exactly such questions. Just such a beginning can prompt a journey that never ends. Part of that investigation is asking: What will always be important to me? What do I value more highly than anything else?

These can be overwhelming questions. But ask yourself this: What would I do with my life if I wasn't a parent? What would I do if no one was relying on me in any way? What would I do if I had a billion dollars? What would I do if I had optimum health? Asking these and many other similar questions, whether alone or with the support of a trusted friend or adviser, allows us to uncover a much deeper and more rewarding sense of who we are.

Clarity of Purpose Demands Clarity of Context: Clarity of Context Liberates Clarity of Purpose

In asking "How shall I live?" we must consider context. We can't know how to live until we know where we are. "No man is an island", as John Donne said.[4] So we need to ask what exactly is the context of my life?

Does our life exist only within the context of our family, our neighbourhood, our country, our continent, or indeed even within the biosphere of this little planet? Thinking about this pulls us away from all that is petty and small-minded. Contemplating this external context lays an intellectual foundation that is independent of our emotional or even our inspirational ups and downs. This is worth emphasizing, for far too often we behave like the fish in a small pond that has no idea there is an ocean. It is a simple point that is almost always forgotten: The larger the context, the fewer the blind spots and the firmer the foundation.

As I describe in very broad brushstrokes, the current scientific understanding of humanity's context, please don't be surprised if you find yourself completely overwhelmed. Please don't be surprised when you want to turn away and go back to the everyday. This is perfectly normal and entirely human. New technology has delivered understanding far beyond what we ever imagined. We are all now being forced to play catchup, and the clock is ticking.

As an important aside, science does not need to negate the powerful conviction derived from direct personal intuition. Indeed, many great scientists have spoken of personal "Eureka! moments" of revelation that have sparked later groundbreaking discoveries. But here is where scientific knowledge is qualitatively different: It can be repeatedly tested; it is rigorously scrutinized and accepted by the world's most respected experts; and the explanation is the simplest currently available. Thus science adds a different kind of confidence that supports our own direct and personal understanding of purpose.

Science is currently leaping ahead in humanity's understanding of our place in the universe. For example, the Hubble Space Telescope, first launched in 1990 and with a resolving power fully ten times any previous Earth-bound telescope, has been able to see far more of our universe. The size and age of the universe is now known in a way that was previously unimaginable. There remain significant gaps in what we know, but the growth in understanding continues at breakneck speed. So far as we know, this tiny blue ball that we call Earth is the only place in the universe that supports life. It appears that humanity is unique in the universe.

The current explosion of scientific knowledge also reveals another essential fact about our universe: It evolves. One of the universe's fundamental characteristics is that it tends to go from simpler structures to more complex. Given a long enough timeframe, science finds endless examples of this ubiquitous developmental curve. Evolution is found amongst all life, but is also observed in the billions of years *before* life appeared. Science tells us that the universe originated with pure energy, later produced matter, and only billions of years later produced the first single-celled examples of life. Then came conscious life, then homo sapiens sapiens, and finally Darwin and his colleagues allowed humanity to recognize the evolutionary process.

Put another way, we can say that the atoms within our body right now also existed within the original Big Bang. But the difference now is that those very same atoms are today able to ponder the significance of evolution. Science tells us that we as humanity represent the universe beginning to become conscious of its own developmental process. Our universe is waking up, and it is waking up through us. Thus we as humanity are now confronted with empirical proof on the grandest scale that, yes, indeed, there is purpose.

Science offers yet more fuel for our own personal quest. Science suggests this century represents a time of the greatest urgency. As one example of many, respected British astronomer Sir Martin Rees, in his book *Our Final Century: Will the Human Race Survive the Twenty-first Century?*[5] argues that the Earth and human survival are in far greater danger from the potential effects of modern technology than is commonly realized. There is no need to pursue this question further here, because many aspects of these dangers are already being discussed in many quarters. Nevertheless, in the face of our strong human tendency to stagnate and to avoid, we can still discover urgent purpose by simply asking one question, "Can I really be so certain of humanity's survival?"

This is all immensely overwhelming. Inevitably we puny humans, with our little brains, struggle with the concept of billions of years and many billions of galaxies. We struggle with the preposterous idea that right now could be so critical to the survival of life for the entire universe. This is completely understandable. As always, technology has raced far ahead of the biological evolution of our brains. Nevertheless, I derive hope in my own teaching work in watching language students progress quickly as they grapple with a strange tongue. Our brains do develop when placed under enough challenge. Similarly, an intellectual understanding can be the first step to a more heartfelt connection. Many people, for example, want to save the Amazon rainforest despite never having been there.

Considering context helps us discover our own purpose as an individual. We now find that the perennial direct intuition of deep purpose can be placed within the biggest scientific context. Heart and intellect can now work together. The result is a huge boost in personal confidence.

How else does this strengthen our resilience? Shocks from left field will always surprise us, but clarity of purpose gives us far greater space to deal with them. By taking the time to seriously consider these perennial existential questions, we discover sufficient internal perspective. This reduces our blinders, reduces the number of truly unexpected events, clarifies our relationship to all that we don't know, and gives us greater acceptance of all that we will never know. In short, we find we have "upped our downside."

Some Examples of Resilient People

So far we have explored the personal discovery of deep intention, and have touched on how science supports that discovery. Now we can look at whether five professional entrepreneurs include purpose within what they do. They have been chosen because they are pursuing their businesses with little reference to national boundaries. Given the more complex global market, given the greater external uncertainty, have these individuals needed to discover internal confidence?

For some readers perhaps living in the town where they were born, this international context may seem very removed from daily life. On the contrary, every day brings further confirmation that we do not have a choice. Like it or not, the rest of the planet is coming right at us.

Gerard Senehi is a true global citizen. I first got to know him in California more than thirteen years ago, and he frustrated me like hell! I simply couldn't pin down his mysterious manner, neither by body language nor by accent. It seems I'm not alone. *New York Magazine* asserts that with "his bedroom eyes and untraceable accent, Gerard Senehi is perhaps the city's most alluring mentalist, and his act bending wineglasses, making cigarettes float, makes even jaded New Yorkers jump. Is he really psychic, or is it just magic? You be the judge."[6]

Gerard is "the Experimentalist" who is "wowing audiences worldwide," according to Fox News. Audiences all over the world—from Prince Andrew of Britain to George Foreman to Kofi Annan—all say the same thing: "mind-blowing." For me, low-key as he is in person, it was only while interviewing him that the story came out. Gerard was born in Paris to two Iranian émigrés. His first school was in Switzerland, then to Iran for three years, then back to Switzerland, and now he lives in the United States. No wonder I couldn't pin him down!

Gerard told me how his international life has shaped his perspective: "My multicultural experience has made me appreciate the unknown.

What seems fixed and accepted in one culture is not always true. It has encouraged me to enquire." He then spoke of the power of purpose in his life: "I see my work as a tool. It allows me the opportunity to engage with influential leaders about deeper matters. My purpose in performing is to give them [audiences] a very engaging, joyful experience, to express the positivity of life, and ideally, to connect with people informally about meaning and purpose and care for our future. . . . Since I have realized purpose, life would be completely empty without it. It is the core of everything. . . . What could be more thrilling than knowing who we are, and why we are here, and having that apply to the way we live?"

Jo Parfitt has made her global wanderings into a definite plus. As journalist, publisher, author, and portable-career coach she has developed a business niche guaranteeing her income and satisfaction no matter where she is. Born in England, Jo spent ten years moving with her husband (who works for Shell) and her children, to Dubai, then to Oman, and finally to Norway, before currently living in the United Kingdom. Jo's various jobs have now culminated in a writing and consulting business focusing on her own experience as an expatriate.

She told me, "I no longer feel I have roots anywhere. I only feel I'm at home when I'm in a multicultural environment. I need to be in the 'expat' bubble." When asked what she offers the world she said: "I offer myself—honest, authentic, and for some reason able to inspire. My international identity helps me to be open-minded, flexible, and broad-minded. I've learnt from all the cultures I've been in. I have a lot in common with my clients. The fact that I've become a cultural chameleon means that I feel comfortable with them, and they with me." "For me *purpose* refers to life purpose, to integrate in a holistic way what I'm doing. I constantly adjust my purpose according to circumstances, environment, age, stage, needs, and what I'm learning." "But in my soul I'm a writer."

I first met **Amir Freimann** twenty years ago in Totnes, England, where we shared an apartment. A "cool cat" Israeli, ex-soldier, and ex-resident of a Japanese monastery, he shared my own pursuit of meaning and purpose. And he still has one thing that I'm jealous about: the perfectly portable job. Amir has specialized in a tiny niche of translating Japanese medical texts into English. With his laptop he can go anywhere at short notice and yet still be available for work by email. He currently switches between bases in Israel and western Massachusetts in the United States. He told me recently by phone, "While my quality of translation is not the best, translation agencies still like me because of my communication skills, which include consistent contact and clear communication. My relationship to my work is very simple. It allows me to do what is important, which is to give my time and energy to spiritual and philosophical development. And especially, it enables me to have the flexibility to engage with a lot of people in a context that is constantly changing. My work is sufficiently well paid to enable enough free time to pursue my other passions."

Shonda Kohlhoff can proudly list her time as an intern at the White House after a childhood spent in Springfield, Illinois. Then nine years ago, she left the States for Europe. She started with research work at the U.S. Embassy in Brussels, Belgium, followed by stints in France and now Germany where she has her own company focusing on intercultural services. "Its mission is to create bridges where there were once walls," Shonda told me. "Most of my clients hire me to mend a rift which has been created in their company." In order to learn firsthand the challenges of culture shock and, in turn, effective cultural adaptation, she spent six months in South Korea learning about its cultural norms, language, and values. "I believe my purpose is—and has been since I was a teenager—to create connections between people. I guess you could call me a matchmaker! This is the constant in my life, no matter where I am geographically. In essence, this purpose of connecting people creates a sense of home for me. It serves as a principle of resilience for me."

In this author's own case, I remained in New Zealand for my first twenty years. Now, at 46 years old, I have been fully established for a period of at least five years in each of four other countries: Australia, England, the United States, and now Germany. At times the shifts between countries have taken place without any forewarning and within a space of days. These leaps happened as I honored my close involvement with one global organization (EnlightenNext) for over twenty years and another (Greenpeace) for over a decade. I currently teach English at a Berlin University and at various German companies. I can truly say I feel blessed as the learning/teaching/learning process I share with my students allows a tangible sense of purpose into the classroom. I will always be a Kiwi, with a strong appreciation for its gorgeous land and its hardy people, but the pull of a much bigger context now holds sway.

In the examples from this chapter, we can see committed people pursuing their passions. They are by no means rootless drifters! Rather it is their clarity of purpose within a global context that continues to energize their daily work.

Conclusion

So what is your ultimate purpose? At this time of increasing diversity, and also the growing appreciation for the value of this burgeoning diversity, I cannot say what your purpose might be. I cannot say how you should live your life. This is something for you to discover in your own way, following your own motivations, and at your own pace. It cannot be imposed by anyone else. But I will again boldly declare: Have no doubt!

It *is* fully possible to discover our own deepest intention, and this deepest intention can certainly meet the challenges we encounter.

The Author

Mo Riddiford, born in New Zealand, has been pursuing the question of existential purpose since early childhood. Through his continuing twenty-year work with EnlightenNext and also later with Greenpeace, his quest has drawn him to live in many countries, requiring ongoing development of personal and professional resilience. Now living in Germany, he teaches English and effective communication at a local university (the Berlin School of Economics) and also within various international companies.

So what is your own purpose?

An important part of this process for many people is the examination of your own motivational makeup. Knowing what you value, and honoring that, will energize your entire life. And it will energize your pursuit of purpose. One of the most powerful tools now available for this process is the Reiss Profile.

If you are interested in using this very reliable, empirically tested tool, whether for yourself or for team development, contact accredited Reiss Master Mo Riddiford (*www.UnderstandWhoYouAre.com*).

Let's journey together into these profound questions . . .

Mo Riddiford, Chair
English Language Teachers' Association
of Berlin and Brandenburg, Germany

moriddiford@yahoo.com
Skype ID: mo-riddiford

Notes

1. Steven Reiss, *Who am I? The 16 Basic Desires That Motivate Our Actions and Define Our Personalities* (New York: Tarcher/Putnam, 2000).

2. Genevieve Clapp, *Divorce and New Beginnings: A Complete Guide to Recovery, Solo Parenting, Co-Parenting and Stepfamilies* (New York: John Wiley & Sons, 2000).

3. This is found in many faiths, but is a foundational aspect of Buddhism.

4. John Donne, *Devotions Upon Emergent Occasions, Meditation XVII* (http://www.phrases.org.uk/meanings/ 257100.html).

5. Sir Martin Rees, *Our Final Century: Will the Human Race Survive the Twenty-first Century?* (London: William Heinemann, 2003).

6. Jennifer Senior, "The Mystery Man," *New York Magazine* (April 21, 2003).

Additional Resources

Cohen, Andrew. *Enlightenment is a Secret: Teachings of Liberation*. Larkspur, CA: Moksha Foundation Inc., 1995. See also www.andrewcohen.org.

Frankl, Viktor E. *Man's Search for Meaning*. New York: Washington Square Press, 1985.

What is Enlightenment? magazine (www.wie.org), which explores the essential human questions. The magazine provides a forum for a wide variety of experts and lay people in science, religion, and other arenas of practice to come together in deep exploration.

Chapter 3

Recognizing Paradoxical Grace in Our Lives

by Richard Freis

The word "grace," like a prism, manifests many meanings when we hold it to the light. To explain the title of this essay—and its connection with resilience—I have to turn to some of those meanings that have a religious root.

In the Christian tradition, *grace* points toward those sources of our life experience that are beyond our control. A grace is a blessing bestowed. It is necessarily a gift, because it is beyond our own power or merit to achieve it. Most deeply, grace is a share in the mysterious life of the divine, which enables us to be, do, have, and become in a measure otherwise beyond us. From this originating depth of grace springs the array of particular graces.

Here is the question of this essay: Do all graces wear the face of obvious blessings? Or are there paradoxical graces that befall us as apparent evils, but through which we more fully come to know and more gratefully to accept that unfolding of things that we call reality?

The claim that there are such paradoxical graces is a core dimension of the Christian understanding of the world [1]:

"The hour has come for the Son of Man to be glorified," says Jesus, referring to a humiliating stripping and crucifixion. "Very truly I tell you, unless a kernel of wheat falls to the ground and dies, it remains only a single seed. But if it dies, it produces many seeds." (John 12:23–24)

This presents an apparent evil as a *paradoxical blessing*. And then:

> Above his head they placed the written charge against him: THIS IS JESUS, THE KING OF THE JEWS. . . . In the same way the chief priests, the teachers of the law and the elders mocked him. "He saved others," they said, "but he can't save himself! He's the king of Israel! Let him come down now from the cross, and we will believe in him. He trusts in God. Let God rescue him now if he wants him, for he said, 'I am the Son of God.'" (Matthew 27:37, 41–43)

Here, against all appearances, we are asked to believe that by a double irony the mocking claims are true and the humiliating death is *a paradoxical grace* for Jesus and all humankind.

As St. Paul writes in a letter: "Jews demand signs and Greeks seek wisdom, but we preach Christ crucified, a stumbling block to Jews and folly to Gentiles, but to those who are called, both Jews and Greeks, Christ the power of God and the wisdom of God." (1 Corinthians 1:21–24) To our natural eye, this is *a paradoxical account of wisdom and power.*

Every major world religion re-sees who we are as human beings, the standards by which we judge what is good and what is bad, and the behaviors that are best because they most align with this vision.

This means that every major world religion tells us there are paradoxical graces, even the greatest of which may wear the face of apparent evil. Yet through them we come to know more fully and more gratefully accept that unfolding of things which we call reality.

Thomas Merton describes the effects of such recognition from a Christian point of view:

For such men [including such women, as the full context of Merton's work makes clear] . . . all things, whether they appear good or evil, are in actuality good. All things manifest the loving mercy of God. . . . God has turned even obstacles into means to their ends, which are also [God's] own.[2]

This view that all things manifest the loving mercy of God parallels the Buddhist view that *samsara*, the ordinary world with its plunging roller-coaster ride of pleasures and sufferings, is identical with *nirvana*, the world of unconditional joy and bliss.

How does this bear on resilience? It does so by inviting us to look at some of the losses, failures, and sufferings in our lives to which we have attributed the character of evil and to consciously shift our perspective and ask whether they have also borne—even in part or whole *are*—paradoxical graces or blessings for ourselves and others. This re-attribution about an event itself or its consequences may allow us to become more reconciled to the past and prepare us to recognize new openings for the future that we would not have recognized otherwise.

Recognizing Paradoxical Grace

I think it's important to sharpen the questions that seeing apparent evils as paradoxical graces raise in us and to give voice to our resistance to it.

Let me begin with two stories, the first Christian, the second Taoist.

The first is the close of a novel, *The Diary of a Country Priest* by George Bernanos, published in 1937.

The young French country priest, who lacks even a name for us in the diary that makes up the novel, is treated high-handedly and even maliciously by parishioners and superiors, and his shyness, humility, and genuinely charitable behavior are misinterpreted in gossip as spiritual flaws.

While on a visit to a doctor in the town of Lille, he discovers that the stomach pain he has been suffering is due to advanced cancer. Looking for a place to spend the night, he turns to Dufrety, a former seminary classmate who has left the priesthood and who lives in a foul apartment with a young woman of the poor who is his mistress. During the night the young priest suffers a hemorrhage and dies. The novel closes with a letter about the death that Dufrety writes to the young man's superior.

> The priest (summoned to perform the last rites) was still on his way, and finally I was bound to voice my deep regret that such delay threatened to deprive my comrade of the final consolations of Our Church. He did not seem to hear

me. But a few moments later he put his hand over mine, and his eyes entreated me to draw closer to him. He then uttered these words almost in my ear. And I am quite sure that I have recorded them accurately, for his voice, though halting, was strangely distinct.

"What does it matter? All is grace . . . "

I think he died just then.[3]

This is close to Thomas Merton's claim that one can rightly recognize God's *loving mercy* in *all* things. Most of us will find a part of ourselves that resists this. At one extreme, the death of a child or grandchild or a young mother or father . . . at another extreme, the large-scale death of war or epidemic or drought and starvation. . . . These not only *grieve* but *outrage* us. We often feel we would do further injury to ourselves if we tried to force ourselves to embrace as good what we truly see as a violating evil.

In reading the novel through, this question confronts us: Can we say "All is grace?" And even more deeply, *should* we say it?

Here is a wisdom story from another part of the world that raises a version of the same question:

A man who lived on the northern frontier of China was skilled in interpreting events.

One day for no reason, his horse ran away to the nomads across the border. Everyone tried to console him, but his father said, "What makes you so sure this isn't a blessing?"

Some months later his horse returned, bringing a splendid nomad stallion. Everyone congratulated him, but his father said, "What makes you so sure this isn't a disaster?"

Their household was richer by a fine horse, which the son loved to ride. One day he fell and broke his hip.

Everyone tried to console him, but his father said, "What makes you so sure this isn't a blessing?"

A year later the nomads came in force across the border, and every able-bodied man took his bow and went into battle. The Chinese frontiersmen lost nine of every ten men. Only because the son was lame did the father and son survive to take care of each other.

Truly, blessing turns to disaster, and disaster to blessing: the changes have no end, nor can the mystery be fathomed.[4]

This story brings us face-to-face with the world of unintended consequences. It makes a less radical claim than Thomas Merton's words on behalf of those who "[respond] to the mercy of God with perfect trust" that "all things, whether they appear good or evil, are in actuality good." In this story the events to which we attribute the meaning "blessing" or "disaster" turn into one another because over time they have consequences in new circumstances that make what was originally harmful now beneficial and what was originally beneficial now harmful.

And what does this story invite us to do in response to a present blessing or disaster? It invites us to not be wed to our attribution of blessing or disaster, but in the unfathomable mystery of things to see a present disaster as a possible paradoxical grace, because it is the possible source of a future blessing. The other side is that a present blessing may be a paradoxical disaster, because it may be the source of a possible future harm. Corn-based ethanol, for example, to point to a conversation currently surrounding us, may appear to be a blessing, because it frees us from nonrenewable and ecologically harmful fossil fuels. But it could turn out to be a paradoxical disaster, if it slows our search for more efficient and sustainable solutions, because of its required use of large amounts of water and agricultural space and its relatively low yield of fuel.

Triple-Loop Learning, Resilience, and Paradoxical Grace

Let me begin by quoting Mike Jay's careful definition of resilience:

Resilience is the differentiated power to persist when things do not work out at first, the capability to navigate ambiguity and uncertainty, the motivation to transcend common problems and barriers and to collaboratively anticipate the future in sustainable ways.[5]

In considering the relationship between the recognition of paradoxical grace and resilience, it will be helpful to start with a couple of framing remarks about resilience.

The first is that the condition of being resilient is a matter of degrees.

The second is that degrees of resilience have a correlation with a framework created by the organizational learning theorist, Chris Argyris, and developed by the business coach, Robert Hargrove, and others to describe levels of learning.[6] In the present context, I will omit some otherwise important factors in the model.

LEVELS OF RESILIENCE

IDENTITY Genetic and Cultural Factors, Motivation Profile, Type, Strengths, Level of Existence Underlying Mental Models	MENTAL MODELS These set the governing variables by which we judge our behavior and events	BEHAVIOR AND EVENTS WITHIN THE MENTAL MODELS Our behavior and events	OUT-COME

↑**Change in BEHAVIOR**
Single-Loop

↑**Change in MENTAL MODELS**
————**Double-Loop**

↑**Change in IDENTITY**
Triple-Loop

Resilience is greater as we become more cognitively flexible in handling increasingly fundamental and comprehensive levels of our thinking about the world and ourselves in it. The chart shows these deepening levels becoming accessible to us as we add to the number and depths of the feedback loops we actually use in relating to the world.

At the single-loop level, we judge behavior, things, events, but cannot go behind the standards we use to examine the mental models our judgments rest on.

Our locus of control consists only in this: We can try to bring about or ward off a certain event or perform or avoid a certain behavior. But we cannot critique and revise the framework that tells us whether a behavior or event is good or bad.

Nor can we take into account our blind spots, core motivation profile, assumptions about ourselves as individuals and members of a society and culture, strengths and weaknesses, or degrees of rigidity and flexibility in different areas and how they may limit or enlarge our freedom and efficacy of response. This structure narrows our ability to conceive and realize more multi-sided and differentiated, hence potentially more broadly resilient, responses.

Our spiritual experience from this perspective is unlikely to arrive at the idea of paradoxical grace, because it is unlikely to bring into awareness the two attributions of evil and grace at the same time. If it did so, we would feel it necessary to decide between them. We might hear and nod with someone else's appeal to a homelier form of this mental model: "Maybe this is a blessing in disguise." But out of ourselves we would hold the straightforward view that God always and only loves us. We could hold this with a great purity, confidence, and tenacity, but without complexity; and we could receive from it a resilience deeply rooted, but narrow in resources and range.

At the double-loop level, we look critically *both* at the behavior or event *and* the mental models that determine our spontaneous judgment of them. Our locus of control thus expands in some degree to the mental models that tell us what attributions we can make about our behaviors and the events that befall us.

The aim of the Taoist story is to lift us from a single-loop to a double-loop perspective by inviting us to change our mental models.

In the single-loop perspective, the meaning of things is simply given and their identity is stable. In the double-loop perspective the events to which we attribute the meaning "blessing" or "disaster" are not stably so, but "turn into" one another as what was originally harmful becomes beneficial and what was originally beneficial becomes harmful.

This is a world in which recognizing paradoxical grace becomes possible to us, a more complex and workable world in which we can look through the simple attribution of disaster to see an event as a possible source of future blessings and to this extent as itself a blessing. Hesitation to name something simply a disaster and greater confidence in the workableness of the world typically make us more resilient. Some confidence in the intrinsic workableness of things, particularly within a perspective that takes into account deeper determining levels, is a condition for arriving at and remaining committed to the view of resilience *as a path* rather than a series of discontinuous events that are finally and undifferentiatedly good or bad.

At the triple-loop level, we look critically at all three levels together—particular behaviors and events, mental models, and now identity. We might say that the identity level involves a special set of mental models that are complex, inter-tangled, held at different degrees of awareness, and with a high emotional charge. At this level we arrive at a form of system thinking that interrelates particular behaviors and events with our valuing and other mental models and our awareness of ourselves.

The addition of this level enables us to notice and take into account the ways our spontaneous assumptions about who we are (and should be) and our native predispositions may bias the ways we frame a problem and conceive and implement possible solutions. Such predispositions would include our characteristic blind spots, particular high and low motivators, strengths and weaknesses, and degrees of rigidity and flexibility in different areas.

Second-loop learning enables us to recognize and live within ambiguity and uncertainty—the way things turn into one another—*in the world*. Triple-loop learning enables us to recognize and live within the ways our thoughts, feelings, and behaviors are ambiguous and uncertain—how they turn into one another—*in ourselves*. Self-knowledge without resistance and acceptance of the self you've come to know enable you to create your particular resilient path by design and keep maturing it as you align your path with yourself and the world in ever deeper and more refined ways.

At this stage there is less a locus of control than loci of control, a fluctuating range of degrees, kinds, and positions. I can control to some extent my inward and outward responses and often find a range of direct and indirect responses to choose from, so I recognize my options for control as highly differentiated in kind and degree. I also acknowledge limits to my control, some of which I may be able to know, others of which are invisible to me. These limits reside both in myself and in other people who are involved or all kinds of external conditions, such as the approach of a category five hurricane or the collapse of a financial market. Also at this stage, my attribution of meaning to events becomes very complex and differentiated, so any outcome will be seen by me as in some ways a success and in some ways as missing full success.

Because I know beforehand that control is distributed and in part incalculable, and that success and failure are always partial and subject to alteration if I take a long perspective over time, I don't have the sort of expectations that can make me throw up my hands as simply a failure when they are not met. This allows me to be more fully resilient.

It is in triple-loop perspective, which follows to the limit our capacity for meaningful differentiation and integration, control and attribution, and calculation of means and ends, and which recognizes the roots and reach of these factors into unknowing, that I believe arises Thomas Merton's radical description of living so that anything—for myself, I must still say almost anything—can become grace for us.

A Practice to Recognize Paradoxical Grace

In this closing section, let me move from theory to a practice you can use to open yourself to the possibility that in some aspect an apparent disaster that has befallen you is a paradoxical grace.

Imagine this scenario.

You are walking along a path—the Path of Life. As you round a corner, you find a box blocking your way. It is tied with a ribbon and bow and has a card on it. You open the card and read, "I am sending this gift because I know it is what you most need at this point on your Path of Life." It is signed by God.

You quickly unwrap the package and what you find is . . . the difficulty that is most troubling in your life at this moment.

Imagine yourself now looking at this difficulty and ask yourself, "In what ways can I see this as a gift of God's mercy, the thing I most need now for myself or the world, a paradoxical grace?"

I first used this practice during the third year that I was incapacitated by chronic fatigue syndrome, and our disability insurer refused to continue to honor my claim. This meant we could no longer meet our house payment.

My mind was thrown into turmoil as I thought of the needs of my family. My first response was to watch everything on television I could find about the homeless, taking notes about how to live out of your car! That "be prepared" attitude was, as I now look at it, a very characteristic clutch for resilience from my personality.

I also repeatedly practiced this exercise, which I was familiar with in both Christian and Buddhist versions. It helped me discern genuine ways that the experience was a gift.

We did in fact lose our house and by that time had already worked out a number of things we could do to keep going. I came to see that the very experience of disabling illness and losing the house and yet making the situation workable gave me confidence in myself. I also recognized that our friends and my family would help us find a way to have a place to live if they knew we needed it, so we wouldn't be left to cope alone.

I came to feel gratitude for the menacing dislocation, because it had pulled me out of my "upper-middle-class ghetto" mentality, whose unconscious assumption was, "I'm a pretty good guy and I pay my taxes, so nothing really bad is ever going to happen to me." It gave me the large, new, and wiser family of all who have experienced the precariousness of life and know anything can happen. It was a wiser and ultimately happier place to be.

I have continued to find the practice a grace-revealing companion, even in the harshest experiences. It is most so when I use it without any attempt to force or manipulate my feelings, with compassion and tenderness for my own and others' sufferings, and with a willingness to recognize all the sides of truth that it reveals to me without denial. Inasmuch as I can do that—and part of the truth it reveals to me may be that I simply can't do it at present—it helps me endure. It frees me to have rather than be had by my experiences. And it fosters the kind of resilience that allows me to inhabit every space as in some degree home.

Try it out.

The Author

Richard Freis has been professor of classical studies, director of the innovative Heritage Program, and designer of the Leadership Seminars in the Humanities at Millsaps College. He has published widely as a scholar, poet, critic, and spiritual director. His pioneering work in developmental and integral frameworks has informed his work as a personal and organizational consultant for the last three decades. He holds a BA from St. John's College in Annapolis, Maryland; an MA and a PhD from the University of California, Berkeley; and a Master of Theological Studies from Spring Hill College. You may contact him at freissr@millsaps.edu.

Notes

1. For biblical passages I quote the *New International Version* for its consistent marriage of clarity in English and fidelity to the Greek.

2. Thomas Merton, *Life and Holiness* (Garden City, NY: Image Books, 1964): 118–19.

3. Georges Bernanos, *The Diary of a Country Priest*, trans. Pamela Morris (New York: The Macmillan Company, 1948): 297–8. I have retranslated the last words of the young priest, since Morris' version significantly misrepresents the original.

4. Jack Kornfield and Christina Feldman, eds., *Soul Food: Stories to Nourish the Spirit and the Heart* (San Francisco: HarperSanFrancisco, 1996): 240–241.

5. Mike R. Jay, CPR *for the Soul 3.0: Creating Personal Resilience by Design* (Mumbai: Leadership University Press, 2006): 62.

6. For Argyris, see Mark K. Smith, "chris argyris: theories of action, double-loop learning, and organizational learning," *the encyclopedia of informal education* (www.infed.org/thinkers/ argyris.htm, 2001). In the bibliography Smith makes available for download the entire book, C. Argyris, R. Putnam, and D. McLain Smith, *Action science: Concepts, methods, and skills for research and intervention* (San Francisco: Jossey Bass, 1985; download at http://www.actiondesign.com/action_science/index.htm). For Hargrove and triple-loop learning, see Robert Hargrove, *Mastering the Art of Creative Collaboration* (New York: McGraw Hill, 1998): 61–71, 165–199. This book is a first step in formalizing triple-loop learning within the framework of collaboration. Building on Hargrove's work, I have developed a more differentiated model of collaboration, which identifies and makes available to the group process the different character types, motivation profiles, and learning styles of the participants and which defines the discussion patterns characteristic of successively higher levels of cognitive development. Those who wish to know more may contact me at freissr@millsaps.edu.

Chapter 4

Embodied Resilience:
Energy Healing and the Resilient Path

by Richard Freis

A Quest for Resilience of Body

On January 26, 1991, one of those summery midwinter days that sometimes occur in central Mississippi, a student stopped by my office at Millsaps College and asked if we could speak about the choices he faced after graduation. It's a conversation I'm always glad to have. But I told him that since it was such a fine day, I'd like to do what I'd been thinking of doing and go over to a nearby nature trail and sit in the sun while talking. On such days I love to see and feel the many preparations toward spring already visible in the winter buds on the trees and the tips of plants just rising from the natural mulch of the woods.

We found a wooden bench, sat down, and began to talk. I had a background awareness that the temperature was dropping and my jacket thin, but I was absorbed in the conversation and didn't register how cold it was getting. When we stood up to return to the campus, I found I was very cold: My body began to shake uncontrollably, and I had to focus on moving my mouth to be able to articulate words. But by the time I reached my office and then drove home, I was warm again.

The next evening I wrote in my journal, "I think I caught the flu yesterday. I'm achy and exhausted. It's hard to get through everything I want. But in a week it will be in the past."

In the fall I found myself forgetting or becoming confused in the classroom and outside it, causing inexplicable and sometimes consequential errors. Finally, the "flu" was given a name, "chronic fatigue syndrome."

Eventually I requested a leave of absence and waited for the condition to run its course. Sixteen years later it persists. For almost a decade I was largely bedridden. I tried everything I thought might heal me, or if not fully heal, that would increase my resilience within the illness.

Toward the end of that time, because of a specialist's medication error, in body and brain I experienced a year of catastrophic shattering intensities of disablement and pain I had never imagined existed. Diabetes erupted. I lost all control of sleeping and waking; the slightest sound or someone moving in my visual field threw me into exhausting episodes of tremors no one knew how to stop. Without forewarning I experienced massive, contentless, whole-being flushes of dread and depression. I learned to have no expectations or wishes. I simply breathed deeply, I thanked God for everything, and I decided on a brief practice that I hoped would restore some resilience to my body: I committed to do one thing daily that would give me an experience of pleasure, however small, thinking that if I intentionally gave my body even a tiny experience of pleasure, it would sooner or later remember how to get there by itself, and that would open up for it a larger margin of resilience.

Energy Healing and the Resilient Path

It was in searching further for a restoration of physical resilience that I came upon energy healing.

Most of us are familiar with one form of energy healing, acupuncture, by experience or reputation. We may call up an image of a woman or man or child lying on a treatment table, while the practitioner inserts fine, very sharp needles into designated points on the client's body. These points lie on meridians, energy loops or circuits that carry a form of bioenergy around the body. The meridians with their interrelations and points accessible to stimulation were mapped in China five thousand years ago. Acupuncture is a form of traditional medicine that has won wide acceptance and some explanation from modern, scientifically trained physicians.

Acu*pressure* is a cousin of acu*puncture*, which stimulates the meridian energy points not with needles, but with tapping or other form of manual manipulation.

Emotional Freedom Techniques (EFT) constitute a form of acupressure. Gary Craig, beginning from the work of psychologist Roger Callahan,[1] designed what we might call a universal tapping algorithm or protocol.

Universal means that this single brief acupressure sequence can be fruitfully applied to a multitude of problems. I will map out its range by examples later.

The remarkable economy of means and scope of effect of Craig's structure arises from his choosing a small number of points that bring into play a wide range of different meridians. Because of its ease of use and range of applications, energy healing became my key to fuller resilience of body.

The Matrix of Healing

Why are EFT and other forms of energy healing such versatile instruments for restoring resilience?

EFT looks at an unhealthy or dysfunctional state through the lens of the body's energy system. The energy system is bound up with every bodily system, as well as with their interlocking activities in the spheres of consciousness, sensing, imaginative associations, feeling, rational thinking and intuitive thinking, and a range of transpersonal states.

Sometimes we ask: "Does this illness have a physical *or* a psychological cause, an environmental *or* an internal cause, a defect of form *or* process in body system X *or* Y?"

The truest answer may be *any or all of the above*: Every unhealthy state expresses itself through many aspects and may have a number of collaborating causes as well as supporting conditions.

The condition may have a physical cause and also a psychological cause. Moreover, it may have an environmental cause and an internal cause. And it may flow from a defect of form and function. To attribute a condition to a single cause—to say, for example, that the *real* cause of these headaches is unconscious emotion—is often reductive, even if stress brought on by unconscious emotion plays some role. This means we can look at a disease or other dysfunctional aspect of ourselves as self-organizing systems through a number of lenses, any one of which, or some combination of which, may open up a path toward healing.

An implication of the interdependence of multiple causes and conditions is that if you want to create change on any level, your chances of success will increase if you address several aspects of the system that supports the present condition. In helping someone recover, for example, from a major wound received in battle, the completeness and rapidity of recovery will increase if you address not only the immediate injuries with appropriate medical interventions, but support them with nutrition, exercise, psychological work, rest, and—often a catalyst for effective, efficient, and sustainable healing in all the other areas—energy healing such as EFT.

The Stress Syndrome

It's hard to imagine a time when nobody answered the question, "How are you?" with "Man, I'm really *stressed out!*" But it was only in the second decade of the twentieth century that the great American physiologist, Walter B. Cannon, who also introduced the term "homeostasis" to physiology in 1932, borrowed the term "stress" from applied physics. In 1936 a research scientist, Hans Selye, named "the *stress* syndrome."

The stress syndrome itself unfolds as a precise sequence of measurable changes in the body. Selye identified three stages in the stress syndrome.

The first stage is the *alarm reaction*, in which neurochemicals and hormones pour forth to prepare the body to fight, flee, or freeze.

If the stressors continue in a diminished degree, the body may adapt to them and the alarm stage symptoms disappear. This is therefore named the *adaptive stage*.

If the stressors continue at too great an intensity for the body, mind, and feelings to adapt, we can become over-sensitive and create ever more intense alarm reactions in response to increasingly small stressors. Stress that is prolonged, unpredictable, and out of our control can prolong the alarm reaction.

In a third stage, the systems of the person so unrelievedly thrown into the alarm response may become exhausted, leading to a suppressed immune system, loss of appetite, muscle wasting, loss of reproductive function, and other conditions that make the body vulnerable. The mind, body, and emotions can't turn this runaway pattern off and ride it into death.

As Selye remarked after reviewing these diminutions in one of his last papers, perhaps with a touch of dark irony, "Apparently the adaptability of an organism is finite."

Stress Syndrome and Energy Healing

In their book *The Promise of Energy Psychology*, which is informed by the perspectives both of contemporary science and the practice of energy healing, David Feinstein, Donna Eden, and Gary Craig outline a mechanism by which manipulating the meridian points may interrupt the alarm response[2]:

1. An image that ordinarily triggers the alarm response is brought to mind while physically stimulating a series of acupoints. Stimulating these points sends impulses to the amygdala that inhibit the triggering of the alarm response.

2. These impulses also cause a reduction, within the amygdala, of the number of neural connections between the image and the alarm response, so the alarm signal is not as "dense."

3. After a number of repetitions of number one, the image can then be brought to mind, or the situation can be experienced directly, without sparking the alarm response.

Energy healing is not only practiced for stress and related problems of individuals. As Dr. Feinstein makes clear in his remarkable study, "Energy Psychology in Disaster Relief,"[3] it has also been used by organizations for events of such massive public trauma as the wars in Kosovo and Rwanda, Sri Lanka following the tsunami, and the United States following the Columbine high school shootings, the terrorist attacks of 9/11, and hurricanes Rita and Katrina.

Again, what energy psychology contributes is this:

It is in its ability to rapidly counter maladaptive hyperarousal in the limbic system that energy psychology may have its greatest advantage over . . . orthodox trauma interventions.[4]

Here are some conditions in which the stress syndrome plays a role following one or all of the patterns I describe above:

- **phobias** of all kinds, for example, of heights; elevators; flapping, darting, and slithering creatures; dental drills; flying; bridges; or your own most familiar terror;

- **afflictive emotions,** such as anxiety, loneliness, anger, guilt, jealousy, grief, or shame;

- **traumas and post-traumatic stress disorder** **(PTSD)** caused by sadistic abuse of children, severe accidents, incidents of war, natural disasters, or rape and other sexual traumas;

- **performance anxiety** in auditions, delivering a speech, making cold calls for marketing, sex, or examinations;

- **physical conditions,** such as unremitting pain, autoimmune diseases, multiple system infectious conditions, acute premenstrual syndrome, morning sickness, or asthma;

- **addictive cravings** for food, drugs, gambling, cigarettes—a classic example of stress feeding stress in a maladaptive feedback loop.

This is also a list of conditions that energy psychology can successfully treat.[5] The close overlap renders plausible the hypothesis of Feinstein, Eden, and Craig that a key mechanism by which energy medicine works is its ability to rapidly counter malregulation of the stress response.

How to Do EFT

Energy healing is a resource not only for trauma-relief workers and other healing professionals. EFT can also be easily learned by individuals who want to know how to help themselves and their families when stress or trauma arise.

> [Note: As always, for serious conditions it is crucial to consult the appropriate medical professional. Even in such cases, EFT often has a contribution to make, but it should be used only in consultation with the medical professional.]

In this section I present the most basic format for EFT practice. There also exist many elaborations that extend EFT's power. In my book, *The EFT Living System: Book I: Foundations*,[6] I discuss them in a way that is accessible to a beginner and, I believe, also offers some fresh insight for the expert. The book tells you how to make your practice of EFT most effective; applies it to a range of concrete issues, from erasing phobias to healing traumatic memories to making affirmations effective to creating peak performance in any endeavor; and it includes case histories that put a human face on the often moving, sometimes funny experience of EFT.

Now to the basic format.

How to Do the Set-up

EFT begins with a brief set-up, which is designed to reduce the potential resistances that often accompany the change process and to direct your attention to the issue you wish to address:

Decide the problem you wish to address.

1. Formulate the set-up statement: "Even though I have/feel/think/do [the problem], I accept and appreciate myself completely!" Some examples: "Even though I have this pulled muscle pain, I accept and appreciate myself completely." "Even though I crave chocolate when I see it, I accept and appreciate myself completely." "Even though I am afraid of heights, I accept and appreciate myself completely."

2. Using a scale from one (low) to ten (high), estimate and write down the number that accords with your present level of discomfort. This is a widely used medical measure of felt discomfort called Subjective Units of Distress (SUDs). Write down your present level of distress as a baseline for you to measure how much the tapping has reduced your distress.

3. Find the "sore spot":

a. Trace the vertical line that runs down the center of your chest.
b. Find the top of the crease between the side of the chest and upper arm.
c. Find the point on your chest midway between points a and b.
d. Move your finger up to a point an inch below your collarbone.
e. Press in that area until you find a spot that is sore.

4. While rubbing the sore spot, repeat the EFT set-up statement three times.

5. Then tap using the basic sequence until the SUD is lowered to one or zero.

Basic Tapping Sequence

Craig's "Basic Recipe" includes thirteen tapping points: eight on the face and upper body and five on the hand.

Experienced EFT practitioners develop a certain freedom in the way they use the basic sequence. If you watch Craig and other EFT masters at work, you will see that at times an EFT practitioner will limit him- or herself to the first eight points, repeated several times. It may also be possible to reach the desired result by using two or three acupoints, perhaps the chin, collarbone, and under-the-arm points in some mixture of repetition and varied sequencing. In general, I find it most effective for beginners to use the eight face and upper body points.

After you tap a round or two, close your eyes, take a deep breath, and exhale slowly, letting your awareness relax into your present state of feeling. Make a new estimate of your SUD and write it down. Continue to tap until your SUD is one or zero or is as low as you are able to bring it.

If you then want to tap on a particular aspect of the present issue (it often helps to zero in on any especially distress-filled aspects) or turn to a related or new issue, format it as a new set-up sequence, write down your SUD, and tap it down.

The picture on the following page shows the acupoints of the basic tapping sequence in order.

Basic Sequence Tapping Points

1. *Inner edge of eyebrow* (EB)	8. *Under breast* (UB)
2. *Outside of ear* (SE)	9. *Outer edge of thumbnail* (TH)
3. *Under eye* (UE)	10. *Edge of index fingernail toward thumb* (IF)
4. *Under nose* (UN)	11. *Edge of middle finger toward IF* (MF)
5. *Between underlip and chin* (CH)	12. *Edge of baby fingernail toward ring finger* (BF)
6. *Collarbone* (CB)	13. *Karate chop* (KC)
7. *Underarm point* (UA)	

The Author

Richard Freis has been professor of classical studies, director of the innovative Heritage Program, and designer of the Leadership Seminars in the Humanities at Millsaps College. He has published widely as a scholar, poet, critic, and spiritual director. His pioneering work in developmental and integral frameworks has informed his work as a personal and organizational consultant for the last three decades. He holds a BA from

St. John's College in Annapolis, Maryland; an MA and a PhD from the University of California, Berkeley; and a Master of Theological Studies from Spring Hill College. You may contact him at freissr@millsaps.edu.

Notes

1. Dr. Callahan developed a form of energy healing he called TFT (Thought Field Therapy), which remains significant.

2. David Feinstein, Donna Eden, and Gary Craig, *The Promise of Energy Psychology* (New York: Jeremy P. Tarcher/Penguin, 2005): 22

3. David Feinstein, "Energy Psychology in Disaster Relief" (www. innersource.net/energy_psych/articles/ep_energy-trauma-treatment. htm).

4. Feinstein, "Energy Psychology in Disaster Relief": 6.

5. For a chart of typical conditions helped by energy healing, see Richard Freis, *The EFT Living System: Book I: Foundations* (Jackson, MS: BODYMINDSPIRITINTEGRAL PRESS, 2006; or www.eftlivingtips.com): 9.

6. Ibid.

Chapter 5

The Hardy Couple:
How to Create Relationship
Resilience for Turbulent Times

by Mari Smith

*Relationships, for most of us, are one of the biggest sources of joy in our lives.
But, they are also one of the biggest sources of pain.*

—Michael Neill

I was thirty-four when I married the love of my life. It took a while to find him, but he was certainly worth the wait. I'd been living in Scotland for the previous twenty years and had no idea my husband-to-be was looking for me in sunny San Diego, California.

A long-lost friend had extended an invitation out of the blue to come visit. I jumped at the offer, and the direction of my life changed forever.

I feel blessed to have a solid, rewarding marriage now. We've taken care to build our relationship resilience over the years . . .

. . . but it hasn't been easy. In fact, it's been a tumultuous ride.

My parents divorced when I was twelve. My father got custody of all five girls and whisked us from Canada back to his homeland in Scotland. I remember that dark night as if it were yesterday—September 4, 1978, at the Greyhound bus station, saying goodbye to Mum. I was wracked with grief, as I didn't think I was ever going to see her again. (I didn't, for ten long years.)

It was a rough and traumatizing time. I spent my adolescence and twenties swearing divorce would never, ever happen to me—the pain was unbearable. (I wonder how many youth go through a similarly difficult time, swearing they'll never divorce, only to find themselves repeating history a few decades later).

My husband and I decided to get married after close to two years of dating. I dreamt of the "honeymoon period," believing any challenges we had would vanish into thin air once we were husband and wife. (A fantasy I likely got from children's fairytale books).

But, although our wedding day was magical, there was no honeymoon period. In fact, our conflicts seemed to intensify shortly after we got married. (We later learned from our relationship expert friends, Paul and Layne Cutright, that each time you deepen a commitment you'll reenter what they call the power struggle phase.)

The Legacy of Divorce

During our first four years of marriage, my husband and I had two very definite NDEs. No, not near death experiences, but near *divorce* experiences.

In *The Unexpected Legacy of Divorce*, Dr. Judith S. Wallerstein writes:

> . . . children identify not only with their mother or father as separate individuals but with the relationship between them. They carry the template of this relationship into adulthood and use it to seek the image of their new family. The absence of a good image negatively influences their search for love, intimacy, and commitment. Anxiety leads many into making bad choices in relationships, giving up hastily when problems arise. . . .[1]

Conflict, anger, projection, and disillusionment infected our marriage. We sought out a competent therapist a couple of times, but that did no good. Poor guy, threw up his arms in despair and told us we were polarized. Great—what now?

As was our habit before we met, my husband and I attended many seminars, workshops, retreats—anything self-help. However, although we found a certain tool or technique that would help for a while, each one had a mere Band-Aid effect. The underlying challenges were still there. And then, worse, we'd use these newfound tools as weapons against each other.

We happened upon a helpful counselor. Then we worked with a coach. Slowly, we seemed to be inching our way towards the marriage we saw in our dreams.

Courage means to keep working a relationship, to continue seeking solutions to difficult problems, and to stay focused during stressful periods.

—Denis Waitley

What finally had the most profound impact on our relationship was immersing ourselves in an extensive array of personality assessments along with developmental coaching. Instead of pointing the finger at each other for our respective shortcomings, we were able to point at the various reports, and the light bulbs went off like the Fourth of July with our newfound understandings.

We learned more about ourselves and each other in six months than we had in the previous six years. It was like learning a whole new language—finally, we were speaking the same one.

Developing the ability to experience the world through your partner's eyes, while holding onto your own perspective, may be the single most important skill in intimate relationships.

—Patricia Love and Steven Stosny
How To Improve Your Marriage Without Talking About It

The Hardy Personality

In nature, it's the hardiest plants and animals—those that are strong, resilient, and adaptable—that thrive. Though we think of the mighty oak as strongest of the trees, it's the resilient willow that survives the storms. When couples face challenges and hard times, the hardy ones—like the willow—fare the best.

Psychologist Dr. Suzanne Kobasa first revealed the "hardy personality" in the late 1970s, when she conducted a long-term study on the impact of stress. She discovered two types of people: those who became increasingly symptomatic and those who rose to meet the challenges with their more stress-hardy personality.

Hardy personalities typically have the following characteristics:

- **Commitment.** Hardy people are actively involved with their jobs and lives, with a strong commitment to self, work, family, and other values. They are often role models for their children and community.

- **Control.** Hardy people believe they can influence the course of events rather than feel powerless. They accept personal responsibility for both "failures" and successes in their lives.

- **Challenge.** Hardy people appraise difficult situations as opportunities for change and development rather than as threats. They see change as an incentive for further growth.

What's Your Resilience Factor?

Dr. Karen Reivich and Dr. Andrew J. Shatté discovered seven factors of resilience as described in their book, *The Resilience Factor.* They scientifically grounded their research in the work of Dr. Martin E.P. Seligman, Director of the University of Pennsylvania Positive Psychology Center and author of *Authentic Happiness.*

Resilience is our ability to rebound from setbacks and challenges we encounter in life. The seven factors of resilience are:

1. **Emotional regulation** is the single most important factor. It is the ability to control response to external events and stay calm under pressure. This factor has a connection to emotional intelligence as examined in the work of Daniel Goleman. Our thoughts create our

beliefs, which create our attitudes, which fuel our feelings, which often drive our actions. We can gain the most leverage over our emotions by examining our beliefs.

Beliefs are a mighty force in your relationships. When things aren't going well, one of the first things you want to consider is, "What beliefs could create this reality?"

—Layne and Paul Cutright

2. **Impulse control,** which is the ability to rein in your behavior under pressure.

3. **Causal analysis,** which is the ability to explain accurately why events happen. Your attributional style drives this factor—whether you see the glass half-full, like the optimist, or half-empty, like the pessimist. There are three sets of attribution:

   - internal vs. external (me/not me)
   - global vs. specific (everything/not everything)
   - stable vs. temporary (always/not always)

Pessimists tend to believe bad events are their own fault, will undermine everything they do, and will last a long time. Optimists tend to believe defeat is not their fault, its causes are confined to this one case, and it's just a temporary setback.

4. **Self-efficacy** is the belief that you have the competence and mastery to solve problems and faith in your ability to succeed in the world.

5. **Realistic optimism** is a belief, grounded in reality, that things can change for the better, there is hope for the future, and you can control the direction of your life.

6. **Empathy** is the ability to tune into other people and accurately read their cues to their psychological and emotional states.

7. **Reaching out** is the ability to seek out new opportunities, challenges, and relationships, and the willingness to stretch and grow in all areas of your life for greater satisfaction, success, and resilience.

Fortunately, you don't need to fully master all seven factors to be fully resilient. Depending on the situation at hand, you may need to tap into one factor more than the others.[2]

> *The true emotionally intelligent person is one who knows how to not trigger another's emotions.*
>
> —Mike R. Jay

The Hardy Couple

The hardy couple, then, are those partners who have hardy personalities and score highest on the Resilience Factor Inventory. The hardy couple is strong and resilient. No matter what challenges they face, they remain committed to each other.

The hardy couple is tenacious. The partners "close all exits"—a strategy recommended by marriage expert Dr. Harville Hendrix, founder of Imago Relationships International. This entails making a solid promise to your partner that you will not threaten any catastrophic end, including divorce, nor will you leak away your time pursuing personal interests only.

When my husband and I declared all exits closed, it was a pivotal moment for me. I felt myself relaxing into certainty at a cellular level; I hadn't realized up to that point how much I subconsciously did not trust that my husband was in for the long haul. (Could this be an old belief from being an adult child of divorce?) This one declaration alone made a huge impact on our relationship resilience.

In their book *The Case for Marriage: Why Married People Are Happier, Healthier, and Better Off Financially*, authors Linda J. Waite and Maggie Gallagher document a twenty-year study that reveals the benefits of staying the course. They write that ". . . the key seems to be the marriage bond itself: Having a partner who is committed for better or for worse, in sickness and in health, makes people happier and healthier. The knowledge that someone cares for you and that you have someone who depends on you helps give life meaning and provides a buffer against the inevitable troubles of life."[3]

We live in an instant-gratification, throwaway society. We think, "If it's broken, throw it away and get a replacement." In Las Vegas, you can get a drive-through wedding and drive-through divorce. But divorce may not be the right solution — not for the vast majority of couples, *if* you're willing to do things differently from the masses.

Dr. John Gottman spent the last twenty-five years studying married couples in his "love lab." Within five minutes of observing a couple interact, Gottman can predict — with 91 percent accuracy — whether the couple is likely to stay together or break up.

Gottman discovered that it's not how *often* couples fight that is detrimental to their relationship, it's *how* they fight. Certain predictors include what Gottman calls "The Four Horsemen": criticism, contempt, defensiveness, and stonewalling. Eradicating these negative patterns will go a long way to making a couple hardier. What also makes the difference, however, is strengthening the friendship at the heart of any good marriage.

> *Let us not look back in anger or forward in fear, but around us in awareness.*
>
> —James Thurber

In a similar vein, Dr. Pat Love, author of *Hot Monogamy, The Truth About Love,* and *How To Improve Your Marriage Without Talking About It,* declares the number one cause of divorce is growing apart. Dr. Love identified three distinct stages that typically occur prior to divorce: withdrawal of interest, resentment, and growing apart.

So, if we know the "divorce missile" launches once we withdraw interest from our partner, what can we do now as a preventive measure to build more resilience into our marriage?

To be a hardy couple, one possible solution you can adopt is to become your partner's number one recreational companion. Dr. Willard F. Harley advocates this strategy in his books, *His Needs, Her Needs; Give & Take* and *Love Busters.* Harley identified ten distinct needs men and women have — five typical for women and five for men. I can say from experience, recognizing and striving to meet those needs goes a long way to fostering relationship resilience.

If your marriage has gone a bit stale, you need to re-romanticize it. Gottman encourages couples who may be experiencing distance from each other to get back in touch with *why* they fell in love with each other, *why* they got married. Get out your wedding album and reminisce. Do some of the things you used to do when you were dating.

My husband and I got married on Valentine's Day, and we make a point of creating a magical day each year on our anniversary, including renewing our vows and watching our wedding video. We also have a nightly habit of saying a blessing before sitting down to dinner together—this is often the highlight of my day. Rituals are a critically important part of the hardy couple's relationship. Rituals are interactions that are recurring, coordinated, and have positive emotional meaning to both of you.

> *The key to growing a marriage that is personal, and not just logistical,*
> *is to be intentional about the connection rituals of everyday life.*
> —William J. Doherty

The Hardy Couple—Born or Made?

Depending on your resilience factor and whether you have a hardy personality or not, it could be argued that hardy couples are born, not made. However, in my experience, it could be either. The key is to focus on your strengths and to deliberately design a relationship that fulfills each partner's desires. It's not about compromise; when we compromise, someone is always in pain.

First, you need to know your own unique strengths, attributes, desires, motivations, and preferences and those of your partner. Then through a process in which you each discover, disclose, and accept—both self and other—you're now in a position to create your own innovative relationship design, if possible, with the help of a competent relationship coach.

You must focus on what's important: What are you committed to as a couple?

It seems essential, in relationships and all tasks, that we concentrate only on what is most significant and important.

—Soren Kierkegaard

Many so-called gurus tout the philosophy of "find your flaws and fix them." But that simply doesn't work. Using your precious life energy to try to strengthen your weaknesses is a complete waste of time.

You'd be far better off discovering your specific strengths and limitations (a less pejorative term than "weaknesses"). Then you can channel your life energy into doing more of what you are *best* at, what comes *naturally* to you. The aim is to build a foundation of wellness, rather than treat symptoms.

Success is achieved by developing our strengths, not by eliminating our weaknesses.

—Marilyn vos Savant

Over time, by deepening self-knowledge and allowing more self-disclosure, these skills can become effective, healthy habits that replace less functional ones. But just as a contractor wouldn't build a house without first having the blueprint from the architect, couples also can benefit from the support of a specialist to create a healthy, strong, resilient marriage.

The Author

Mari Smith is a marriage educator, relationship coach, speaker, and author. Her expertise and passion are helping couples build extraordinary relationships and take control of their financial future together as a partnership. Mari has written many e-books, articles, and special reports on the topics of love of money. She based her signature program, Attract Love & Build Wealth Ultimate System for Singles, on her personal journey of going from single and broke to happily married and creating wealth with her husband.

Free valuable information and resources for couples are available at *www.TheHardyCouple.com* and for singles at *www.MillionDollarRelationships.com* and *www.AttractLoveBuildWealth.com*.

Are you a hardy couple?

Find out now! Take a quick self-test online at *www.TheHardyCouple.com*.

Support for building relationship resilience

Visit Mari's website for details of products, services, and recommended sources of support for couples and relationship-minded singles: *www.TheHardyCouple.com*.

Notes

1. Judith S. Wallerstein, Julia M. Lewis, and Sandra Blakeslee, *The Unexpected Legacy of Divorce: A 25 Year Landmark Study* (New York: Hyperion, 2000): xxxv

2. To find out your resilience factor, take the free Resilience Factor Inventory test at www.TheHardyCouple.com.

3. Linda J. Waite and Maggie Gallagher, *The Case for Marriage: Why Married People Are Happier, Healthier, and Better Off Financially* (New York: Doubleday, 2000): 77.

Chapter 6

Upping the Downside of Being a Stay-at-Homer

by Tim Condon

All the time folks say to me: "How can you do what you do?" or "I could never do that." I don't climb the world's highest mountains, nor do I take off and sail solo around the world. I'm not risking my life hunting tigers, nor am I risking millions of dollars playing the markets. In a world that is filled with high-power thrill seekers and career-driven dollar-chasers, I choose to be a stay-at-home dad.

It's not for everyone, and it may not even be a perfect fit for me. It offers a busyness that I have never known before. It offers joy and frustration. Its rewards are secured only through abdication of personal freedom. It sounds a lot like life.

Once we learned my wife was pregnant, we decided that one of us should be at home with our baby. To decide who, we took into account our general personalities and what we seemed more drawn to do. The choice was clear that I was the more likely candidate. Little did we know that my preference for self-study in fields such as psychology and philosophy would thrive during this period of relative seclusion. And that those interests would lead us both to insights into just how much I am cut out for this work and, on a larger scale, how preferences, interests, and what we are "cut out for" are deeply rooted in the core of our being. I'm glad I am the one home caring for our daughter. I have learned quite a bit in the first year, and I'm sure that much more will become evident in those that follow.

The Up and the Downside

I anticipated this new role to be a wonderful opportunity to nurture and care for a dynamic, growing, changing, learning, little baby. But once our baby arrived, I was suddenly under a kind of house arrest and subject to the unpredictable demands of a needy human. This left me busy, but lacking mental stimulation. To balance out the intellectual deficit, I turned to the fountain of knowledge and nonsense that is the internet. And through connections forged there, I found community and opportunity that led me to a rather surprising place: very real knowledge of myself. I had often encountered advice along the lines of "know thyself" and "an unexamined life is not worth living," but I never realized that there were so many tools available to help a person do just that. These tools aid in looking into the ways and whys that a person leads his or her life; they can even help in discovering how a person's life has been leading him. The internet lays such tools at the feet of every self-searcher who has online access.

I had the access and the time. Thanks to the asynchronous nature of the internet, I'm freed from the times and schedules of the traditional educating institutions, and I'm able to attend when the time is available. Which, as anyone who is a stay-at-homer knows, is vital to getting things of import checked off the list. Use time when it is available. The internet also gives me access to information in many different forms. I can listen to audio while playing with the baby or scrubbing the floor; I can read a white paper or take an assessment when baby decides to nap. With this random free time and internet connectivity, I started to dig. Instead of feeling tied down to the house and needs of a child, I used technology to bring freedom to me. If you are at all like me, you may shy away from the "opportunity" offered by computers. I was a basic user, no whiz at all. I used the computer to check email, and that was about it. But I can say that finding a purpose such as learning about one's own self is a great motivator. I have learned more about computers in the last year, just because I was truly motivated, than I had learned in years of dabbling with it.

As an initial step, I took about ten personality assessments, though as few as three might serve a person, depending on what he is looking to learn about himself. The assessments allow self-knowledge to come into a person's frame of reference. They allow us to see, in a non-threatening way, how we tick and why we do some of the things that we do. Types of assessments abound: assessments that tell about our preferences, worldviews, learning styles, conflict modes, motives, traits, and typologies. These are all ways to dig into our hard-wired natures. Most are relatively simple tests that reveal, for our scrutiny, preferences and structures that drive us. As we identify them and make them objects of our scrutiny, we are more capable of operating on them or with them or at least not fighting against them. Some assessments are more easily accessible and understandable than others, but there are plenty available, depending on what you wish to learn about yourself.

Just the process of taking the assessments taught me something about myself, because I watched myself as I answered the questions. I learned much as I caught myself heading toward an answer that was less of what I truly am and truly do and more of what I wish I was and would like to do. That insight was just from the *process* of taking the assessments. It is as important to have a clear picture of your capabilities as it is to have a clear picture of what is required of you in your life.

Even more insights into my nature became clear as I studied the initial data that the assessments generated. They inspired a profoundly reflective frame of mind. I found myself watching and observing my behavior in daily life and comparing it to the results from the assessments. Sometimes I saw accuracy and sometimes incongruence. Often I traced back the incongruence and found that it was me that misled the assessment and not the assessment that failed. This observing also made space for a very natural righting of myself—a sort of innate accepting of how I am and why I do what I do. I could judge it with less concern and more dispassionate honesty and see myself with refreshing objectivity. And this was just the initial reading of the feedback. Many of these assessments offer extensive depth and nuanced information that can be studied and learned from as deeply as one wishes to dive. The results may be accessed in different ways. There are recordings that can be listened to online, that walk you through example data; there are papers that lead you through the results; there are even phone calls in which you can participate in order to get help working through the details.

Taking the time and spending the money to get to know myself has been a valuable investment. A realistic picture of my strengths and capabilities, as well as my weaknesses and needs, prepares me to play to my strengths and create systems that design around my weaknesses. As I compare my capabilities to the requirements in my day-to-day life, I have insight into where I can apply my energies to get the most leverage. And looking forward, piecing together what really drives and draws me will help me have a clearer picture and actionable plan for reentering the work world when our baby goes off to school.

As it becomes more and more clear to me what drives me from the inside, I am realizing how unaware I have been of the external forces put upon me. Examining the demands society places upon me in my new, unconventional role as a stay-at-home dad is the second wonderful opportunity now available to me.

My experience has shown me that raising a child can be a crucible to all the cultural assumptions I have, for the most part, so readily accepted. If you have an inquiring and critical mind, if you are the type who analyzes before making choices, then having a baby may cause you to question not just what rises up to meet you, but also the many things that are pushing you from behind.

Being a parent has allowed me to question and investigate the techniques and beliefs that were used and instilled when I was raised—everything from how children should be dressed, what they should be fed, or how to react to a baby's cry, as well as many deeper issues. It's a time to decide which traditions and customs I wish to adopt for my new family and pass on. It allows me to weigh more critically what cultural and religious beliefs I wish to make my own. Are the ones passed down by my family appropriate in meeting the needs of the three of us, or do I need to find new culture, different communities, different belief structures or forms of discipline and guidance? I'm at a crossroads: Do I carry on what I was taught? How do I add to what I have learned? These types of questions, when truly investigated, offer fertile ground for assessing belief structures and what undergirds them. Sometimes it's quite astounding to see how tenuously they are supported, how quickly they fall, or how surprisingly important they are to one's sense of self.

It is one thing to hold something to be true and important to oneself. It is often a wholly different matter to consciously transfer an aspect of meaning-making onto a trusting child.

As a stay-at-home dad, questions also arise about gender roles. We are a small but growing group, mostly because of the growing numbers of woman who choose to pass on the traditional role and pursue a career and the growing belief that children benefit from spending their early years home with a parent. Suitability for staying at home does not fall along gender lines. Some are more fit for it than others. How can a person be sure? Well, in our case, we had a clue I might be the one, but the questioning continues. Now that being at home is my reality, how do I feel about not bringing home the bacon and instead being the one who fries it up in the pan? I'm comfortable with it, though I meet and speak to people who are not. It's easier because we chose to live in a more liberal city, where gender roles are more flexible and stay-at-home dads are more common. Yet, I'm challenged every day.

Thankfully, all these issues are opportunities. I can move through them blindly or use them as leverage points to decide not just what really matters, but to investigate why something matters. Reflection offers the chance to generate stronger ties with that which matters and to let go of that which slows us down.

For an extra measure of strength, think of scenarios that would rock your world: financially, health-wise, in your relationships, or work-related. How can you prepare for shakeups in these fields? Use your time at home to increase your family's resilience. It's like taking vitamins or getting regular exercise: worth doing no matter what. Being prepared for something that doesn't occur is infinitely better than being unprepared for something that does occur. We are still stronger for having taken the action to be prepared. Knowing what strengths you have to rely on in tough times is a resource in itself. Knowing where your limitations lie allows you to design in systems to support that area if and when stressful times find you.

Learning what truly drives you from within is powerful knowledge. Satisfying intrinsic motivations offers a deeper happiness. Knowing yourself increases your ability to know what you truly need, instead of chasing after what you think you want or are conditioned to want. Knowing yourself also means knowing your limitations. Only by knowing them can you design them away.

The Author

As an itinerant traveler and uncommon laborer, Tim Condon spent two decades of his life struggling to not only understand the language and culture of the people around him, but to understand himself. Now, happily settled in Madison, Wisconsin, with a wife and small daughter, Tim's traveling days are over, but his journey of self-knowledge continues. Having studied a synthesis of Eastern spiritual and Western developmental teachings, Tim enjoys applying a wide range of explanations to the world around him. Despite being fanatically passionless, he participates regularly in discussions of how the world works and what makes people tick.

Chapter 7

Optimal Health: The Foundation of Your Professional Practice

by Phil Faris

What would happen to you and your business if you couldn't work six months or longer due to a health challenge? It happened to me, and what I learned changed my life forever. Let me tell you how.

It's said we don't appreciate things until we don't have them. This is especially true when it comes to our health. As a professional, any health challenge that lasts over an extended time can impact every aspect of your life. I know this only too well.

My Health Challenge

In 2001, I had sold a business and was in the process of starting up a consulting practice. My middle daughter was enrolled in a private, out-of-state school, and I was looking forward to my oldest daughter's upcoming wedding. Then it happened.

It was a pleasant Sunday afternoon, and I was scraping paint off the house. I was finishing up the last areas near the roof of the garage, and the ladder slipped out from under me. I crashed face first towards the ground. Instinctively, I used my hand to brace my fall and protect my face. My face was unharmed but both my wrists were fractured.

What followed was a period of rehabilitation and personal reassessment. For the next six months I would be unable to work, drive a car, or engage in my normal physical activities. I lost the few clients I had left, because I couldn't service them. My cash reserves were depleted within ninety days. Credit cards and savings accounts were used to keep myself and the family afloat. I had been self-employed for over twenty years and had prided myself on being self-sufficient. Now I was dependant on others just to make it through the day. Unfortunately, I had taken my health for granted, and I paid a price. I learned that having an extended health challenge didn't just impact me physically. It impacted me emotionally, socially, intellectually, financially, and spiritually. My world was turned upside down. I had always seen myself as a person who could fix anything. Now I couldn't even fix myself.

This may sound like a tale of woe, but it's not. The experience taught me about what I had that allowed me to survive and what I needed so that I would never be in the same situation again.

> *Adversity introduces a man to himself.*
>
> —Unknown

The Journey of Recovery

My journey of recovery became a journey of revelations and discovery. When the realization of the severity of my injuries set in, my thoughts became filled with anger and frustration. Although to others I kept a positive facade, inside I was filled with self-doubt and fear that my life had taken a permanent turn for the worse. Fortunately, this period of "poor me" was short-lived, because I started to become aware of *what was happening around me and for me, instead of only what had happened to me.* This simple change in perspective helped me focus on what was truly important.

Although I could never accurately express the gratitude I felt for what others did for me during the period, I can summarize the events that I was fortunate enough to experience.

- My wife cared for my every need, until I was able to get some use of my hands.

- The first three weeks I was home from the hospital, neighbors took turns making dinner for me and the family.

- When I started my therapy, family members and neighbors volunteered to drive me thirty minutes to the therapist's office, wait for an hour, and then drive me home. I had therapy three or four times a week.

- When my finances became dire, my sister and brother-in-law loaned us money.

- I received constant visits from family and friends, who encouraged and supported my personal recovery while bolstering my spirits.

- My daughters gave me strength because they believed me when I told them, "Everything will work out" and "I'll be fine." Their belief in me made it difficult for me to seriously entertain my own self-doubts. Knowing I was recovering for them, as well as for me, reinforced my commitment to a successful recovery.

At first my life revolved around just getting through the day and managing pain. Soon I began to focus on my rehabilitation. I started setting goals so that I could see progress each day. For instance, my initial goal was to move all my fingers. Next it was to touch my thumb to my index finger on the same hand. Eventually, my goal became touching my thumb to my pinky finger. As my rehab progressed I started setting longer-range goals around what I wanted to do *after* my recovery. This shift in focus seemed to allow me to become more aware of all the support I was getting from others. Because I was so focused on my goals and uplifted by those who were supporting me, I never had time to worry about the fact that I was out of work, out of money, and facing the possibility of being limited physically from the injuries.

When the swelling in my hands went down, I began working with an occupational therapist. Because therapy was the key to my recovery, I wasn't going to settle for anyone less than the best. Finding the right one wasn't easy. The first therapist was outstanding, but was so booked up, he could only see me twice a week, not the four times I needed. The second was nice, but her approach wasn't aggressive enough. Finally, the third therapist was available and felt comfortable pushing my therapy sessions to the max. I put my recovery in her hands, and I'm glad I did.

After a few months, I started getting some use of my hands. This enabled me to function somewhat independently. I could brush my teeth, feed myself, dial a phone, peck on the computer, and write (sort of) with my opposite hand. I took this newfound freedom to engage in activities that would nourish both my mind and body. To complement the therapy for my hands, I started walking every day. To stimulate myself mentally, I started doing research on the internet and taking tele-classes on coaching, personal development, and business.

With savings dwindling and my ability to function growing, I decided to relaunch my consulting business and started sending letters to prospective clients. Within several weeks my efforts paid off, and I had a prospective client who wanted a meeting. This success, however, presented a new dilemma, because with both hands in casts I still couldn't drive. Fortunately, fate stepped in, and a neighbor volunteered to give up half her day so she could chauffeur me to and from the meeting.

The call went well, and within a month I had my first client. By that time, I was able to drive, and I was beginning to get interest from other prospects. Finally, my financial fortunes were starting to look up. Having achieved some initial success gave me the confidence to switch from setting only survival goals for the business and my finances to ones that would inspire me.

Although my wrists and hands will never be the same, they recovered well beyond my doctor's expectations. I'm proud of the fact that I achieved several key goals that I set for myself during this period of recovery and realignment. I achieved two key physical goals by playing basketball and tennis within a year. Financially, I achieved the goals of having my consulting practice up and running within eighteen months and my financial ship righted in two years.

During this period of recovery I also discovered that my blood pressure was high, and so was my cholesterol. These conditions were attributable to both family history and lifestyle. Again, I was fortunate because without all the checkups from the accident, I probably wouldn't have discovered that I had these two silent killers knocking on my door.

Lessons Learned

They say experience is the best teacher. This is probably true. In many cases, however, the tuition is prohibitive! So my goal here is to share what I learned so that others may benefit without paying the price I paid.

> *Learning is not compulsory . . . neither is survival.*
> —W. Edwards Deming

I didn't plan on having an accident and not being able to work. Nobody does. That's the point. Life happens. I have since learned that I am not alone in not being prepared for such a challenge. According to the Council for Disability Awareness, three out of ten workers between the ages of twenty-five and sixty-five will experience an accident that will keep them out of work for three months or more. About one in seven can expect to be disabled for five years or more. They also state that although accidents and workplace injuries are a significant cause of disability, the primary causes are degenerative disease like cancer, heart disease, and diabetes. These diseases cause major limitations for twenty-five million Americans.

This dilemma isn't limited to the United States. John Robbins points out in his book *Healthy at 100*: "Throughout the industrialized world people are living longer, but get sick sooner. So the number of years they spend chronically ill is actually increasing at both ends." The Center for Disease Control and Prevention also says that 60 percent of all deaths worldwide are a result of chronic diseases.

What is most disconcerting about these numbers is the fact that as many as 50 percent of these diseases can be eliminated with changes in lifestyle.

The Resilience Factor

When events knock you off your path, I learned, it's your resilience that determines how fast and successfully you recover. From my studies on resilience, I learned, as Mike Jay points out (*www.uppingthedownside.com*), that my capacity to recover was determined to a large extent by where I had invested my attention and energies *before* the accident. For example:

- You can't save more money when there isn't any coming in.

- You can't get more physically fit if you've lost the ability to exercise.

- You can't ask for referrals if you don't have a client.

- You can't get interest on a savings account if you never make a deposit.

The key is to have reserves and a plan for the areas of your life that are vulnerable to disruption and unexpected events. For me, the areas where I had ample reserves (i.e., family and friends) helped me overcome challenges caused by not having enough in others (finances, transportation, etc.).

Throughout the ordeal I learned different ways to survive physically, emotionally, financially, mentally, socially, and spiritually. These processes taught me how to accept responsibility for what I could control and accept what I couldn't. Since I couldn't control the events happening around me, I trusted in my faith in God and in the kindness of others. Without both, it would have been easy for me to have "thrown in the towel" and persist in some version of "poor me."

Since the accident, I've gained a new perspective on my health and its impact on everything around me. I realized how fragile good health can be and how quickly reserves of cash, self-confidence, positive attitude, and energy can be depleted. I decided that I could no longer take my health for granted and committed myself to treating it as if my life depended upon it. To do this meant I needed to develop a different framework for looking at health and all that it entailed.

The Optimal Health Model

After considerable research, I started my model by borrowing a commonly used label, "optimal health." I then constructed my own working definition and model of it, because I needed a model that reflected the scope and depth that would ensure that the requisite resilience would be built in. Next, I developed a plan for achieving and sustaining optimal health. I wanted a plan that would provide the resources necessary for me to not just survive, but to thrive in years to come. Although still a work in progress, here is my model for developing an Optimal Health Plan. (For more details, visit: *www.antiagingoptimalhealth.com*.)

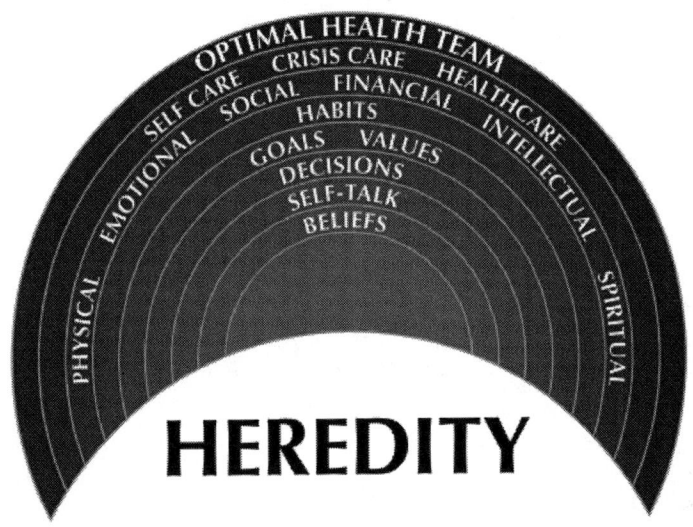

Following are the definitions for each of the components in the model:

Heredity. At the core of any plan is heredity. This is the blueprint that determines one's natural capacity and areas of strength, as well as areas that are more at risk.

Beliefs. Beliefs shape how a person views the world. My belief that I would recover fully gave me the perseverance to "hang in there" when giving up seemed like it might be an option.

Self-talk. We all have an inner dialog that focuses our attention and constantly fuels our view of the world and ourselves. By consciously listening to what and how I talked to myself, I was able to direct the dialog in a positive direction.

Decisions. What we say "yes" and "no" to is determined by the decisions we make. One of the most difficult, yet rewarding, decisions I made was to ask others for help.

Goals/Values. Our goals and values help clarify what is important and give direction to our decisions. Aligning our goals and values insures that our actions support our intention. Setting goals around things I value (playing sports) made it easier to do my physical therapy every day.

Habits. Habits are the repetitive actions we take to get things done. By being clear about my intentions, I was able to develop habits that directly supported my goals and values.

Six Domains of Optimal Health. I learned that optimal health is made up of six separate, yet interrelated, domains. Each one is important in its own right, yet susceptible to the influences of the other domains. The six domains are:

- **Physical.** This relates to how the body functions.

- **Emotional.** This relates to how we feel and respond to the world around us.

- **Mental.** This refers to how we engage and stimulate our mind.

- **Social.** This represents how we interact within the communities to which we belong.

- **Spiritual.** This is the personal domain of how we connect with the universe.

- **Financial.** This is the domain that reflects our ability to afford a certain level of health care.

I didn't find this last domain in other models of optimal health. The fact of life in the United States is that people's financial situation has a direct impact on their options in achieving optimal health. If my wife hadn't been working, and if I hadn't been covered by insurance, I would have lost everything I owned. According to the Council for Disability Awareness, 50 percent of all mortgage foreclosures are a result of disabilities, compared to 2 percent by death. In addition, half of the bankruptcies that affect 2 million Americans annually are caused by medical bills and other effects of illness. When I look at my physical health long-term, I now know that my financial health directly impacts the quality and number of health-care options available to me. If I want to live to be a healthy one hundred, I will need the financial support system to get me there. This doesn't mean I need to be wealthy to achieve optimal health. It means that my financial reality (including insurance) needs to be aligned with my optimal health goals.

The Three Optimal Health Strategies

- **Self-care.** What I must do myself to achieve and maintain my health.
- **Health Care.** What I do with my health-care providers to achieve and maintain my health.
- **Crisis Care.** What I do and the people I rely on in a health-care crisis.

Optimal Health-Care Team. These are the people and services you utilize to implement your Optimal Health Plan. As I came to understand, this team is not just doctors and nurses. The full team that helped me survive my health-care challenge included:

- my wife and children
- other family members
- neighbors and friends
- primary care physician
- orthopedic surgeon
- occupational therapist
- pharmacist

- insurance company
- accountant
- insurance agent
- personal trainer

Summary

If you're like me and want to live a long, healthy, happy, and productive life, I suggest that you leverage my experience and begin developing your own Optimal Health Plan. To help you to assess where you are right now, ask yourself these questions:

- How long do I plan to live?
- What is the quality of life that I want?
- To what extent is my current lifestyle and financial reality supporting my health goals?
- What changes do I need to make to achieve my life and health goals?

Your honest answers will show you a path to better health and happiness. The key to your success, however, is to start taking action now.

After all, isn't it time that you started treating your health as if your life depended upon it?

The Author

Phil Faris is an optimal health coach dedicated to helping Baby Boomers develop strategies for leading longer, healthier, and happier lives. He is the author of "Strategies and Tips for Optimal Health and Anti-Aging," "Take Command of Your Health," and numerous other articles on health, fitness, and anti-aging. Phil believes that people need to start treating their health as if their life depends on it . . . because it does. By adapting healthier lifestyle strategies, Baby Boomers can extend their life expectancy, while significantly improving the quality of their life. He feels that the journey created with aging is one that should be enjoyed and not endured.

If you should need help in developing your Optimal Health Plan, check out my website at *www.antiagingoptimalhealth.com* for resources.

Chapter 8

Reflections on a Personal Journey
by Lesley Parrott

Resilience. I feel I earned a PhD in it!

In 1986, our eleven-year-old daughter, Alison, was lured from our home in an idyllic neighborhood in Toronto. Two days later, her naked body was found in a secluded ravine. She had been brutally raped and murdered. Needless to say, my life started all over again from that point in time. I've been on an incredible journey taking me to the depths of the human experience. I've learned a lot and grown a lot. Now, more than twenty years later, I'm proud to often hear myself say, "I have not only survived, but thrived."

If anyone had told me this was possible, I would have taken them for the village idiot or the most insensitive and unknowing human being ever to set foot on this planet. Yet today, my marriage has survived, our beloved son is in no doubt about his own personal values and integrity, and my career has flourished.

Reflecting on my own resilience, I believe I was blessed by my childhood upbringing and my inherent personality. I was brought up in Scotland, a daughter of the manse. My father was a minister, and when I was a young child, we lived in a small seaside town. Later when I was a teenager, my family moved to inner-city Glasgow. The small town gave me my innocence and naïveté and the slums of Glasgow, in the sixties, my street smarts. Quite a useful combination.

My parents were always involved in the community and called upon to make a difference in the lives of others. They were extremely busy and, frankly, had neither the time nor interest to be overly involved or fussy parents. There was a lot of unconditional love, but not a lot of worry over our every move. Early on in life, therefore, I learned to fend for myself.

Given my own extraverted personality with a keen interest in people from an early age, I, too, became involved in reaching out to help others. As a youngster, I learned how to speak to people arriving at the manse door after a death in their family. I volunteered to teach cooking (another lifelong passion) to a bunch of brash and what could be described as underprivileged Glaswegian teenagers only a couple of years younger than me. And then, through their wild curiosity, I ended up giving them sex education lessons—I hasten to add, despite my own lack of experience on this topic!

I was fortunate that, in my formative years, I was well aware of the adversities faced by people in their lives, and also discovered in myself coping and social skills that became invaluable as I matured and had to deal with my own challenges. I often feel that parents today are so eager to be fully present and involved in their children's lives that they rob them of the ability to develop and build their own inner resources.

As I discovered, our individual and inherent personality, which is developed from a very early age, is a clue to how we deal with life's adversities. This became abundantly clear to me when tragedy struck. I needed to *talk*, and talk I did. My husband said to me very early on in this journey of grief, "it's not real to you unless you talk about it." He, being as strongly introverted as I am extroverted, couldn't imagine why every thought had to be processed out loud. Fortunately, it did not take losing Alison to discover that we dealt with life quite differently.

I had many patient and loving friends who became saints in the art of listening. They selflessly listened endlessly with empathy and without judgment. One of my big lessons was to accept that rather than helping others, for once I had to ask for, and accept, help and support.

As Alison's murder had a high profile in the Canadian media, there was a need and an opportunity to speak in a larger arena. The case remained unsolved for ten years, and then there was an arrest and, three years later, a conviction of first-degree murder.

During the ten-year period, I used my communication skills to keep the case in the public eye in order to help solve the crime. I also reached out to others through the media and talked about the process of grief and healing. I became deeply involved in the charitable organization Bereaved Families of Ontario, which offers self-help and mutual support to families who have lost a loved one. I also cofounded the street-proofing program Stay Alert . . . Stay Safe to help educate children and their families, in a positive way, on how to stay safe. Like many families that face tragedies, these actions helped relieve the feeling of powerlessness. Many people have a real need to help others and to do something to prevent similar tragedies. This is all part of the process to help make sense of the senseless—another building block on the road to resilience.

I have learned a few other things about resilience: how to develop it and what it can do for you. When you face adversity, you must allow yourself to fully acknowledge it and feel the impact of what has happened. Inevitably, there are feelings of pain so acute you often feel sick to the stomach, you shake, your heart aches, and you certainly weep. When this happens, be fully present and allow yourself to be with that pain. Rather than denying or distracting yourself from it, the more you can actually absorb it, the quicker it dissolves.

Deep and painful feelings have returned to me over the years and, frequently, intensely. Whenever I allow myself to acknowledge and take the time and create the space to feel the impact of this pain, the quicker the feelings dissipate and I am, once again, able to fully participate in life. This completely flies in the face of what I believed prior to my own journey through the minefield of deep and seemingly insurmountable grief. I, like many other well-intentioned people, believed that constructive distraction and always being positive were the best course of action. I have also learned not to indulge in "what ifs." I think most of us come sooner or later to the realization that today is all we have—not yesterday, not even tomorrow.

One of the hardest lessons to learn is to forgive others and to forgive ourselves. This is vital to letting go and moving forward. Ironically, by not forgiving those who have wronged us, we allow them to have a hold on us. This can be incapacitating and overwhelming. And the person who has the hold on you isn't even aware of your internal struggle! By setting them free you set yourself free. This does not mean condoning unacceptable behavior or diminishing its impact, significance, or as in my case, downright evilness. It is, however, an acknowledgement that you cannot change what has happened, and to wish healing for the perpetrator is also to wish healing for yourself. In other words, it is a desire to clear the way forward and involves the necessary step of letting go and wishing for healing for us all.

To forgive yourself can be the hardest part. Guilt and self-blaming come all too easily, often concealed in anger and a feeling of diminished self-esteem. Yet ultimately, to forgive yourself opens up your universe into a place of deep compassion, with the possibility of a life filled with true understanding and meaning of the very complexities and purpose of life itself. If you can arrive at this place, you have an incredible gift to offer others you meet along the way. By confronting and overcoming your greatest vulnerabilities, you are truly free to live life to the fullest, and to share that life with love, understanding, and compassion for others.

An optimistic nature has also been a key ingredient of my own resilience. I can attest that in the midst of incredible darkness, the very goodness of life kept peeking through: a touching gesture from a thoughtful friend, a spring flower, discovering a lovely painting, seeing a newborn baby, and even a smile from a stranger. I have learned to search for, and celebrate, the many small, everyday joys in life.

This brings me to the ultimate learning — *live fully in the present moment.* Seek out all the little moments of joy, beauty, and happiness in your life. I have. People often say to me, "Lesley, you are one of the happiest people I know." Little do they know my story, but I accept with grace and understanding that they are seeing me fully engaged, and I take that as a compliment of just how far I have come from the depths of despair.

Yet sometimes the way forward, regardless of our personality, our positive disposition, and our best intentions, does not seem clear and certainly is not easy. That's when you need faith in yourself and in life itself. You must trust that the uncertainty won't last, that the present situation will change and evolve, and by living in the present, you will always have a new perspective and new opportunities. By regularly checking in on and focusing on our resilience, we are also actually building that very capacity within ourselves.

I think the major hurdles in life return us to our core, whereas we can sometimes be totally derailed by an apparently lesser setback. The process is much the same whether it is a life-changing event or the minor irritations we face on a daily basis. Managing our working life with balance between who we are and who we are expected to be is a constant challenge. So here is my hard-earned "to-do" list for engaging the resilience within us all, whether it be in a personal or professional context:

- Know who you are and, if necessary, do some work to overcome your childhood obstacles.

- Understand your own personality and coping mechanisms and be ready to engage them.

- Reach out to others for help when adversity calls, and be ready to reach out to them when they need you.

- Acknowledge and allow yourself to absorb the impact of the occurrence, big or small.

- Forgive others and, more important, forgive yourself. This opens up a world of possibilities.

- Be optimistic, live in the present, and seek out the small joys presented to you every day.

- Hang in there when all seems bleak and remember the sun *will* rise tomorrow and with it another perspective.

The opportunity to live this life, with all its ups and downs, highs and lows, challenges and opportunities, is a great gift. To live only the upside is to experience half the journey. A profound understanding of the downside allows you to know what it is to be truly human.

The Author

Lesley Parrott is a facilitator, leader, humanitarian, and a friend to many. She is a renowned veteran of the Canadian advertising and communications industry, where she worked in senior leadership positions. Her beloved daughter, Alison, was murdered in 1986, and through learning to live with this loss, she has reached out to help others dealing with tragedy and loss. In her consultancy, Lesley brings together her corporate and personal experiences to help those in the corporate world communicate effectively. She's the recipient of many awards, including the prestigious Spiess lifetime achievement award and the YWCA Toronto Women of Distinction award for Communications and Community Service. See *www.lesleyparrot.ca*.

Backstory

I would like share with you how I came to write this essay. During these past twenty years, I've spoken publicly on many of the personal issues I've faced. I have also been featured in many articles and programs focusing on people dealing with loss and tragedy. The latest is a wonderful documentary film titled *Forgiveness—Stories for our Times*, which features four people, all of whom have dealt with violent personal loss, confronting and exploring forgiveness from their own perspective.

Through both my personal and professional experiences, I arrived at a point when I felt not only ready, but compelled to take my message of "surviving and thriving" into the realm of keynote speaking. I have a specific interest in reaching those in the corporate world, as I have had a successful career working in the private sector. I also have a real passion to help people cope with the many difficulties presented by their professional lives and the often unacknowledged or misunderstood challenges they face. My dilemma, and one I struggled with, was how to position and make relevant to business people the learning from my own overwhelmingly sad, personal story.

This is where Mari Smith and resilience came in. I had been chatting about the wonders of Facebook with Sandy McMullen, one of the other essayists, and discovered she, too, had recently joined the popular social-networking site. We immediately became Facebook friends, and on looking at her profile, I found she was a member of the Upping the Downside Group hosted by Mari Smith. Reflecting on the question posed by Mari on the site—"What does resilience mean to me?"—I realized this was the very topic on which I could communicate with relevance to those in the corporate environment. Once again, an example of how the universe unfolds. Thank you, Sandy and Mari, for bringing me to this place.

Chapter 9

Emotional Intelligence for Resilience: How to Know What You Really Want and Stay Focused on It

by William Murray

Two capabilities of emotional intelligence are clarity of intention and collaboration. Having clarity of intention and collaborating with others results in more energy and resourcefulness. And that means more resilience in the face of problems, change, and turbulence. Resilience means we can handle turbulence and bounce back.

To be resilient and resourceful, we need to ask ourselves in each new situation:

- What do I really want? Or,

- What matters?

- What is important?

- What values do I want to preserve in this situation?

Knowing our answers at a deep level gives us great energy to be resilient—to deal with life's setbacks. Usually our first answer is not the final word. We need to dig deeper.

Dig Deeper: A Story

For example, a woman in a workshop of mine on emotional intelligence said, "What I want is for my teenage daughter to clean up her room. It's horrible!"

I coached her to ponder what she really wanted. I said, "OK, then here is how you can get that wish to come true. Give your daughter all sorts of cleaning equipment, lock her in her room, and tell her she cannot come out until the room is clean."

The woman was shocked. "Oh, I couldn't do that."

"Why not?"

"Because she would hate me. She would be angry with me for months."

"OK," I replied, "then you must want something else in addition to a clean room. What is that?"

The woman pondered and said, "I also want to keep a good relationship with her."

"Well, then you could hire someone to clean the room," I replied.

"No, no. That won't do either."

"Why not?"

"Because I want her to learn to take responsibility for cleanliness. She needs to learn to do that before she leaves home in two years for college."

"Now you have dug deeper into what you really want," I summed up. "You want three things:

- a clean room,

- a good relationship with your daughter,

- your daughter to learn to take responsibility for cleanliness."

The woman grew excited, "Yes, yes, that's it!"

Emotional Intelligence

Emotional intelligence means that you know what you really want, at a deeper level than your first inclination. In this situation, for example, the woman really valued cleanliness and wanted her daughter to learn to share her value. You can see from her excitement that this process of digging deeper energized her. After that, she had more energy to craft strategies to get what she really wanted.

A simple strategy often will not get you what you really want. You must be resourceful. When you dig deeper, new alternatives will come to mind. *Knowing what you really want at a deeper level makes you more resourceful.*

Collaboration

One way to be resourceful is to ask the other person what they really want and help them to dig deeper. For example, the woman could ask her daughter what she really wants. Maybe the daughter needs a sense of independence and control over her environment. Meanwhile, if the daughter senses that her mother genuinely desires to meet not only her own needs but also those of her daughter, she will be more likely to join her mother in brainstorming for solutions—strategies to meet both of their needs. If the mother can create a sense that both of them are a team facing this problem of cleanliness, success is more likely. Your ultimate success in difficult situations will depend on whether you can keep both your needs and the other person's in mind and seek strategies that satisfy both of you.

Clarity of Intention

The principle here is that you have the most energy if you work in alignment with what you really want. Keep asking yourself what you really want and dig deeper in each situation. Then you will be energized and resourceful in finding strategies to get what you really want and in collaborating so that the other person gets what they want, too.

Knowing what you really want is a form of emotional intelligence needed to face changes, complexity, ambiguity, and turbulence in your workplace and in the world. In his book *Coach2 the Bottom Line*, Mike Jay asserts: "One of the most critical roles of a leader is centered in establishing clarity of intention." If you are a leader of your company, you must know what you really want. Then you can set goals accordingly and plan appropriate actions.

When turbulence blows you off course, you can correct your course by remembering what you really want. If you have clarity of intention, you have a sense of direction no matter what happens.

Mission Statement

Clarity of intention is important in both big-picture and small-picture views. The big picture is about your true values that guide your life. The small picture is about what you want in a given situation, such as the above example. Ideally, you should get clear about the big picture values so that they inform what you want in daily situations. A good way to get clear about the big picture is to write a personal mission statement.

I wrote my personal mission statement years ago, and it has kept me focused. I refer back to it to remind myself of my deeper values so that I express them in daily challenges. For example, a deep value in my personal mission statement is to help people develop professionally. Sometimes doing that may pull a person out of their comfort zone, and they may react negatively. Then I remind myself of my value and stay the course, but possibly with a different approach. This gives me a sense of integrity, which is another goal in my mission statement.

I noticed years ago that people don't seem to get around to writing their personal mission statement. Since then I have coached over one hundred people through writing their own personal mission statement. All have been energized by the process. Some have told me later on that they kept on referring to their personal mission statement and were able to stay focused on their major goals. They were performing better as a result.

Stephen Covey, in his book *The 7 Habits of Highly Effective People*, advocates strongly for writing a personal mission statement. I have twice attended long workshops sponsored by Covey Associates. The workshop leader asked us each time to raise our hand if we had written our personal mission statement. In each workshop, I was the only one who had written one. I was shocked. Covey's book gives so many good reasons for doing this. Why would someone sign up and pay for these workshops if they had not done this? The workshop leader guided us through writing our personal mission statement right then and there.

The personal mission statement is crucial for the big picture. I believe, however, that other forms of detailed planning are a matter of personal preference. Some people like more detailed goals and action steps planned out in advance. They make a plan and work the plan. Others prefer to stay flexible and react to needs in the moment. Either way may be more effective for a given person or in a certain work environment. Some work environments require a lot of planning. Others require fast shifting around. Some require both at different times.

Clarifying Process: Story of John and Bob

I have coached dozens of leaders and professionals through this process of clarifying what they really want, to have clarity of intention. Here is another example.

A client of mine, let's call him John, was angry that his colleague, Bob, kept bringing in a report late. John had to take numbers from Bob's report every Thursday and put them into a report that he gave to the president on Friday. The president used John's report to write a memo he sent out every Monday. Because Bob was late, John often had to work all Thursday night to get his report ready for the president. Being late with the president was not an option.

I asked John, "What have you done to date with Bob?"

John replied, "I keep telling him to get his blankety blank report in on time! He says OK, but a week or two later, he is back to being late."

Bill: "What do you really want here?"

John: "To get the report on time."

Bill: "Then why don't you complain to the president?"

John: "Because Bob and I work together on lots of other things, and I don't want to get him riled up and uncooperative."

Bill: "So, in addition to getting the report on time, you want to keep a good working relationship with Bob, right?"

John: "Yes, that's right. So I keep my frustration to myself."

Bill: "Is there anything else you really want?"

John: *Ponders.* "Yes, for Bob to take responsibility for himself and not make me have to keep reminding and pushing him. For him to value timeliness and teamwork, just as I do."

Bill: "OK, you have now named three things you want in this situation:

- the report on time,
- a good working relationship with Bob,
- for Bob to take responsibility."

Anything else?"

John: "No, that's it."

Bill: "In that case, you are in a better position to look for strategies that will get you what you really want. If you had settled for just number one, the report on time, your strategy would be flat, not good enough to get you two and three. Now call on your resourcefulness to craft a comprehensive strategy."

John: "Seems like a tall order. I don't have any great ideas."

Bill: "Want me to help? Two heads are better than one."

John: "Yes, indeed."

Bill: "What I recommend is to get Bob involved. You need to invite him to help solve this problem. I could assist you in setting this up and be present for your meeting with Bob. I think I can help you collaborate to come to a good outcome."

John: "Great idea. So you can kind of mediate this?"

Bill: "Exactly. I'll strive to have you each go for a win-win, to see what the other really wants and try for strategies that give you both what you really want. Can you do that? Ask what he really wants and keep that in mind, too?"

John: "Yes, I like collaboration. We are, after all, on the same team. These reports are important to both of us."

Bill: "Good. I think we can get a discussion in which you both see each other as on the same team in trying to solve a problem of timeliness. I expect that three heads are better than two. We should be able to increase our resourcefulness and find a good strategy that meets both your needs."

As a result of this discussion, these two were able to see together that an organizational problem was causing Bob to be late, not any personal problem of Bob's. Then they went to the correct person to solve that problem. A new computer system was developed that produced the needed information faster and satisfied both men's needs.

I have helped several clients through this process of clarifying what you really want and collaborating with others to get it.

Collaborative Process Summary

1. Know what you really want.

2. Dig deeper.

3. Ask the other person what they really want.

4. Collaborate with them to find strategies for you both to get what you want.

Having clarity of intention and collaborating with others results in more energy and resourcefulness. And that means more resilience in the face of problems.

Stay Focused on What You Really Want

Unfortunately, problems, stress, and turbulence sometimes get us upset so that we temporarily forget what we really want. Then we shift to some lesser goal instead. Therefore, we need to consider what to do when turbulence blows us off course and things do not go as planned.

In the above case, for example, what if Bob says to John, "I don't have time for any such meeting. I told you I would get that report in on time. So get off my back!" John might lose sight of what he really wants. He might shift to the goal of letting off steam to express his anger at Bob. He might fire a zinger at Bob, "You're not a team player. You are just out for yourself!" Later, John might regret what he said. Lack of impulse control has been cited as the number one problem leaders are coached to improve. So what would I coach John to do here?

Impulse Control

I might start with some facts about impulse control. We humans have a biological problem. For most of our species' existence, life was relatively simple. One of our most important challenges was to react very quickly to any threats of physical danger, in order to stay alive. We were and are equipped with a part of the brain called the amygdala that reacts very quickly to danger. In the past, if someone saw a tiger, the amygdala sprang into action, sending blood to the legs to run and the arms to fight.

The blood is taken from the brain. You see, the brain has done its job. It recognized danger. Now the limited supply of blood must be channeled to legs and arms. This is what gets us into trouble today—lack of blood in the brain at a crucial moment in a conversation. When someone says or does a dumb thing, we may say, "He lost his head." Right, the brain is not functioning well in many stressful situations because it lacks blood.

The fight-or-flight syndrome helped people when the crucial choice was simple. All someone had to do was spot something and determine if they should fight it or flee from it. Fast reactions saved their life. But today this same amygdala gets you into trouble in the office. It may save your life if you step off the curb in front of a truck. You see the truck, and your amygdala will take over and cause you to jump back onto the curb. No thinking is involved. Only reacting.

But in the office this fast reacting often spells trouble. It might spell trouble if John reacts without thinking to an unwelcome comment from Bob. Now what can we do about this reaction problem? When stress has made you reactive, here are some ways to recover yourself.

Recovery Process

1. Train yourself to notice your physical symptoms of being upset, such as: tense muscles, shallow breathing, heart racing, face flushed, making fists, perspiring, tightness in chest, etc. These sensations tell you that you are reacting, and it is time to get your focus back.

2. Calm yourself with techniques such as deep breathing and meditating.

3. Remember to ask yourself the question, "What do I really want?" This asking a question will make your brain come back into action, and more blood will flow into it so it can work on the question.

4. If necessary, take time out. Say you will come back later.

We have less resourcefulness when stress gets us off course, especially if the amygdala takes over at the wrong times. Try the above ways of staying focused on what you really want, and invent your own.

A Story of an Exccutive

Here is a true example of this recovery process. An executive I'll call Sam joined a company. After some months, he noticed that he was being left out of key meetings that he should be in. He wondered what had gone wrong. Sam asked for a meeting with four people who he hoped would tell him.

Sam was clear about what he really wanted from this meeting—feedback about what he had done to be left out of these meetings. He confided that he was concerned about being left out and asked for their frank feedback. Silence followed. Then one woman blurted out, "It's because you're a backstabber!" Sam reacted strongly. He almost got out of his chair to challenge the woman and set her straight. Then he noticed how hard he was gripping his chair arms. White knuckles showed.

He realized that he was upset and angry. He decided to calm himself down before he said anything. He breathed deeply several times. He pondered what to say as all eyes watched him. He remembered his initial goal of getting feedback and got focused back on that. Finally, he said, "I must have done something to make people believe that. Can you tell me what I did?" The woman calmly told him.

This executive noticed his plight—that he had forgotten what he really wanted. He relaxed and got refocused on his goal. Once he regained his focus, he was able to say something that got him what he really wanted, frank feedback.

Conclusion

Use your emotional intelligence to increase resilience by knowing what you really want and staying focused on it. As we have seen, this results in more energy and resourcefulness to solve problems. This works best if you involve other people in a collaborative approach to reach win-win goals.

The Author

William R. Murray is a Master Certified Coach and graduate of Corporate Coach University. He began as a line manager with bottom-line profit responsibility. Then in 1976, he began training and coaching managers in leadership and communication skills in JCPenney's corporate headquarters in New York City. Since then he has trained and coached business owners and leaders in companies ranging from large companies like IBM to family businesses. In 1993, William founded Eagle Alliance Executive Coaching. He also leads Tele-Workshops on emotional intelligence. He holds an MBA from Harvard University and an MDiv from Yale University.

To explore your own possibilities . . .

If you would like more information, please see my website (*www. eaglealliance.com*), and its Blog on Emotional Intelligence. I assist leaders, business owners, and professionals to improve their performance and results, as well as their resilience. Results include powerful leadership, better decisions, increased communication, and improved work relationships, all leading to more effectiveness at work and greater profits. To explore possibilities for getting these results, please contact me at 919-419-9460 or send an email through the website (from the home page, click on Contact Us).

Chapter 10

Consumeritis and the Resilient Earth

by Richard Freis and Harrison Sheppard

A Culture of "More"

The deliberate transformation of American culture into a consumer culture before all else began in the early 1900s, particularly following the First World War. Sigmund Freud's American nephew, Edward Bernays, invented a new profession that he named "public relations."[1] Its purpose was to adapt his uncle's discoveries into a method for convincing the public that buying an advertised product will lead them to happiness, because it will fulfill their deepest dreams. Figures for the consumption of goods and services with the correlated figures for consumer debt rise through the century and take off exponentially in the early 1980s.[2]

No message other than the consumer-dream-fulfillment message has ever been communicated to the public in such volume by any private or public institution, secular or religious. Young people today know no time when this message was not the main influence infusing—indeed, dominating—their consciousness.

We can measure how radical the change is by noticing that what was for millennia described as one of the seven deadly sins has now become a virtue. Here are some lines from a fourth century portrait of the thoughts and behaviors of a *monk* who is in the grips of avarice:

If someone gives something first to another who has nothing, the avaricious one is inflamed with burning rage. "I'm treated like a stranger." . . . He only wants, he feels, to supply his daily wants. . . . [H]e fans the fires of covetousness, while believing it will be extinguished *by possessing more and more. . . .* His God is now things. . . . [Yet t]he things he wants so desperately don't even exist because they are images in his mind.[3]

Why has this happened? Because, as the writer, Evagrius, says, there is a lack of fitness in the impulses that govern what he says "yes" to (*epithymia*) and what he says "no" to (*thymos*), a lack of fitness caused by and further causing deceptions in his thinking (*nous*).[4]

Today the principal voices of our culture say of the unfettered consumption of goods and services things like: It's good for the economy. It's healthy for us to care for ourselves by satisfying our desires; and besides, we need the best and most recent versions of things. Living in habitual and increasing debt is prudent—or at least not imprudent—because of our ability to secure easy credit.

From the earlier perspective, this sounds wholly paradoxical, and to the religious, blasphemous. It's as if to say: Being an unfettered consumer and run by the desire for more is the principled and prudent practice of greed. It is also the principled and prudent practice of instant gratification. The sense of non-sense in hearing these statements should alert us that something's going on here that we need to investigate.

What we now have culturally is a condition so familiar that we scarcely ever stand back and notice it; and so varied and pervasive in its manifestations that they are never looked at as springing from a single core. Harrison Sheppard and his coauthor, Alex Aris, have done this work in their movement-starting book, *Too Much for Our Own Good: The Consumeritis Epidemic and Good Movies,*5 which documents in detail the positions taken in this essay.

What they bring startlingly to our attention is that consumeritis is threatening the resilience for survival of humankind and the world.

Consumeritis and Its Effects

We'll begin by quoting the formal definition of *consumeritis* from *Too Much for Our Own Good* (with internal numbering added), and then we'll discuss it.

> Consumeritis is a species of excessive materialism, now a pathological condition of epidemic proportions, with which many Americans are actively or passively afflicted, and which is spreading to other countries. It is characterized by addiction to the purchase of consumer goods and services, (1) beyond what is needed to satisfy personal needs broadly understood, (2) often beyond the victims' financial means, and (3) commonly diverting victims' energies and resources from more fulfilling activities and pursuits of happiness.[6]

In medicine the word ending *itis* indicates an inflammation of the part of the body it is attached to, as tonsillitis is an inflammation of the tonsils or phlebitis an inflammation of the veins. *Consumeritis is an inflammation of the desire to consume.*

The comparison of our consumption of goods and services, and of the world's available resources, with a disease doesn't work in every way, but it brings some aspects of our present situation into sharp clarity.

Imagine that consumeritis is a meme-borne plague infecting the entire population of the United States. The demands this plague makes on the resources that support the genuine health of this country are ever greater, and the methods we use to try to diminish the feverish anxieties the plague brings with it exacerbate the inflammation rather than reducing it. In the grip of the epidemic we have lost the ability—and the energy of will—to see what *we* should say yes to and what we should say no to for our well-being.

Meanwhile, the evidence plainly reveals that the same plague is increasingly infecting other countries around the globe. Many of these populations have the desire and, increasingly, the ability to claim available resources at the level we do. Yet the world can only supply so many goods and services. And the population of the world, which reached six billion in 1999, is projected to reach seven billion in 2013 *and* 10 *billion by* 2030. This means that rapidly increasing demand is devouring decreasing resources around the globe at a pace that may lead to environmental breakdown and economic, social, and political system failures, including aggressive wars triggered by the scarcity of resources.

The effects of consumeritis are already degrading our own lives and the lives of our families, our nation, and the globe. Here are a few examples:

First, effects on the family: American children now see on average forty thousand commercial messages a year and as many as one million by the time they are twenty. The internet, where they are spending increasing amounts of time at early ages, is as laden as other media with commercial advertising aimed at children. The increase in childhood obesity has been shown to be directly and indirectly linked to consumeritis. Complications in overweight children include hypertension, type 2 diabetes, respiratory ailments, orthopedic problems, and sleep disturbances. The link between consumeritis and child and teen depression, impaired emotional growth, juvenile crime, and alcoholism is well documented. Financial pressures are the leading factor contributing to divorce. College and graduate students, whose education the United States needs if we wish to maintain our position in the increasingly knowledge-based and complex world society, are dropping out of college because they can't pay their credit-card debt.

And then, the environment: "The major cause of the continued deterioration of the global environment is the unsustainable pattern of consumption and production, particularly in industrialized nations," stated the United Nations Agenda 21 in 1992.[7]

Meanwhile, the nonrenewable resources on which our well-being and that of the rest of the world now depend are indeed being used with a wastefulness that might alarm Ebenezer Scrooge no less than Rachel Carson. It is as if we should saw off the limb we are standing on—without first making sure we have another limb to support us. Environmentalist Bill McKibben has written, "Fossil fuel was . . . a one-time gift that underwrote a one-time binge of growth."[8] Yet we treat it as if it were replaceable at will. Of the total U.S. work force, 78 percent—more than one hundred million people—commute to work daily *driving alone.*

Where are we heading? McKibben puts this in concrete terms, so we cannot miss the meaning:

> If we do try to keep going, with the entire world aiming
> for an economy structured like America's, it won't just

be oil that we'll run short of. Here are the numbers we have to contend with: Given current rates of growth in the Chinese economy, the 1.3 billion residents of that nation alone will, by 2031, be about as rich as we are. If they then eat meat, milk, and eggs at the rate that we do, calculates ecostatistician Lester Brown, they will consume 1,352 million tons of grain each year—equal to two-thirds of the world's entire 2004 grain harvest. They will use 99 million barrels of oil a day, 15 million more than the entire world consumes at present. They will use more steel than all the West combined, double the world's production of paper, and drive 1.1 billion cars—1.5 times as many as the current world total. *And that's just China; by then, India will have a bigger population, and its economy is growing almost as fast.* And then there's the rest of the world.[9] (emphasis added)

He adds, "Trying to meet that kind of demand will stress the earth past its breaking point in an almost endless number of ways.[10]" *We are approaching the limits of resilience.*

To be sure, there are rational bases for a degree of hope. In their recent book *Revolutionary Wealth*, for example, Alvin and Heidi Toffler elaborate pictures of what they call Second Wave, or industry- and product-based wealth, and Third Wave, or knowledge-based wealth. They describe how our historical moment stands with one foot in the first and one foot in the second, and hold out hope that solutions will emerge or may be emerging as we move further into the Third Wave.[11]

Again, Ray Kurzweil argues that despite our assumed intuitive view that technological change is linear, it is actually exponential; so the twenty-first century will bring us not one hundred years of progress but twenty thousand years of progress at today's rate. This law of accelerating returns points to *eucatastrophe*, if I may use a word coined by J.R.R. Tolkien, a culminating turn of events, as in the Christian last days or the Marxist end of history, which leads to universal good. Kurzweil names the turning point the Singularity, an acceleration of technological change so rapid and profound it will soon outpace our capacity to foresee it, understand it, and plan for its effects, yet through it intelligence will increasingly saturate the matter and energy of the universe.[12]

Here is a small example of the bearing of Kurzweil's law on our concerns: "The economic models used for the social security projections are entirely linear, i.e., they **. . .** assume a fixed rate of growth of 3.5 percent per year for the next fifty years!"[13] In the perspective of the law of accelerating returns, this way of arriving at a prediction is, as Kurzweil calls it, "ludicrous."

We will be in a better position to evaluate Kurzweil's arguments in a decade. However, his arguments are so decontextualized from the factors governing the full texture of individual and group human life that it is hard to grasp from them what impact the technological advances and their economic sequels might have across the whole human race. And if this is so, it is necessary to take seriously the imminence of global collapse made probable by so many indicators and urgently, in whatever ways we can, to shore up whatever strengthens a resilient life and a resilient world.

Recovering Resilience

There is another side to the comparison of consumeritis with a diseased state, for *to say that there is an unhealthy condition of consumption suggests there is a healthy condition of consumption from which it departs.* How, then, can we foster effective, efficient, and sustainable forms of right consumption for a resilient earth?

Discerning a need for resilience is not the close of a process. Once we are aware of the danger, it is time to act. At this point, as Dr. Don Beck, the codeveloper of Spiral Dynamics, points out: "There are no prizes for predicting the rain, only for building the ark."

The effective ark will be built by many hands constructing its many parts with many different and collaborative aims on personal and institutional-systematic levels.

To do this comprehensively would require us to create an Integral World Resilience Project. But it is not being done. It was encouraging to see writer and ethical futurist Jamais Cascio, in his blog "Open the Future," recently write about the greater appropriateness of the word "resilience" over "sustainability" for environmental discourse:

When applied directly to environmental strategies, resiliency may appear similar to sustainability in superficial ways. Both sustainability and resilience would encourage aggressive moves to greater energy efficiency, for example. The similarity of tactics belies a divergence of [strategic] intent, however; for sustainability the purpose is to reduce our impact to below a certain threshold, while for resilience, it's to increase the resources available to meet [uncertain] future problems.

"If we're to survive the twenty-first century," he concludes, "we need to be striving for environmental and civilizational resiliency."[14]

In the absence of a shared Integral World Resilience Project, each of us is bound to identify somewhat haphazardly the areas where we believe we can make a contribution to a resilient world.

Analyzing the responses to the publication of *Too Much for Our Own Good*, coauthor Harrison Sheppard, together with Richard Freis (see other chapters in this volume) and Mike Jay, found both that people acknowledged the diagnosis of consumeritis in a world of diminishing resources as true of themselves and a cause of fear on behalf of their children and grandchildren, and at the same time did not trust they would be able to sustain the transition from consumeritis to a resilient path of consumption.

Sheppard, Jay, and Freis therefore asked: How would we design an effective, efficient, and sustainable intervention to help human beings reach a resilient state of right consumption on the personal level?

Here are our assumptions about such a design. Some of them are readily adaptable to other areas that require change to a more resilient state. These are directing our further work.

1. Consumeritis, with its many shape-changing forms and its many tentacles stretching into multiple areas of life, is now among the most decisively dangerous memes on the planet.

2. If you want to reduce the dangers that arise from the overuse of limited resources and from the secondary, tertiary, and further consequences of this overuse, you amplify your leverage first when you lower your own resource consumption. You gain this result in two ways: directly by using fewer resources yourself and indirectly by your example of successfully and comfortably doing so. In Gandhi's famous phrasing of the need to walk our talk if we hope to be effective, "You must be the change you want to see in the world.

3. For a consumption-reduction program to be efficient, effective, and sustainable, it has to have a *personally customized design, rooted in your particular leading motives and strengths*, with *support as needed over time*.

This suggests the model for mapping and establishing a resilient path developed by developmental and integral thinker Mike Jay in his book CPR *for the Soul: Creating Personal Resilience by Design*. This model is scaleable, which means it can be used to develop a resilient path at any level, from a personal issue to a project to a lifetime to a transnational corporation to an issue that touches the entire planet. It is not possible to give a detailed account of the structure, rationale, and instrumentation of this process in a few paragraphs. Let us close, however, by referring to some of the key elements:

1. At whatever scale we are working, we begin by mapping the demand environment—what the project requires—and the available capability—what those carrying out the project bring as resources. The assessment used to carry out the mapping is a spiral-on-spiral instrument, developed by Mike Jay and based on the work of Claire Graves and the developers of Spiral Dynamics. It embraces eight levels of existence defined by increasing situational complexity and the complexity of thought needed to resolve the complex situation.

2. Where there is a gap between the personal resources each of us brings to a change process and the demand environment, it is probably *not* efficient, effective, or sustainable for us to try to make large-scale and elaborate changes in ourselves—in our own personal capabilities—to meet what is demanded. A resilient

design will add capability complementary to that which we bring, for example, by hiring and through other forms of collaboration.

3. Among the resources we bring to whatever we do are our strongest personal motivating desires as well as our knowledge of what we find motivationally neutral or even demotivating. For clarity about these questions, we use the Reiss Desire Profile and, if it appears helpful, a strengths assessment.

4. In supporting the process of reducing our resource use, we use a coach trained in the processes to help us design our customized resilient path and perhaps as an accountability person and trouble shooter in the event we need further help in making the design effective. A key to making the path resilient is to find a way to link reduced resource use with our strongest motivators, as well as with our greatest strengths.

5. As each of us comes to increasing awareness about what really satisfies our strongest motivating desires and engages our greatest strengths, we begin to recognize spontaneously what is truly rewarding to us, as opposed to the pseudo-desires for what we unthinkingly believe we want or need—namely, to indiscriminately consume more stuff—because of the confusing "noise" of advertising.

6. The cost of this intervention program must be made affordable for those at low as well as median and high income levels and use minimal resources.

These assumptions are guiding our present work in designing an efficient and effective intervention process to reduce our personal overconsumption of resources and thus to contribute to recovering a resilient earth.

The Authors

Richard Freis has been professor of classical studies, director of the innovative Heritage Program, and designer of the Leadership Seminars in the Humanities at Millsaps College. He has published widely as a scholar, poet, critic, and spiritual director. His pioneering work in developmental and integral frameworks has informed his work as a personal and organizational consultant for the last three decades. He holds a BA from St. John's College in Annapolis, Maryland; an MA and a PhD from the University of California, Berkeley; and a Master of Theological Studies from Spring Hill College. You may contact him at freissr@millsaps.edu.

Harrison Sheppard is a member of the California State Bar and is admitted to practice in federal District Court and the U.S. Supreme Court. After a twenty-two-year career as a U.S. government attorney and principal of an international visual arts agency, he founded Harrison Sheppard Law & Conflict Resolution in San Francisco in 1993, specializing in negotiation, business law, private trust administration, government regulation, and intellectual property. His writings have been widely published in the mass media and scholarly journals. Harrison received a BA from St. John's College in Annapolis, Maryland, and a JD from the University of California, San Francisco. His website addresses are http://voicesoflife.com and http://whatsrightwithlawyers.com.

Notes

1. For a remarkable account of Bernays' work and its influence, see Adam Curtis' four-part documentary for the BBC, *The Century of the Self*, particularly part one: "Happiness Machines." There is an illustrated account of Bernays' widely diverse projects and influence at the website of the Museum of Public Relations (www.prmuseum.com/bernays/bernays_1915). See also Larry Type, *The Father of Spin: Edward L. Bernays and the Birth of Public Relations* (New York: Owl Books, 2002).

2. See the figures and tables in Harrison Sheppard and Alex Aris, *Too Much for Our Own Good: The Consumeritis Epidemic and Good Movies* (San Francisco: Aristotle & Alexander Press, 2006): 307–16.

3. Mary Margaret Funk, *Thoughts Matter* (New York: Continuum, 1998): 57–59. For a complete version of the "thoughts," radically condensed by Funk, that express and further foster avarice and the other

eight deadly sins, see John Cassian, *The Monastic Institutes*, trans. Jerome Bertram (London: St. Austin Press, 1999). Cassian's Latin version was an elaboration of a Greek original by Evagrius (see n.4 below).

4. For Evagrius and the codification of the eight deadly sins, see: Bernard McGinn, *The Foundations of Mysticism: Origins to the Fifth Century* (New York: Crossroads, 1991): 144–157.

5. Purchase this book at: www.too-much-for-our-own-good.com.

6. Sheppard and Aris, xxiii.

7. Sheppard and Aris, 165

8. Bill McKibben, "Reversal of Fortune," *Mother Jones* (http://www.motherjones.com/news/feature/2007/03/reversal_of_fortune.html, March/April 2007): 1.

9. McKibben, "Reversal of Fortune," 1.

10. McKibben, "Reversal of Fortune," 1.

11. Alvin Toffler and Heidi Toffler, *Revolutionary Wealth* (New York: Knopf, 2006).

12. Ray Kurzweil, *The Singularity is Near: When Humans Transcend Biology* (New York: Viking, 2005).

13. Ray Kurzweil, "The Law of Accelerating Returns," section on "Software Price Performance Has Also Improved at an Exponential Rate" (http://www.kurzweilia.net/articles/art0134.html?printable=1).

14. http://www.openthefuture.com/2007/02/the-resilient-world.htm.

Chapter 11

What's It All About?
How Does Living Artfully Contribute to Your Professional Resilience?

by Sandy McMullen

Over the years of talking and working with artists, only a handful I've known rise to the level of making a living by doing the creative work they love. The level of success in the arts isn't necessarily directly related to skill, talent, or effort. There isn't one easily discernable path that people can take, and artists habitually struggle because the time required to make a living interferes with the time they get to spend practicing their craft. The stereotype of the "starving artist" is alive and well, and while I would never recommend the life of an artist to people concerned with ensuring resilience in their lives, there is something to be learned from looking at processes that artists use that foster resilience. Moreover, living artfully creates a rich and robust foundation that promotes resilient responses to a variety of interesting and challenging life conditions.

In this chapter I will explore what living artfully is all about and why it's worth investigating. I will also illustrate processes and behaviors that enhance resilient capacities based on real-life examples.

Masterpieces from every age and continent have inspired generations with their beauty and truth. These paintings show the full expression of the genius and spirit of the individual, and they not only inspire us in times of upheaval, but also motivate us to reach deeper or go further to step fully into our potential. What survives from any culture are artifacts and mark-making that afford us a window onto the people who lived in a particular place and time and a view of their reality. Accessing the quotient of the unknown is what makes us fully human and is one place where living artfully plays a role in our resilience. Why is that important? As human beings, we have a depth and range of possibility that goes beyond what is immediately apparent. That is not to say that all things are possible to all people. Rather, the question to ask is, "To what extent am I in tune with my gifts, talents, strengths, and passions and living life fully and with ease as a result of this attunement?"

Four Levels of Competence

To demonstrate different levels of attunement, here is a simple model adapted from the work of Dan Sullivan of Strategic Coach and Gay and Kathlyn Hendricks of the Hendricks Institute.

4	Artful living
3	Excellence
2	Competence
1	Incompetence

1. Incompetence

- Things that almost anyone can do better than you.

- Lack of skills, aptitudes, and interest in this area.

2. Competence

- Things that you can do fairly well but others can do just as well.

- Some learned skills but not in alignment with your preferences, desires, or key motivations.

3. **Excellence**

- Things that you can do better than most people.

- You get feedback that other people admire this ability in you.

- You get jobs given to you or requested of you because you do them so well, BUT they drain you.

- While you may have developed skills and agility in this area, it is not connected to your purpose.

4. **Artful Living**

- Fully utilizing your preferences, gifts, talents, and unique abilities.

- Doing what lines up with your intrinsic motivation, desires, interests, and passion.

- This is the zone where you forget about time. You are fully absorbed in a way that is effortless. You're in the "flow state."

- This is the skill or quality that nobody else brings to the table. If it were missing the organization and the people in your network would miss it.

Author, researcher, and international trainer L. Michael Hall refers to this as our "genius state": "This . . . state is at the same time so very special and yet so common. We were born for it and naturally experienced it as children when we would get so lost in experiences. This . . . captures our attention and fits with our highest values and intentions."[1] Living artfully involves the kind of total absorption that blocks fear. It is a place where we trust ourselves and the Universe. We are open and receptive and naturally adopt a "learner's mind." There is an integration of one's full being that has benefit for ourselves and those we come into contact with. Imagine the ease and flow if we designed our lives to spend most of our time and resources living artfully. Rather than investing our energy in trying to fix ourselves in areas where we are incompetent or even competent, we ought to be rigorous in saying *no*, delegating those functions for which we are inept to others or finding automated systems for them.

The larger challenge may occur in areas of excellence. People give special recognition for a job well done, not realizing that it may be an energy drain. Mary Stacey, for example, is artful at helping organizations realize their strategic aspirations; however, she can work as well in the trenches to align teams by facilitating learning.[132] She is so excellent at facilitating groups that she is in high demand, but energetically drained. When she stays focused at this third level of excellence, she is not working "in the zone" that is true to her intuitive, analytic abilities of being a thinking partner with senior leadership. As Mary so aptly puts it, "My excellence was killing me." Mary decided to collaborate with a gifted facilitator, and this symbiotic relationship has allowed them both to grow and flourish.

The Path to Artful Living

How can we distill what artful living means to us? Self-knowledge is key to the choices we make, the things we know to say YES to and those things we say a clear NO to. There are various ways that we gain self-knowledge, some of which are out of our control. Disruptions of various kinds can teach us things about ourselves, and we generally love stories of the heroic journey where people learn how to overcome obstacles such as illness, natural disasters, accidents, and other external misfortunes. Learning does not have to involve suffering, however. It can be intentional and self-directed. Five ways that we can begin to gain self-knowledge include: assessment tools, self-observation, self-directed investigation, requesting feedback, and of course, coaching.

Some particularly useful assessment tools are the Myers Briggs Type Indicator, which looks at our conscious preferences; the Reiss Desire Profile, a trait-based assessment that looks at our intrinsic motivation and can be used to predict behavior; and the Enneagram, a model of nine intrinsic motivational styles and resulting worldviews. There are many good assessment tools, but the key factor of value to me is the time and focus I invested to learn how to work with what I discovered about myself. This is where self-observation plays a valuable role. For instance, from the Reiss Desire Profile my results show a low score on Power. This has huge implications for someone running their own business, a prime example being the internal barriers to asking for business from potential clients or customers. Over time, as I noticed my reluctance to actively go out and ask for business, I also noticed my ease and natural ability in creating relationships and supporting others. This is part of who I am at my artful best, and so I incorporated this ability into the design for building my business by focusing on creating mutually beneficial cooperative endeavors with other professionals.

Actively seeking feedback is a hallmark of people who excel in their field. Associates or more experienced colleagues are generally willing to provide high-quality feedback if they are asked for their professional opinion. When you ask for feedback, take the time to find out what's below the surface. You may find some nuggets of insight that can anchor you in your work. One coaching client commented that I ask the questions that they are afraid to ask themselves. That kind of response gives me the courage to continue to ask the next hard question.

Finally, to identify the elements that contribute to artful living for you, investigate your path and explore how you got to where you are. What are the messages from your family of origin, your cultural heritage, your circle of friends, and your spouse? How are they impacting your decisions today? A prime example of these subtle messages occurs around our educational decisions. Do we feel pressure to get credentials, such as another degree? Is that a piece of the equation that will make the difference to our work?

Another interesting question to ask is, "What metaphors am I living by, and are they supporting my gifts and talents?" For example, some people "do battle," "make a killing," "launch a campaign," or use other war imagery in how they talk about their business. This has a different impact from the language of "flow," which inspires ease.

Questions that take us beyond our rehearsed scripts expand our self-knowledge. We thrive or stagnate according to the quality of questions we ask ourselves. We don't learn from our experiences, but from our reflections about our experiences. The better the quality of the questions we ask, the more resilient we become.

Cultivating Resilience

Resilience, by definition, relates to how well individuals and systems bounce back from disruptions to current conditions. These disruptions can knock people into a different reality, shifting their relationship to time, money, sense of security, even their sense of self. Certain practices can help an individual process disruptive change and make sense of where they are now in the landscape. Artistic practices, for example, include such things as sketching different perspectives, taking time to reflect and consider subject matter, and spending time replenishing the creative well by visiting galleries and other similar experiences that provide inspiration. Buddhist thought teaches that what we resist persists. Rather than being reactive and trying to fight or fix things in a knee-jerk fashion, engaging in artful experiences can allow us to stay in the new experience long enough to help us begin to process its new conditions. This isn't an endorsement of nonaction, but rather taking the pause required to be proactive rather than reactive. Life need not be a two-step of event and react, but rather can be a waltz of three steps. We get a better result when we take the pause to put our next "right step" into action.

Linda Lundstrom is an award-winning entrepreneur and Canadian fashion designer.[143] She is a true entrepreneur with a huge capacity, doing the work of ten people everyday. Linda is a hardy soul who has led her business back to robustness after a close skirmish with bankruptcy. She used this setback as a learning experience to improve her business and her life.

Linda is a highly creative artist using fabric and scissors as her medium. There is also artistry in how Linda runs her business. Brenda Zimmerman, author and scholar in complexity, has written about how Linda finds simple solutions on the other side of chaos to navigate her international manufacturing and retail enterprise through ever-changing reality. One thing that contributes to Linda's resilience is her daily swimming ritual. Her indoor "Swimex" is like a water treadmill in a personal-sized pool in a beautiful, spa-like setting with a vibrant, beautiful painting in her line of sight. Linda uses her time in the water to just BE—in a moving meditation. "I get my best ideas when I am in the water." The repetitive nature of stroke after stroke has a calming effect on the nervous system, triggering the relaxation response. It also creates the space required to integrate past and current events so that the end result is restorative. When we don't reflect on and integrate past experience, the lingering effects can build and become a mental, physical, and spiritual drain that robs us of whatever resilience we might have.

Integrating a swim into her hectic life is very intentional on Linda's part. It is not merely about building capacity to handle more stress. It is a way to create the necessary expanded space required for the creative process to occur. It is also a choice for a certain way of living that is integrated, artful, and connected to something larger than herself. Linda does not simply design and manufacture clothes; she gets out of bed every morning eager to help make women everywhere feel really good about themselves. The time in the water allows Linda to connect to the core of who she really is and always has been. The discipline to return to this connection fosters the resilience she needs to lead a business and in the fashion world, perilous at the best of times.

There are many ways to find this connection to self, and each of us can find our own unique approach. From one perspective, this is critical to an artist's work. On the other hand, some people cook or garden or putter with vintage cars as their way of slowing down and reconnecting with themselves. The question I invite you to ask yourself is, "Are you making time and space to simply BE?" or have you filled your time with frenetic busyness or with downtime that is merely numbing out, such as watching TV or surfing the internet?

As another example of artistic practices and their contribution to building resilient capacities, artists are a perfect example of the resilient motivational dynamic that is set up when people live according to their mental, spiritual, and psychological DNA. Motivation is intrinsic, so painters sketch, draw, and paint, and musicians, actors, and dancers rehearse over and over again. The work has a natural rhythm, and even when it is demanding, it is ultimately affirming and enlivening and not depleting. This discipline builds trust in their abilities. The magic of unconscious competence brings a total commitment on the part of the artist that refuses to allow tentative gestures. Immersed in the work, artists are generally focused and grounded. They learn to *see*, not just look—to notice angles, spatial relationships, intensity, to see what is actually there. In one sense they are intimately connected to what is REAL in paint, gesture, or tonality. Experienced artists trust that mistakes or unexpected events can be used as a catalyst to create something new. They also develop the clarity to know when a disruption is of a scale that a fresh direction is a better choice.

Resilience in Action

Leif Benner is a masterful goldsmith and designer making one-of-a-kind pieces for his discerning clients.[154] He is one of a handful of young designers and artists who have a strong client base and who approach their work in a way that integrates their gifts and talents with a successful business model. Three years after establishing his own studio in Toronto's newest arts center, the Historic Distillery District, Leif's studio space was brutally ransacked, destroying everything he had built in one devastating blow. Leif had a young family to support and from an outsider's perspective, he had a hard choice to make about his next step.

Leif is naturally resilient, a result of his self-proclaimed combination of bull-headedness and unrelenting optimism. To him he had no choice but to carry on. The work was integral to who he was, and no external event was going to be the arbiter, putting choices for his future out of his control. Leif has been manipulating materials in some creative endeavor all his life and, in particular, as a goldsmith, he has developed a refined sense of what he can control and what he cannot. He knows when to call it a day and when to trust his skill and capacity to stay the course.

In addition to this tangible, practical sense of awareness, Leif also has a bigger sense of purpose: He is more than a designer and goldsmith. As Leif explains, "I like people and making personal connections. The couples who come to me to design their engagement and wedding rings get attached, and I get the occasional invitation to the celebration. What it's all about for me is being part of that optimistic moment where people enter into that union."

As much as Leif's natural resilience helped him to start again, this alignment with his passion, talents, and larger purpose is what keeps him going. Leif turned things around, and in six months had recouped his losses and reestablished his business with systems and strategies to protect him in the future.

Conclusion

My final thoughts return to the phrase, "What's it all about?" When we open ourselves through self-knowledge and making choices to design our life to be true to who we are, it is amazing what naturally falls away and what opens up for us and for others. To quote Joseph Campbell: "When you follow your bliss, doors will open where you would not have thought there would be doors and where there wouldn't be a door for anyone else."

Living artfully is connected to purpose, and purpose is the core to motivation and resilience. Perhaps Friedrich Nietzsche said it best: "He who has a *why* to live for can bear with almost any *how*."

The Author

Sandy McMullen offers a unique combination of professional coaching expertise, hands-on business experience, and a strong reputation as a professional artist. She creates open and inviting environments that help clients maximize their performance and leadership capabilities, while staying connected with the energy and passion that come from their innate creativity. Sandy is a recipient of the 2006 Prism Award for Business Excellence through Leadership Coaching. She received training from the Coaches Training Institute and Business Coach certification through the International Consortium of Business. She is a Master Practitioner of Neurolinguistic Programming, accredited in the Myers-Briggs Type Indicator, the Emotional Competency 360 Inventory, and qualified in the Enneagram, a model of nine motivational styles.

Notes

1. http://www.self-actualizing.org/articles/maslow_on_genius_state.pdf.

2. I know Mary Stacey through her consulting company where I am an associate. See http://www.contextconsulting.com/associates.php.

3. Linda Lundstrom is a friend, a fellow traveler on the path of learning, growth, and development, and also has been a consulting client of mine. See http://www.lindalundstrom.com/

4. Leif Brenner is a colleague and neighbor in the artists complex where an art gallery is located in which I am a partner. See http://www.leifbenner.com.

Chapter 12

Key Tool for Understanding Personal Resiliency

by John H. Richards

This article is about a powerful model for understanding the structure of human behavior through introducing you to the Enneagram personality type system. The article is structured to provide you with an overview of the Enneagram system as well as assist you in identifying your own most probable Enneagram type (EnneaType).

Working with hundreds of people over the years, I have found that gaining an understanding of the motivational and behavioral aspects of your EnneaType is like being presented with a detailed manual or map of how you mentally operate yourself—including understanding what motivates or de-motivates your behavior.

Discovering a Tool for Developing Increased Resilience

Up to and including the present, I have been either the CEO or in a senior-level management position with more than a dozen companies, including management positions with The Readers Digest and Capitol Records, and president and CEO of a division of Ogilvy & Mather Advertising International. I have launched and owned six different enterprises, with one of these businesses reaching over $18 million in sales in less than six years. I am currently CEO of three businesses, including Horizon Business Systems Corporation, a business consulting and executive coaching company I launched in the 1980s.

In the early 1970s, I became deeply interested in human behavioral systems when doing est and several other Werner Erhard and Associates trainings. After the Erhard trainings, I became involved with Jim Newman and his PACE (Personal and Company Effectiveness) training and then with Paul Larsen's Summit Workshops. In the early eighties I was a senior JDL workshop leader with The John-David Learning Institute and also went through a dozen Neuro-Linguistic Programming (NLP) trainings out of which I received my NLP Practitioner, Master Practitioner, and NLP Provisional Trainer certifications.

> *The more clearly and specifically we have insight into ourselves, the more possible it is to let go of old debilitating patterns of behavior from the past.*
>
> —Don Richard Riso

In 1987, a friend invited me to a weekend training on the Enneagram personality typing system. The training was presented by Don Richard Riso, who had just published his first book on the Enneagram system titled *Personality Types*. Riso's introduction to the Enneagram system that weekend awoke something in me, and I became deeply motivated to learn more about this model of personality. It is my hope that this article will do the same for you.

As I continued to study and integrate the use of the Enneagram into my business consulting and coaching work, I have become more and more impressed with the uncanny accuracy of the Enneagram as a tool for identifying the structure of people's patterns of behavior. As a result of my studies and deep interest in the system, in 1993 I developed and published the Nine Keys EnneaType Assessment (9KETA), and in 1994 I presented the 9KETA Enneagram assessment at an international conference held at Stanford University. In 1997 The Nine Keys EnneaType assessment was validated at the University of Kentucky and the assessment instrument has gone on to distribution in three languages in the United States, Canada, Europe, Australia, and Asia.

The Enneagram personality model provides an effective platform for developing a better understanding of yourself, the structure of your personality, and your patterns of behavior, as well as those of the other people in your life. It is currently being used in dozens of fields, including business management, marketing, advertising, education, psychotherapy, consulting, coaching, entertainment, medicine, sales, and law. Thousands of organizations have found the Enneagram system useful including the Federal Reserve Bank (which was a client of mine), the Central Intelligence Agency, the Walt Disney Company, and IBM. In addition, the Enneagram is being heavily used for character development by fiction writers and movie screenwriters, as well as thousands of real estate agents in identifying buyer personalities, doctors and chiropractors in identifying patient personalities, and defense lawyers and prosecutors in their jury selection. In short, today you can find the Enneagram being used in almost every field imaginable.

> *The word "personality" comes from the Latin word "persona," which means "mask." Your personality is the face you wear in public and the image you prefer to have of yourself in private. It is a specific set of habitual attitudes and their resultant behaviors that influences your beliefs, opinions, and interactions with others.*
> *—Robert Tallon, business consultant*

The Question Is, Do We Have a Personality Or Does Our Personality Have Us?

The Enneagram personality typology model defines nine distinctly different personality styles or strategies for interacting with the world. It all got started for each of us when, early on in our lives, we made a nonconscious choice of how best to survive in our environment. As a result of our core decision, we took on the ontological structure of one of the Enneagram types to the exclusion of the other eight types.

It was as if, when our lives were just beginning, each of us was led to a rack that held nine very different costumes. And we were told that putting on any one of these nine different costumes would give us what we wanted and needed—such as getting love and nurturing by our parents or caretakers. So we each selected and put on one of the nine costumes, and then we totally forgot that we were not the costume.

As we took on the habitual structure of behavior patterns of our selected EnneaType, we each learned how to best use that structure of behaviors as a set of strategies to successfully survive in the world to the point where you are now reading this chapter.

The Enneagram is one of the most comprehensive models currently available for understanding human nature. This chapter will provide you with a basic understanding of this model of personality that, in turn, will help you in understanding yourself and others in ways that are both practical and profound.

> *Our behavior in the world is the perpetual revealing of ourselves. The observable patterns of a person's behavior tell us who they are.*
> —Paul Larsen, *Summit Workshops*

The great advantage of being able to identify your EnneaType is that you will gain a composite and highly accurate overview of your personal structure of dealing with the world around you. Developing a better understanding of what motivates your own and other people's behavior will allow you to recognize the being/doing/having that brings you happiness and to have greater resiliency when change inevitably occurs. The Enneagram is dynamic in that it not only identifies your EnneaType habitual behaviors, it will also allow you to see how you can change your behavioral patterns in ways that will greatly enrich your life and your relationships.

The remainder of this article is presented in two parts. Part One provides a set of short self-assessment surveys that, when completed, should provide a fairly accurate indication of your Enneagram personality type. Part Two is a short but highly descriptive outline of many of the aspects of each of the nine Enneagram types from which you can get further confirmation of your EnneaType.

In an appendix you will find three additional interesting correlations that I have produced: the individual EnneaTypes (1) relative to their Myers-Briggs Type Indicator (MBTI) preferences, (2) correlated with the four main Steven Reiss basic desires or motivational traits, and (3) as correlated with their Buckingham-Clifton Strengths designations.

More than forty books have been written and published in dozens of languages on the Enneagram, with six of these books coauthored by the most well-known authors on the system: Don Richard Riso and Russell Hudson. I highly recommend the Riso-Hudson books, as well as others I have listed in the appendix. I also invite you to visit the *Horizon9Keys. com* website where you will find a great deal more information on the individual EnneaTypes, as well as on the Enneagram in general.

PART ONE: EnneaType Assessment Survey

EnneaType Statement Group A

Score each statement:
5 = Strongly Agree; 4 = I Agree; 3 = Partially Agree/Disagree;
2 = I Disagree; 1 = Strongly Disagree

____ I see myself as being a strong, self-reliant, and resourceful person.

____ Most people would say that I get things done, no matter what the obstacles.

____ It's not my nature to be a follower, and I don't like taking orders and directions from people I don't respect.

____ If there is a lack of leadership with something I'm involved with, I'll tend to move toward taking the leadership position.

____ I tend to make fast decisions when I am faced with important situations and challenges.

____ I usually react with a show of self-confidence when I'm confronted with tough situations.

____ I'll do what's necessary to overcome the challenges I'm faced with.

_____ I tend to take action believing that I can handle whatever problems come up if something unforeseen should go wrong.

_____ I'm straightforward and direct in my communications, and I prefer people to be direct with me.

_____ I consider myself a realist and tend to tell it the way I see it.

_____ I'm willing to fight for what is important to me.

_____ When I get angry, I find it difficult not to show my anger. But it is usually a short burst that is over quickly, and then I'm ready to move on.

_____ If I had to choose, I would prefer that people respect me rather than like me.

_____ People need to prove that they're reliable before I'm willing to put a lot of trust in them.

_____ I'm usually able to persuade people with my show of confidence and the strength of my personality.

_____ **Total Group A Score**

EnneaType Statement Group B

Score each statement:
5 = Strongly Agree; 4 = I Agree; 3 = Partially Agree/Disagree;
2 = I Disagree; 1 = Strongly Disagree

_____ I think of myself as being special and unique.

_____ I have very good intuition and imagination, and I tend to be quite creative.

_____ It's very important to me that my life and work have meaning.

_____ I prefer my work to be stimulating to my creative nature and to support my sense of purpose and vision.

___ When my work does not allow me to express myself and my talents, I look for other ways to express my creativity.

___ I tend to make decisions based on what I'm experiencing and feeling internally, rather than on what is going on externally.

___ I think I'm much more sensitive and in touch with my emotions than most people.

___ I'm very idealistic about some things, and it is difficult for me to compromise my ideals.

___ I prefer working and doing things with people who understand me and appreciate my individuality and unique qualities.

___ I can be quite sensitive to other people's interactions and communications with me.

___ I tend to be much more productive when my creativity and feelings are respected.

___ My working style tends to be somewhat different than others, and it's important that I understand how I fit into a particular job or work group.

___ I tend to do my best when I'm given the freedom to authentically express my imagination and creativity.

___ There always seems to be something missing in my life and relationships.

___ It's easy for me to reveal my feelings and emotions.

___ **Total Group B Score**

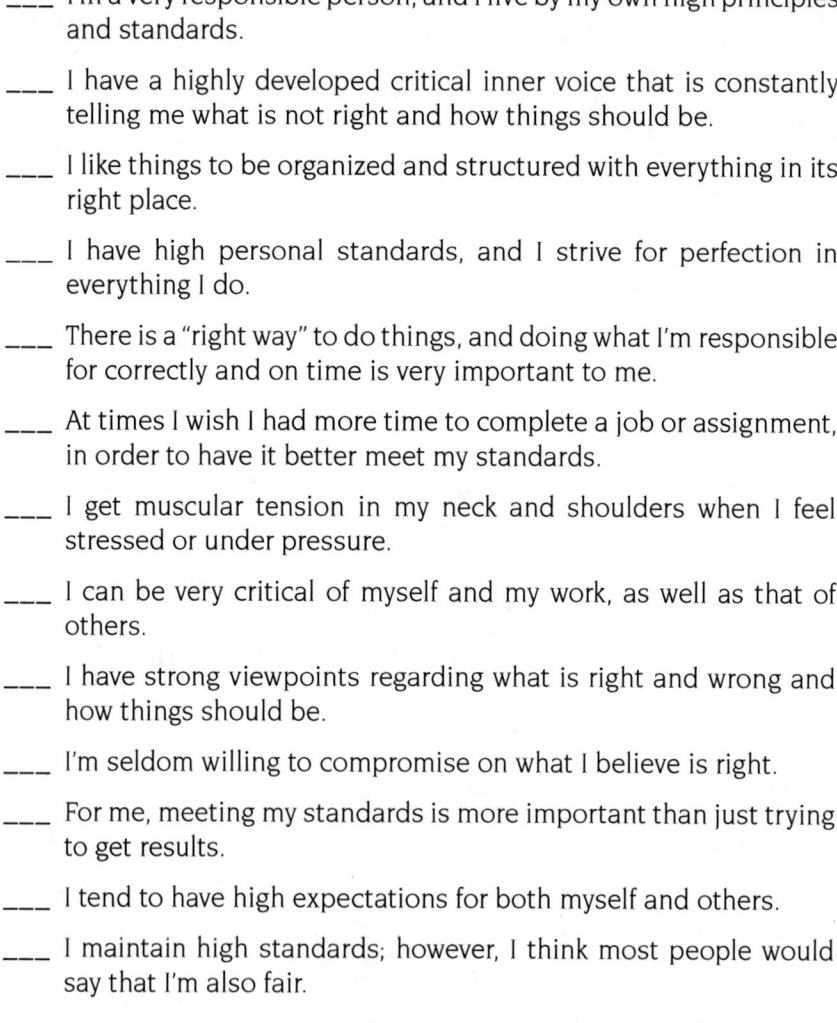

EnneaType Statement Group C

Score each statement:
5 = Strongly Agree; 4 = I Agree; 3 = Partially Agree/Disagree;
2 = I Disagree; 1 = Strongly Disagree

____ I'm a very responsible person, and I live by my own high principles and standards.

____ I have a highly developed critical inner voice that is constantly telling me what is not right and how things should be.

____ I like things to be organized and structured with everything in its right place.

____ I have high personal standards, and I strive for perfection in everything I do.

____ There is a "right way" to do things, and doing what I'm responsible for correctly and on time is very important to me.

____ At times I wish I had more time to complete a job or assignment, in order to have it better meet my standards.

____ I get muscular tension in my neck and shoulders when I feel stressed or under pressure.

____ I can be very critical of myself and my work, as well as that of others.

____ I have strong viewpoints regarding what is right and wrong and how things should be.

____ I'm seldom willing to compromise on what I believe is right.

____ For me, meeting my standards is more important than just trying to get results.

____ I tend to have high expectations for both myself and others.

____ I maintain high standards; however, I think most people would say that I'm also fair.

____ I'm fair and honest with others, and I will take a stand for what I believe to be ethical and right.

____ I expect myself and other people to act responsibly and fairly.

____ **Total C Group Score**

EnneaType Statement Group D

Score each statement:
5 = Strongly Agree; 4 = I Agree; 3 = Partially Agree/Disagree;
2 = I Disagree; 1 = Strongly Disagree

____ I enjoy the experiences I get from being able to do a lot of different things.

____ Having a lot of interesting experiences and enjoying life is very important to me.

____ I tend to like most people, and most people usually like me.

____ I totally agree with our country's founding fathers on what they said about our having "the right" to our personal freedom and the pursuit of happiness.

____ I like to do things that stimulate and motivate me and create enjoyable new experiences for myself.

____ I enjoy expanding my knowledge of many different things.

____ It's not difficult for me to be involved with several tasks or projects at the same time.

____ I have a highly active mind that quickly moves back and forth between different things.

____ I find it easy to become enthusiastic about new possibilities and projects.

____ I like the planning phase at the beginning of a project when there are lots of interesting options.

____ I don't enjoy having to do boring repetitive work or having to deal with a lot of details.

____ When I feel pressured or something is bothering me I tend to easily get distracted with something else that is more interesting.

____ I tend to work best in short spurts, rather than in single, long, focused periods of time.

____ If I'm in a leadership position I encourage others in my team or group to participate by making their own individual contributions.

____ I like to get the big picture of how things work together, and I enjoy being able to connect concepts that initially appear to be unrelated.

____ **Total Group D Score**

EnneaType Statement Group E

Score each statement:
5 = Strongly Agree; 4 = I Agree; 3 = Partially Agree/Disagree;
2 = I Disagree; 1 = Strongly Disagree

____ Stability in my personal relationships and financial security are very important for me.

____ I prefer predictability and stability in my life, and I can become stressed when things get unstable or there is a lot of change going on.

____ I'm a practical person, and I tend to rely on the tried and true.

____ I can be resistant to accepting unproven new ideas and unnecessary change.

____ Most people would say that I'm responsible in doing what is required of me to do my job.

___ I prefer to have clear rules and direction, and it's important that I know what is expected of me by those I consider to be in authority.

___ There are many times when I tend to be too overly cautious, and then there are other times that I'll proactively take something on just to get past my anxiety over it.

___ I tend to look to others I trust for input and advice when making important decisions; however, I don't like others making decisions for me.

___ Although most people would consider me to be dependable and hard working, I still tend to worry about the judgments of my performance.

___ I can be very loyal to a person or group once I have committed myself to them.

___ I tend to be very observant and to notice potential problems before most others do.

___ It can be difficult when people want a closer relationship as I tend to allow only a chosen few who have gained my trust to enter my personal realm of close friends.

___ When faced with what I consider to be a dangerous or difficult situation, I will either avoid it to protect myself or challenge the situation head on to get past it.

___ I prefer not to be the person in charge or in a position of authority over others.

___ If I'm put into a leadership position, I will try to foster an atmosphere where everyone feels that they're contributing to the overall outcome.

___ **Total Group E Score**

EnneaType Statement Group F

Score each statement:
5 = Strongly Agree; 4 = I Agree; 3 = Partially Agree/Disagree;
2 = I Disagree; 1 = Strongly Disagree

___ I'm a goal-oriented person, and I'm proud of my successes.

___ I feel most successful when I'm working toward, and moving toward, achieving the goals that I've set for myself.

___ My job, work, and career are the most important part of my life.

___ My accomplishments and achievements are a major part of how I view myself.

___ I know that I'm being successful largely based on what I'm accomplishing and the positive recognition that I'm receiving.

___ Being recognized and acknowledged for my successful accomplishments is very important to me.

___ I can be flexible with changing my attitude and strategies when it is necessary to achieving my goals.

___ Positive recognition from others is a strong motivator for me to strive to be the best at what I do.

___ I can influence and motivate others to help me in moving toward accomplishing the results I want to achieve.

___ Making a good impression on others is important to me, and I can be quite social and charming when I want to be.

___ I try to present the right image, and sometimes it's necessary for me to "sell" myself in order to achieve my desired outcome.

___ My ability to project an "I can do it" attitude has been one of my major assets.

___ I can be quite competitive; however, I can also be a good team player.

____ I work hard to achieve my goals, and I'm successful in almost everything I take on.

____ I always have more to do than will fit into the time available, and I often have to take time from my personal life to get things done.

____ **Total Group F Score**

EnneaType Statement Group G

Score each statement:
5 = Strongly Agree; 4 = I Agree; 3 = Partially Agree/Disagree;
2 = I Disagree; 1 = Strongly Disagree

____ I'm a people-oriented person, and I like to be helpful and supportive of others.

____ Feeling needed and appreciated and showing others that I care about them is very important to me.

____ Many times I can sense other people's needs without their telling me, even when I hardly know them.

____ My ability to assist others comes easily and naturally to me.

____ I have a tendency to consider the needs of others before my own.

____ I put a high priority on friendship and devote time to supporting my friends.

____ I tend to be more strongly people-oriented than goal-oriented.

____ I'm good at giving people my one-to-one attention and making them feel special by responding to their individual needs.

____ It makes me feel good when others acknowledge and appreciate my support and assistance.

____ Communicating with others is important to me, and I devote a lot of time to phone calls and email.

____ I tend to accept others easily at face value, and people generally tend to see me as being friendly and approachable.

____ People generally find it easy to reveal their personal thoughts and feelings to me—even those whom I have just met for the first time.

____ I'm usually sympathetic to what others tell me about themselves and their lives.

____ I see myself as being warmhearted and generous with others; however, sometimes people take advantage of my good-natured willingness to help.

____ When I'm a member of a team, I tend to focus on the needs of the team members.

____ **Total G Group Score**

EnneaType Statement Group H

Score each statement:
5 = Strongly Agree; 4 = I Agree; 3 = Partially Agree/Disagree;
2 = I Disagree; 1 = Strongly Disagree

____ I'm curious, analytical, and logical.

____ I consider myself to be an insightful and knowledgeable person.

____ I devote as much time as possible to expanding my expertise in the specialized areas that I am most interested in.

____ I can concentrate my attention for long periods of time without any need for involvement with others.

____ I can become highly focused when I'm mentally focused on something that I'm doing—sometimes so much so that I lose the sense that time is passing.

____ I tend to resist direct supervision of my work or unwanted demands on my time.

____ I'm usually highly perceptive and analytical of what is going on around me.

____ It has always been important for me to have my own private spot where I can spend time by myself to reflect and think about things.

____ I like to be able to see the big picture and to understand the structure and patterns of the situations that I'm involved in.

____ I value my privacy, and I need to have private time to myself to analyze and think about the significant issues in my life.

____ I require time to analyze and work things out clearly in my own mind before I'm comfortable communicating my thoughts or conclusions to others.

____ I do not enjoy networking and tend to avoid being involved with a lot of people contact.

____ I enjoy communicating with people who are objective and analytical in their thinking and who are good at expressing themselves clearly and intelligently.

____ In meetings and group situations, I usually prefer to be in the background and observe what is going on before getting directly involved.

____ It is important for me to have regular time to myself to review and sort things out and to reflect on what is going on in my life.

____ **Total Group H Score**

EnneaType Statement Group I

Score each statement:
5 = Strongly Agree; 4 = I Agree; 3 = Partially Agree/Disagree;
2 = I Disagree; 1 = Strongly Disagree

____ I think that most people would consider me to be an easygoing and nonconfrontational type of person.

___ I'm pretty undemanding and easy to get along with.

___ I try my best to maintain as much harmony as possible in my relationships and with the people I work and associate with.

___ I tend to avoid or minimize conflicts and tension in my life.

___ In general, I'm willing to just accept the way things are.

___ I consider myself to be a good listener, and I can appreciate and accept differences in other people's viewpoints.

___ I can usually see both sides of people's arguments in a situation.

___ It's okay with me if other people initiate things, and it' easy for me to go along with what others want to do.

___ I don't like to feel pressured and prefer to be able to work at a pace that is comfortable for me.

___ When I'm faced with multiple tasks to do, it can be difficult to decide which is more important.

___ I'll often see different alternatives as being equally desirable or to have equal priority.

___ I can easily be swayed over to other people's positions and priorities other than my own.

___ I tend to disregard little problems until they become big problems that I can no longer avoid.

___ I sometimes have difficulty taking a strong stand against opposition, even when I think I'm right.

___ If I feel that I'm being pushed into doing something when I'm not ready to do it yet, I can easily distract myself with doing something else to ease the pressure.

___ **Total Group I Score**

EnneaType Total Scores

Fill in your total score for each of the letters from the questionnaire above. The number associated with each letter corresponds with one of the nine EnneaTypes that are described below.

A-EIGHT ___   B-FOUR ___   C-ONE   ___

D-SEVEN ___   E-SIX   ___   F-THREE ___

G-TWO   ___   H-FIVE ___   I-NINE   ___

PART TWO: Some Descriptive Aspects of the Nine EnneaTypes

The Enneagram personality system clearly delineates that there truly are different strokes for nine different folks. Each of the nine EnneaTypes has a different set of worldviews, core inner drives, core motivations, and values. This means that each of the nine EnneaTypes has an entirely different structure for making meaning for every aspect of their relationships, communication, and operating behavior in the world.

In effect, each of the nine EnneaTypes is so ontologically different that it is almost as if we came to Earth from nine different planets. As a result, we are all continually trying to figure out how to relate in our work and our relationships to those people who have EnneaTypes that are different from our own.

Please read the descriptions of the three EnneaTypes that you gave the highest scores in Part One. As you do, circle any words or phrases that you highly identify with. Then note each of your three top EnneaTypes as number one for the type that you gave the highest score to, number two for type that you gave the second highest score to, and number three for the type that you gave the third highest score to. Below is some data on each of the nine EnneaTypes. In reading this descriptive information, pay particular attention to the three types you gave your highest scores to and note which of the three EnneaTypes you most identify with. Also see the appendix for a listing of books on the Enneagram that will give you a much deeper understanding of the Enneagram system, in general, and EnneaType(s) you most identify with in particular.

EnneaType ONE

I am a very responsible person, and I live by my own high principles and standards. I have a highly developed critical inner voice that is constantly telling me what is not right and how things should be. I like things to be organized and structured, with everything in the right place. I have high personal standards and I strive for perfection in everything I do. There is a "right way" to do things, and doing what I'm responsible for correctly and on time is important to me. At times I wish I had more time to complete a job or project to have it better meet my standards. I get muscular tension in my neck and shoulders when I feel stressed or under pressure. I can be very critical of myself and my work, as well as that of others. I have strong viewpoints regarding what is right and wrong and how things should be. I'm seldom willing to compromise on what I believe is right. For me, meeting my standards is more important than just trying to get results. I tend to have high expectations for both myself and others. Although I maintain high standards, I think most people would say that I am also fair. I am honest and straightforward with others, and I will take a stand for what I believe to be ethical and right. I expect myself and other people to act responsibly and fairly.

Worldview. I see imperfection everywhere. There is a right way, and I need to do what I can to correct and improve myself and the world.

Core Inner Drive. I strive for perfection and to make sure that things are correct and right.

Core Motivation. I move toward perfection in both myself and the world and away from being irresponsible.

Some ONE Key-Value Words. Appropriate, Authority, Completion, Conscientious, Consistent, Controlled, Correct, Correcting, Disciplined, Efficient, Ethical, Exacting, Honest, Improving, Inspecting, Integrity, Managing, Moral, Neat, Obligations, Objective, Orderly, Organized, Perfection, Planned, Principled, Quality Control, Reliable, Responsible, Rules, Self-Disciplined, Stable, Standards, Structure, Supervising

At *Their* Best. ONEs are at their best when they're completing or have completed a project or task and it meets THEIR standards.

ONE *Resiliency in Overcoming Obstacles, and How They Typically Respond to Change.* ONEs tend to be rigid and inflexible when faced with change, unless they're able to clearly see the change as being an improvement over the current situation. When they do see that a change will bring about improvement, they can become strong advocates for the new way. They can also be champions of change to overcome what they view as wrong situations. ONEs are the rulebook makers; it is as though their whole lives are a strict set of rules that tell them which direction is the right one to take. In most situations they tend toward pessimism. They expect problems to occur, and they're usually prepared to handle them when they do occur. They see obstacles as a normal part of life and verification of the imperfections in the world. In the face of obstacles, they tend to thrive on achieving what they think is right, and they solve problems and overcome obstacles logically. ONEs have the ability to make clear, logical decisions about the most appropriate action to take in a situation.

Type ONE *Exemplars.* Julie Andrews, Dr. Joyce Brothers, Jerry Brown, Cesar Chavez, Dick Cheney, Hillary Clinton, Harrison Ford, Jodie Foster, Rudy Giuliani, Katherine Hepburn, Dr. Jack Kevorkian, Aetolia Komani, John McCain, Ralph Nader, Leonard Nimoy and as Mr. Spock of Star Trek, Colin Powell, Vladimir Putin, Mit Romney, Donald Rumsfeld, Meryl Streep, Margaret Thatcher, Emma Thompson, Harry Truman

EnneaType TWO

I'm a people-oriented person, and I try to be helpful and supportive of others both at home and work. Feeling needed and appreciated and showing others that I care about them is important to me. Many times I can sense other people's needs without their telling me, even when I hardly know them. The ability to assist others comes easily and naturally to me.

I have a tendency to consider the needs of others before my own. I put a high priority on friendship and devote time to supporting my friends. I tend to be more strongly people-oriented than goal-oriented. I'm good at giving people my one-to-one attention and making them feel special by responding to their individual needs. It makes me feel good when others acknowledge and appreciate my support and assistance. Communicating with others is important to me, and I devote a lot of time to phone calls and email. I tend to easily accept others at face value, and people generally tend to see me as being friendly and approachable. People generally find it easy to reveal their personal thoughts and feelings to me—even those whom I have just met for the first time. I'm usually sympathetic to what others tell me about themselves and their lives. I see myself as being warmhearted and generous with others; however, sometimes people take advantage of my good-natured willingness to help. When I'm a member of a team, I tend to focus on the needs of the team members.

Worldview. People need and depend on my help and support; they can't do it without me.

Core Inner Drive. I want to assist and be supportive of others, and I need to be appreciated for my contributions to others.

Core Motivation. I move toward being connected to and appreciated by others and away from being physically or emotionally isolated.

Some TWO Key-Value Words. Assisting, Attentive, Caring, Compassionate, Considerate, Concerned, Dependable, Empathetic, Encouraging, Friendly, Generous, Giving, Helpful, Kind, Loving, Moral, Nurturing, Openhearted, Pleasing, Reassuring, Relating, Sharing, Supportive, Sympathetic, Thoughtful, Understanding, Warmhearted

At Their Best. TWOs are at their best when they're doing things for others and are being acknowledged and appreciated for their contribution.

TWO Resiliency in Overcoming Obstacles, and How They Typically Respond to Change. TWOs tend to be open and receptive and to view obstacles as opportunities to give help and support to others. When change is seen as an opportunity to be supportive of others they handle the change well. A major problem for TWOs is taking care of their own needs, as they tend to be able to see the needs of everyone else, but not their own. They have a sincere desire to help their friends, coworkers, and in their relationships and to be rescuers when problems arise. On the other hand, when personal conflicts arise they tend to have difficulty facing their own obstacles and making hard decisions. As problems are exacerbated, they may need to rely more and more on others to show them what to do. TWOs usually hesitate to ask for help, however, and often resent having to do so. They prefer that help be offered voluntarily.

Type TWO Exemplars. Alan Alda, Pat Boone, Barbara Bush, Glenn Close, Bill Cosby, Barbara de Angelis, John Denver, Sally Field, Kathie Lee Gifford, Andy Griffith, Melanie Griffith, Monica Lewinsky, Barry Manilow, Florence Nightingale, John Ritter, Mr. Rogers, Richard Simmons, Mother Teresa

EnneaType THREE

I'm a goal-oriented person, and I'm proud of my successes. I feel most successful when I'm working toward—and moving toward—achieving the goals that I've set for myself. My job, work, and career are the most important part of my life. My accomplishments and achievements are a major part of how I view myself. I know that I'm being successful largely based on what I'm accomplishing and the positive recognition that I'm receiving. Being recognized and acknowledged for my successful accomplishments is important to me. I can be flexible with changing my attitude and strategies when it is necessary to achieving my goals. Getting positive recognition from others is a strong motivator for me to strive to be the best at what I do. I'm able to influence and motivate others to help me move toward accomplishing the results I want to achieve. Making a good impression on others is important to me, and I can be quite social and charming when I want to. I try to present the right image, and sometimes it's necessary for me to "sell" myself in order to achieve my desired outcome. My ability to project an "I can do it" attitude has been one of my major assets. I can be quite competitive; however, I can also be a good team player. I work hard to achieve my goals, and I'm successful in almost everything I take on. I always have more to do than will fit into the time available, and I often have to take time from my personal life to get things done.

Worldview. Life is a competition, and I can win if I accomplish my goals and avoid failure.

Core Inner Drive. I strive to accomplish my goals and be seen as successful by others.

Core Motivation. I move toward being successful and accomplished and away from being mediocre or average.

Some THREE Key-Value Words. Accomplishing, Achievement, Acknowledgement, Admired, Ambitious, Awards, Career, Committed, Communicating, Delegating, Enthusiastic, Flexible, Goal-oriented, Good Image, Hardworking, Impressive, Marketing, Motivated, Organizing, Performance, Productive, Recognition, Self-assured, Self-starter, Successful, Winner

At Their Best. THREEs are at their best when they're accomplishing their goals and being acknowledged for their accomplishments.

THREE Resiliency in Overcoming Obstacles, and How They Typically Respond to Change. THREEs adapt well to change. They tend to be the most adaptable of all the nine types; they're able to change as fast as they see a new and better way to achieve their goals. They can be quite competitive and see obstacles to their success as challenges to be overcome as quickly as possible. They're doers and have a strong belief in themselves and their ability to achieve what they want. They tend to be pragmatic and always focused on end results. They will do whatever they need to do to solve problems, overcome obstacles, and avoid failure—or any appearance of failure. And they don't mind showcasing what they've accomplished against the odds.

Type THREE Exemplars. Tony Blair, Bill Clinton, Joan Crawford, Tom Cruise, Rebecca DeMornay, Werner Erhard, Michael Jordan, Mary Kay, Reba McEntire, Joe Montana, Demi Moore, Anna Nicole, Norman Vincent Peale, Summer Redstone, Tony Robbins, Arnold Schwarzenegger, Cybill Shepherd, O. J. Simpson, Sylvester Stallone, Brian Tracey, Jack Welch, Oprah Winfrey

EnneaType FOUR

I think of myself as being special and unique. I have good intuition and imagination, and I tend to be quite creative. It's very important to me that my life and work have meaning. I prefer my work to be stimulating to my creative nature and to support my sense of purpose and vision. When my work does not allow me to express myself and my talents, I look for other ways to express my creativity. I tend to make decisions based on what I'm experiencing and feeling internally, rather than on what is going on externally. I think I'm much more sensitive and in touch with my emotions than most people. I'm very idealistic about some things, and it is difficult for me to compromise my ideals. I prefer working and doing things with people who understand me and appreciate my individuality and unique qualities. I can be quite sensitive to other people's interactions and communications with me. I tend to be much more productive when my creativity and feelings are respected. My working style tends to be somewhat different than others, and it's important that I understand how I fit into a particular job or work group. I tend to do my best when I'm given the freedom to authentically express my imagination and creativity. There always seems to be something missing in my life and relationships. It's easy for me to reveal my feelings and emotions.

Worldview. Even with all my talent and authenticity, no matter what I do, there always still seems to be something missing.

Core Inner Drive. I strive to express my originality and to be appreciated for my uniqueness.

Core Motivation. I move toward being unique and special and away from being plain or typical.

Some FOUR Key-Value Words. Aesthetic, Artistic, Authentic, Beauty, Compassionate, Creative, Feelings, Depth, Dramatic, Emotions, Expressive, Idealistic, Imaginative, Individuality, Insightful, Inspired, Introspective, Intuitive, Melancholy, Original, Passionate, Poetic, Romantic, Self-expression, Sensitive, Special, Style, Unique, Vision, Warm

At Their Best. FOURs are at their best when they're able to express themselves and when others appreciate their uniqueness and make them feel special.

FOUR *Resiliency in Overcoming Obstacles, and How They Typically Respond to Change.* FOURs tend to respond to change depending on how they view it. They will welcome any change that allows them more freedom to express themselves, their uniqueness, and creativity. On the other hand, they can quite stubbornly oppose any change that they see as restrictive to their freedom to express themselves in their own way. FOURs tend to not fit well in structured or hierarchical working environments. They approach problem solving as a creative challenge and will usually find ways to solve the problem differently than anyone else has done before.

Type FOUR Exemplars. Ingmar Bergman, Marlon Brando, Prince Charles, Judy Collins, Robert De Niro, Bob Dylan, Michael Jackson, Janis Joplin, Jennifer Lopez, Madonna, Stevie Nicks, Nick Nolte, Prince, Anne Rice, Winona Ryder, Paul Simon, Elizabeth Taylor, James Taylor, Vincent Van Gogh, Alan Watts, Oscar Wilde, Tennessee Williams, Virginia Woolf, Neil Young

EnneaType FIVE

I'm a curious, analytical, and logical person. I consider myself to be an insightful and knowledgeable person. I devote as much time as possible to expanding my expertise in the specialized areas that I'm most interested in. I can concentrate my attention for long periods of time without any need for involvement with others. I can become highly focused when I'm concentrating on something that I'm doing—sometimes so much so that I lose the sense of time passing. I tend to resist direct supervision of my work or unwanted demands on my time. I'm usually highly perceptive and analytical of what is going on around me. It has always been important for me to have my own private spot where I can spend time by myself to reflect and think about things. I like to be able to see the big picture and to understand the structure and patterns of situations that I'm involved in. I value my privacy, and I need to have private time to myself to analyze and think about the significant issues in my life. I require time to analyze and work things out clearly in my own mind before I'm comfortable communicating my thoughts or conclusions to others. I do not enjoy networking and tend to avoid being involved with a lot of people contact. I enjoy communicating with people who are objective and analytical in their thinking and who are good at expressing themselves clearly and intelligently. In meetings and group situations, I usually prefer to be in the background and observe what is going on before getting directly involved. It's important for me to have regular time to myself to review and sort things out and to reflect on what is going on in my life.

Worldview. I'm a world unto myself, and I need to protect my privacy and resources from intruders.

Core Inner Drive. I strive to expand my knowledge and understanding of the world in general and my specific interests and/or expertise in particular.

Core Motivation. I move toward being autonomous and independent and away from being emotional or uncontrolled.

Some FIVE Key-Value Words. Analytical, Big Picture, Conceptual, Curious, Detached, Expert, Focused, Independent, Individualist, Insightful, Intellectual, Intelligent, Intuitive, Knowledgeable, Logical, Mental, Objective, Observant, Perceptive, Private, Profound, Research, Reserved, Self-sufficient, Specialized, Synthesizer, Theoretical, Thinking, Wise

At Their Best. FIVEs are at their best when they're privately involved researching or working on something that they're deeply interested in expanding their expertise on.

FIVE Resiliency in Overcoming Obstacles, and How They Typically Respond to Change. FIVEs are information gatherers and will want to research all the various aspects of a situation before making a change to their own environment. They pay little attention to standard operational policies and procedures; however, they work hard at building their own routines and procedures. Having their own processes and patterns both on and off the job allows FIVEs to be able to spend less time having to think about anything outside of what they're working on. In general, FIVEs are emotionally detached from what is going on around them and do not take problems and obstacles very seriously. They tend to address problems and obstacles to action by observing and analyzing them, but do not get emotionally affected by them. They will dissect the obstacle and handle things in digestible pieces, rather than tying to smash through barriers.

Type FIVE Exemplars. Isaac Asimov, the Buddha, Tim Burton, Agatha Christie, Michael Crichton, Albert Einstein, Bobby Fischer, Sigmund Freud, Bill Gates, J. Paul Getty, Al Gore, Stephen Hawking, Anthony Hopkins, Howard Hughes, Stephen King, John Lennon, George Lucas, Friedrich Nietzsche, Georgia O'Keefe, Jackie Onassis, Michelle Pfeiffer, Susan Sontag, Bob Woodward, the Uni-bomber

EnneaType SIX

I tend to be a practical person, relying on the tried and true. Stability in my personal relationships and financial security is important for me. I prefer predictability and stability in my life, and I can become stressed when things get unstable or there is a lot of change going on. I can be resistant to accepting unproven new ideas and unnecessary change. Most people would say that I'm responsible in doing what is required of me to do my job. I prefer to have clear rules and direction, and it's important that I know what is expected of me by those I consider to be in authority. There are many times when I tend to be overly cautious, and then there are other times when I'll proactively take something on just to get past my anxiety over it. I tend to look to others I trust for input and advice when making important decisions; however, I don't like others making decisions for me. Although most people would consider me to be dependable and hardworking, I still tend to worry about judgments of my performance. I can be very loyal to a person or group once I have committed myself to them. I tend to be highly observant and to notice potential problems before most others. It can be difficult when people want a closer relationship, as I tend to only allow a chosen few who have gained my trust to enter my personal realm of close friends. When faced with what I consider to be a dangerous or difficult situation, I will either avoid it to protect myself or challenge the situation head on to get past it. I prefer not to be the person in charge or in a position of authority over others. If I'm put into a leadership position, I will try to foster an atmosphere in which everyone feels that they're contributing to the overall outcome.

Worldview. The world is a dangerous place, and it is becoming ever more chaotic. Finding loyalty is difficult as everything is suspect.

Core Inner Drive. I strive for stability and security in my life.

Core motivation. I move toward being safe and secure and away from being vulnerable.

Some SIX Key-Value Words. Anxious, Careful, Cautious, Committed, Cooperative, Courageous, Dependable, Devoted, Dutiful, Faithful, Friendly, Hardworking, Heroic, Hesitant, Loyal, Practical, Pragmatic, Prepared, Prudent

At Their Best. SIXes are at their best when they're in an environment in which they can trust those around them and are feeling secure and appreciated—and also when they're proving that they're able to stand on their own.

SIX Resiliency in Overcoming Obstacles, and How They Typically Respond to Change. SIXes tend not accept and adapt well to change, as they prefer stability and the tried and true and prefer working under set rules and procedures. When changes are made that affect them, they're usually slow to adapt to the new changes. They tend to believe that everything will be much worse than they anticipated. Trust is a major issue for SIXes, and they tend to trust only people, policies, and procedures that they know and have found they can depend on. They habitually plan for worst-case scenarios and therefore are able to foresee potential problems and handle obstacles fairly well. It is rare for them to encounter an obstacle that they have not already anticipated and mentally planned for. Their habit of worrying all the time about what can go wrong prepares them for any unpredictable negative situations that might arise. When faced with a problem, however, they immediately begin looking for what else could go wrong.

Type SIX Exemplars. Woody Allen, Kim Bassinger, Albert Brooks, George Bush, Sr., Mia Farrow, Sally Field, Mel Gibson, Gene Hackman, J. Edgar Hoover, Tommy Lee Jones, Diane Keaton, Ted Kennedy, Jay Leno, Gordon Liddy, Penny Marshall, Marilyn Monroe, Bob Newhart, Richard

Nixon, Oliver North, Robert Redford, Julia Roberts, Meg Ryan, Stephen Wollinski

EnneaType SEVEN

I enjoy the experiences I get from being able to do a lot of different things. Having a lot of interesting experiences and enjoying my life is very important to me. I tend to like most people, and most people usually like me. I totally agree with our country's founding fathers about our having the right to personal freedom and the pursuit of happiness. I like to do things that stimulate and motivate me and create lots of enjoyable new experiences for myself. I enjoy expanding my knowledge of many different things. It is not difficult for me to be involved with several tasks or projects at the same time. I have a highly active mind that quickly moves back and forth between different things. I find it easy to become enthusiastic about new possibilities and projects. I like the planning phase at the beginning of a project when there are a lot of different interesting options to explore. I don't like having to do boring repetitive work or having to deal with a lot of details. When I feel pressured or something is bothering me, I tend to easily get distracted with something else that is more interesting. I tend to work best in short spurts, rather than in single, long, focused periods of time. If I'm in a leadership position, I encourage others in my team or group to participate by making their own individual contributions. I like to get the big picture of how things work together, and I enjoy being able to connect concepts that initially appear to be unrelated.

Worldview. The world is full of many interesting possibilities and opportunities for me to explore.

Core Inner Drive. I explore as many interesting and enjoyable experiences as possible.

Core Motivation. I move toward interesting and exciting experiences and away from being tied down or bored.

Some SEVEN Key-Value Words. Carefree, Curious, Enjoyment, Entertaining, Enthusiastic, Excitement, Experiencing, Extroverted, Flexible, Free, Fun-loving, Happy, Imaginative, Independent, Innovative, Inspiring,

Lighthearted, Likable, Networking, Optimistic, Options, Playful, Pleasure, Positive, Possibilities, Proactive, Spontaneous, Upbeat

At Their Best. SEVENs are at their best when they're feeling free of pressure and are enjoying experiencing things that stimulate them.

SEVEN Resiliency in Overcoming Obstacles, and How They Typically Respond to Change. SEVENs tend to be the most flexible of the nine EnneaTypes, and because they're constantly on the lookout for new possibilities, they're able to see creative options unseen by others. They're masterful change agents and see change as inevitable, positive, and necessary in whatever enterprise they're engaged in. When they're faced with unexpected change or problems, their optimism gives them the ability to shift from the negative to the positive and remain resilient in overcoming obstacles. Their quick and agile minds assist them in finding their way around obstacles—they will find options and possibilities that others are unable to see.

Type SEVEN Exemplars. John Belushi, Richard Branson, Mel Brooks, Carol Burnett, Michael Caine, Jim Cary, Chevy Chase, Joan Collins, Ram Dass, Malcom Forbes, George Foreman, Michael J. Fox, Cary Grant, Tom Hanks, Goldie Hawn, Hugh Hefner, Bob Hope, Magic Johnson, Michael Keaton, President John F. Kennedy, Larry King, Eddie Murphy, Jack Nicholson, Linda Ronstadt, Steven Spielberg, Howard Stern, Lily Tomlin, Robin Williams, Robert Anton Wilson, Shelly Winters

EnneaType EIGHT

I'm a strong, self-reliant, and resourceful person. Most people would say that I get things done, no matter what the obstacles. It's not my nature to be a follower, and I don't like taking orders and directions from people I don't respect. If there is a lack of leadership with something I'm involved with, I'll tend to move toward taking the leadership position. I tend to make fast decisions when I am faced with important situations and challenges. I usually react with a show of self-confidence when I'm confronted with tough situations. I'll do what's necessary to overcome the challenges I'm faced with. I tend to take action, believing that I can handle whatever problems come up if something unforeseen should go wrong. I'm straightforward and direct in my communications, and I prefer people to be direct with me. I consider myself a realist and tend to tell it the way I see it. I'm willing to fight for what is important to me. When I get angry, I find it difficult not to show my anger; but it is usually a short burst that is over quickly, and then I'm ready to move on. If I had to choose, I would prefer that people respect me, rather than like me. People need to prove that they're reliable before I'm willing to put a lot of trust in them. I'm usually able to persuade people with my show of confidence and the strength of my personality.

Worldview. It's a jungle out there, and I need to be strong, proactive, and resilient to protect my territory and possessions.

Core Inner Drive. I have to be a self-reliant and a take-charge leader who is in control of things.

Key Motivation. I move toward being strong, independent, and in control and away from being vulnerable or dependent on others.

Some EIGHT Key-Value Words. Action, Aggressive, Assertive, Authoritative, Challenge, Champion, Command, Confront, Control, Courageous, Determined, Direct, Expansive, Extroverted, Fairness, Independent, Invincible, Justice, Leader, Negotiator, Power, Powerful, Protective, Respect, Risk Taker, Self-confident, Self-directed, Self-reliant, Strength, Strong, Take Charge

At Their Best. EIGHTs are at their best when they're being courageous, overcoming challenges, and feeling in control.

EIGHT *Resiliency in Overcoming Obstacles, and How They Typically Respond to Change.* EIGHTs tend to be highly effective in creating and initiating change, provided they're the initiators, as it tends to strengthen their sense of control. They do not, however, respond well to change that is forced on them without their consent. EIGHTs expect that there will be obstacles and their motto is: "When the going gets tough, the tough get going." They take pride in their ability to overcome obstacles; they tend to be the most hardy and resilient of all the EnneaTypes, and they enjoy proving that they can handle whatever is thrown at them. EIGHTs believe in allowing people to make mistakes and that you have to make mistakes in order to make progress. Their modus operandi is "ready–fire–aim"; they're proactive in taking charge and getting things handled when problems arise, believing that if something happens to get screwed up along the way, they can figure out how to clean it up later.

Type EIGHT Exemplars. Margaret Albright, Lucille Ball, Al Capone, Johnny Cash, Fidel Castro, Sean Connery, James Dean, Kirk Douglas, Dr. Phil, the Godfather, G. I. Gurdjieff, Leona Helmsley, Ernest Hemmingway, Charlton Heston, Saddam Hussein, John Huston Mike Jay, President Lyndon Johnson, Rush Limbaugh, Golda Meir, Bette Midler, Aristotle Onassis, George Patton, Sean Penn, Janet Reno, Telly Savalas, George C. Scott, Frank Sinatra, Joseph Stalin, Barbara Streisand, Donald Trump, Darth Vader, John Wayne, Mike Wallace, Barbara Walters

EnneaType NINE

I think most people consider me to be an easygoing and non-confrontational type of person. I'm pretty undemanding and easy to get along with. I try my best to maintain as much harmony as possible in my relationships and with the people I work and associate with. I tend to avoid or minimize conflicts and tension in my life. In general, I'm willing to just accept the way things are. I consider myself to be a good listener, and I can appreciate and accept differences in other people's viewpoints. I can usually see both sides of people's arguments in a situation. It's okay with me if other people initiate things, and it's easy for me to go along with what others want to do. I don't like to feel pressured and prefer to be able to work at a pace that is comfortable for me. When I'm faced with multiple tasks to do, it can be difficult to decide which is more important. I'll often see different alternatives as being equally desirable or to have equal priority. I can easily be swayed over to other people's positions and priorities rather than my own. I tend to disregard little problems until they become big problems that I can no longer avoid. I sometimes have difficulty taking a strong stand against opposition, even when I think I'm right. If I feel that I'm being pushed into doing something when I'm not ready to do it yet, I can easily distract myself with doing something else to ease the pressure.

Worldview. Everything will work out as long as I stay in the background, go with the flow, and don't make waves.

Core Inner Drive. I strive to have peace and harmony in my life.

Key Motivation. I move toward having peace and harmony in my relations and away from being confrontational or in conflict with others.

Some NINE Key-Value Words. Accepting, Accommodating, Agreeable, Amiable, Calm, Cheerful, Content, Diplomatic, Easygoing, Fair, Friendly, Gentle, Harmonious, Humble, Laid Back, Mediator, Nonjudgmental, Patient, Peaceful, Peace Loving, Receptive, Relaxed, Selfless, Soothing, Trusting, Undemanding, Understanding, Warm.

At Their Best. NINEs are at their best when everything is going smoothly and there are no conflicts or problems.

NINE Resiliency in Overcoming Obstacles, and How They Typically Respond to Change. NINEs tend to be the least prepared of the EnneaTypes for handling change and overcoming any obstacles they're faced with. They have a fundamental belief that things will work out for the best in the long run. They tend to go with the flow, focusing on the positive and accepting any obstacles that come along as a necessary part of life. They don't tend to take things too seriously, and with their optimistic nature they either handle things or put them off to a later date, when they may or may not handle them. Over time NINEs create an environment that is comfortable for them; and they will drag their feet and passively resist any change or disruption to the comfortable life style they've become accustomed to. It is difficult for them to have to change and learn something new and different from what they're used to.

Type NINE Exemplars. Loni Anderson, President Jimmy Carter, Rosalynn Carter, Julia Child, Gary Cooper, Kevin Costner, Bing Crosby, Jeff Daniels, Doris Day, Walt Disney, Dwight Eisenhower, Peter Falk, Henry Fonda, Gerald Ford, Buckminster Fuller, James Garner, Whoopi Goldberg, John Goodman, Woody Harrelson, Michael J. Pollard, Dan Quayle, Ronald Reagan, Keanu Reeves, Roy Rogers, Marge Simpson, Jimmy Stewart

The Author

John Richards is founder and president of Horizon Business Systems Corporation and its operating division, Musicom Communications. Under HBSC he provides executive coaching services, and Musicom Communications is a respected leader in the development and production of corporate-employee, audio-communications programs. John is also founder and executive director of Nine Keys International, which provides personal-development trainings and publishes educational and training materials, mostly related to personality typography systems. He has been president and CEO of nine companies, five of which he founded. He has also held executive management positions with The Reader's Digest, Capitol Records, Ogilvy & Mather International, and Republic Corporation. John is a certified Master Practitioner and Provisional Trainer in NLP. John is the author of more than a dozen articles on the Enneagram typology system and author or coauthor of five books.

Appendix A

Correlations with Other Assessment Tools and Bibliography

by John Richards

EnneaType with Predominant Myers-Briggs Type Indicator (MBTI) Preferences[1]

ONE: Tend to be predominantly **Introverts**, mostly **T** and always **J**
TWO: Tend to be predominantly **Extroverts** and almost always **F**
THREE: Tend to be predominantly **Extroverts** and mostly **S**
FOUR: Tend to be mostly **Introverts** and predominantly **NF**
FIVE: Tend to be mostly **Introverts**, mostly **N** and always **T**
SIX: Tend to be predominantly **Introverts** and mostly **SJ**
SEVEN: Tend to be predominantly **Extroverts** and mostly **P**
EIGHT: Tend to be mostly **Extroverts** and **TJ**
NINE: Tend to be mostly **Introverts** and **FP**

EnneaType with main Steven Reiss Basic Desires (motivational traits)[2]

ONE: Idealism, Order, Honor, Power
TWO: Acceptance, Family, Social Contact, Status
THREE: Status, Power, Acceptance, Vengeance
FOUR: Independence, Status, Acceptance
FIVE: Curiosity, Independence, Saving, Order
SIX: Order, Tranquility, Honor, Acceptance
SEVEN: Independence, Curiosity, Social Contact, Saving
EIGHT: Power, Independence, Vengeance, Curiosity

NINE: Tranquility, Saving, Acceptance, Honor

EnneaType with Marcus Buckingham-Donald Clifton Strengths Designations[3]

ONE: Belief, Discipline, Responsibility, Analytical
TWO: Woo, Includer, Consistency, Developer, Harmony
THREE: Achiever, Maximizer, Focus, Adaptability, Arranger, Competition
FOUR: Significance, Empathy, Relator, Connectedness
FIVE: Analytical, Input, Strategic, Intellection, Ideation, Discipline
SIX: Context, Deliberative
SEVEN: Adaptability, Communication, Positivity, Futuristic, Developer, Learner, Ideation
EIGHT: Self-Assured, Command, Strategic, Activator, Maximizer, Competition
NINE: Harmony, Consistency

Notes

1. This section is drawn from research conducted in 1995 and 1996 by John Richards and Tom Flautt with more than one thousand participants around the United States. The researchers presented their Enneagram/MBTI correlations at both the International Enneagram Conference and the Association for Psychological Type conference in 1999. See John H. Richards and Tom Flautt, *A Test of Myers-Briggs/Enneagram Theories with Data from the EM's Survey* (Portola Valley, CA: *The Enneagram Monthly*, June 1997).

2. Steven Reiss, *Who Am I? The 16 Basic Desires That Motivate Our Actions and Define Our Personalities* (New York: Tarcher/Putnam, 2000).

3. Marcus Buckingham and Donald O. Clifton, *Now Discover Your Strengths* (New York: The Free Press, 2001).

Additional Resources

David, Oscar. *The Enneagram for Managers: Nine Different Perspectives on Managing People.* Lincoln, NE: Writers Press Club, 2001.

Goldberg, Michael J. *The 9 Ways of Working: How to Use the Enneagram to Discover Your Natural Strengths and Work More Effectively.* New York: Marlowe & Co., 1999.

Lapid-Bogda, Ginger. *Bringing Out the Best in Yourself at Work: How to Use the Enneagram System for Success.* New York: McGraw Hill, 2004.

Linden, Anné, and Murray Spalding. *The Enneagram and NLP: A Journey of Evolution.* Portland, OR: Metamorphous Press, 1994.

Mattone, John, and Richard Andersen. *Success Yourself: Using the Enneagram to Unleash Your Personal & Business Potential.* New York: MasterMedia Limited, 1996.

Palmer, Helen, and Paul B. Brown. *The Enneagram Advantage: Putting the 9 Personality Types to Work in the Office.* New York: Harmony Books, 1997

Richards, John, with illustrations by Charles Harris. *The Illustrated Enneagram: An Animated Look at the Nine Enneagram Personalities.* Huntington Beach, CA: Horizon Nine Keys Publishing, 1994.

Richards, John H., and Lyudmyla I. Richards. *The Nine Keys EnneaType Personality Selector Instrument,* Version 5.5. Huntington Beach, CA: Horizon Nine Keys Publishing, 1993–1997.

Richards, John H., and Lyudmyla I. Richards M.D. *The Nine Keys EnneaType Assessment,* Version 5.6. Santa Barbara, CA: Horizon Nine Keys Publishing, 1993–2007.

Riso, Don Richard, with Russ Hudson. *Personality Types: Using the Enneagram for Self-Discovery.* New York: Houghton-Mifflin, 1996.

Riso, Don Richard, and Russ Hudson. *The Wisdom of the Enneagram: The Complete Guide to Psychological and Spiritual Growth for Nine Personality Types.* New York: Bantam, 1999.

Tallon, Robert, and Mario Sikora. *From Awareness to Action: The Enneagram, Emotional Intelligence, and Change.* Scranton, PA: University of Scranton Press, 2004.

Vallentino, Albert J. *Personality Selling: Using NLP and the Enneagram to Understand People and How They Are Influenced.* Iselin, NJ: Vantage Point Publishing, 2000.

Part Two:
Creating Professional Resilience
By Design

Introduction to the 64 Strategies for Creating Professional Resilience By Design

by Mike Jay

Before we jump right into the sessions that created this second part of the book, we want to remind the reader that this is a spoken book. With a spoken book come many challenges, most of which we managed, though a number of them we didn't, as you'll see. We ask your indulgence with the style of the book, continuing to remember we edited a spoken transcript and did our best to get you the ideas and their worth in as few sentences as possible. Be sure to get involved in our resilience club and get access to the audio recordings so you can play the material over after you've done the read-through. It will work in tandem as you integrate the materials.

We begin as Mike Jay is talking about the introduction of the resilience system:

One of the cool things about what I teach is how to use a combinatorial system, which brings in motivation and development, uses multiple assessments as a portfolio of self-knowledge, and incorporates Spiral-NEXT: identifying efficient, effective, and sustainable solutions. Then, once you mix that all up in a pan, what you get is a multicolored, multidimensional, *emergent* cake. This kind of cake is a lot more fun to eat. That is really the gist of what I try to do. It's difficult in the beginning, because there is so much jargon, and so many different models are being thrown in that sometimes you don't know which one I'm using.

If a person stays with this for a while, though, it really becomes interesting to look at adult behavior and the richness of just being alive. To me, the true richness in aliveness, and especially having the opportunity to work with people developmentally, is to see this extraordinary diversity that creation and evolution have produced in what we call human life, human experience. It's fascinating stuff for some of us.

The professional resilience model we roll out in this book is a straightforward model. It's different from personal resilience, which I wrote about in my first book in this series, CPR *for the* Soul: *Coaching Personal Resilience by Design*. The model here is not as hard to use as the personal resilience model, which almost always will require interaction with a trained coach, facilitator, or mentor. In the professional resilience model, the requirements are already outlined. It's a matter of modifying them to your own personal situation, which I will show you how to do, and then working to get what it is you need. So it's very straightforward.

It's almost a prescriptive process. We'll show you here how to set it up as a structured or standardized approach. It's timely, too, I think. We definitely have uncertainty, turbulence, and ambiguity coming at us, and the range of responses with which people can handle these problems will demonstrate their resilience challenge.

We've got a professional resilience system that I know works and a model we can teach to other people. That will open the door to other kinds of intervention, other kinds of coaching, which means it will open the door to the personal resilience model, which is much more complex. It will open the door to whatever it is you do. If you are relationship oriented or inspirationally oriented or Enneagram oriented or emotional-intelligence oriented like various authors in this book, whatever your flavor is, you can work with that area in this resilience paradigm. That's what I mean by *upping the downside*, which is exactly what we're doing here. I'll tell you a story behind that.

This is supposed to be the time of my life when I go into my second high-energy phase, the second *good* phase of my life. My first phase was amazing and had all kinds of wonderful things happen to me. Then I went through a different phase. Now I have made it out of that, and I'm going into my second high-energy phase.

In astrology, normally people do not have more than one energy phase in their life. Some people don't have any. I have been interested in astrology since traveling to India several years ago and seeing so much work being done in that area. I am not an astrologer. In fact, if you had said to me ten years ago that I would be open to astrology, I would have said you were nuts. But the thing about astrology, especially when you get into Chinese and Vedic astrology, is that it can be pretty accurate at the core of our unconsciousness. You look at it and say, "Golly, how can they say this?" I got my latest Vedic astrology report recently. I had done one when I was in India a few years ago. They first told me about this second energy phase coming at fifty-five. I've been priming myself, so you have to take that into consideration as you read this book. Parts of my enthusiasm for life now are going to show through.

In any case, if you go to *Indastro.com*, you can get a free reading. It's a birth chart, as Vedic astrology is different from Chinese astrology. The reason I'm bringing it up is it's another assessment that I think that you would enjoy. I'm not saying yours will be as right on as mine is, but I'm saying that it may be helpful to you.

How can they know this kind of stuff? Are we living karma? Are we living a deterministic life? I don't know, but my report is scary as it is pretty much right on. There were only a couple things I would argue with. I always considered myself to be a bit of a fluke, but this astrology report pegged me pretty well. After seeing this mini-report, I went ahead and bought the full reading, which has all of the details about your life.

Matt Ridley, in his book *Nature Via Nurture, says*—"If you do not want to be a victim of nature, then the best thing is to know your nature."

In other words, when I look at this astrology, it is my nature. It is a programming that exists in the world. Now, if I want to be subject to that, then I should not learn it and know it. If, on the other hand, I want to hold it as object and have a relationship with it, THEN I have some choice. Choice, that's the key. So I'm not saying get your astrology, because that's what is going to be your life. I'm saying get your astrology, because you want that information in your life in some cases.

I feel really lucky. I feel like I was a winner in nature's lottery. I was talented and not only that, I had the kind of heart to go along with the talent. I've been able to do almost everything I wanted to do in my life. I feel very fortunate, especially in the latter years as I begin to understand that not all of this has to do with Mike Jay. It has to do with my ancestry, with karma, or stuff that's already been in place—if you believe in that. I'm not sure I do, but there has to be something out there as a creative force that is working with us. I am very grateful.

When I look at others who are not so lucky, I wonder why they ended up poorly in nature's lottery. This is why I think we need to rewire our whole society. Our society is built on meritocracy, which means those who got great lottery tickets are always going to be the ones who do the best. How does our society make up for the fact that not all of us were in the front of the line when the tickets were passed out? How do we compensate for that? We haven't learned as a people, as a society, as a civilization to compensate for that fact. We're so afraid that somebody will lose their hope or desire if they think they're going to be *disposed* to depression their whole life. Well, some people are! And we pretend by telling them stories about how they are not. What kind of societal joke is that?

Why am I not predisposed to depression? Well, it's because of my personality. I'm optimistic. I can't be depressed. It's impossible for me to be depressed for very long with my attributes. That is the resilience savant. Yeah, and it's just the luck of the draw. It's not like these guys who get up and say, I'm a self-made person. I did all this. I learned all this. I'm this smart. There was a guy, my mom's boss, who talked to her one day. He had a huge ranch. The subject came up of whether a person was lucky or not in having inherited a ranch compared to the work it took to build up a ranch. The guy turned to her and said—this is how wise he was—"It's a whole lot easier to keep a pot boiling, than it is to bring it to boil."

See, that's the whole thing we have to understand with the book and the film called *The Secret*, which says, "You can have, be, or do anything you want" (see *thesecret.tv*). We're all different. We all were endowed with gifts, but in our society, business reality says we're going to reward people who do X, Y, and Z. It just so happens that some people are in direct alignment with that. Those are our exemplars. That's a Warren Buffet. Warren Buffet is perfect for business reality. Every one of his skills, everything he does, everything he believes is a perfect match. Would you not expect him to do well? It's the same with Bill Gates, who scored 1600 on his SAT. Yet for each one of us to look at what they do and how they do it and conclude that through the law of attraction I can do that too. . . . I've read Buffet's books and I've read Gates' book. I can't do what they do. For one thing, I'm not as smart as they are. The second thing is, I just can't do some of the things they do because I'm not motivated to do them. I won't keep doing it. I'm a risk taker, not like Buffet who says, "Why take risks, just do the math?"

One thing that we have to understand, that our society needs to understand, and this goes beyond liberal and conservative, is there is something to this nature stuff. If nurture is going to help nature as much as it can, we need to change the way we do things. We need to provide more solutions than a meritocracy. I'm not saying stop it, but I'm saying don't make it an end-all. Some people are not endowed with these kinds of gifts. I know a lot of people whom I respect a lot, and they have hardly any gifts. They just do their job every day. They're the salt of the earth.

One time I was in Colombia, up early because I used to run early. Now, if I say I'm running, it looks like I'm rolling. The point is that *people* sweep the streets in Colombia. They don't have machines to do it. People do it because it gives them jobs. These people don't make much money sweeping the streets every morning, but one thing I loved about Colombia is the streets are always clean. One time I went out and talked to one of street sweepers. He said, "I look forward to every day, because I have a job. My family depends on me to make a little bit of money. I come out here. I get to do this job, and I'm happy."

That point in time, back in 2000, is when I wrote *Now What*, which is now titled *Right Action — Right Results*. That was the beginning of a turning point for me, to realize each one of us has gifts. If we're forced to work in a society where you are only rewarded for having X gifts, and we have other parts of the alphabet, then we're going to spend the rest of our lives chasing X. I don't want to stop rewarding X, because we've shown that X lifts people out of poverty. But at the same time, what we have to figure out in our society is what about A, B, C, D, E, F, G? That's what is missing in our society today. That's how this resilience formula came about, by looking at the question, can we help people?

So, part of what I've done with *upping the downside* is I've looked through all the means (memes)—those ways of doing things—that say if you do this, there's a good chance that no matter what happens in the future, you'll be okay.

There's a good solid set of means in this professional resilience model—tried and proven. So even if a person is not going to be a resilient personality, which 99 percent of people are not, we teach them that these are the requirements for resilience in the reality that we live in today. If people want to have a more successful life—I'm not saying happy, but more successful—then these are the things that they need to find some kind of competence in. And they don't have to change themselves; they can get it by collaborating with others—by *reaching out*.

Does that mean that they do all of the things in this model? No. But if you're motivated, you will do some of the things on the list naturally. If you're not motivated, you won't do some of these things, which means you won't be resilient *unless* you seek out and develop a strengths-based design that mitigates some of these existential requirements.

What we're saying to people is, first we're going to find out what things you're capable of. Next we're going to find out what kinds of things you like to do. Now the things that you like to do and the things you're capable of, those are the things we're going to assign to you. The other things, the ones you may be capable of but won't do and the ones you are not capable of and won't do, we're going to find help for you through design.

See, the model is built to produce resilience by resilience—by modeling the solution. By doing what the model shows, *it forces you to reach out and collaborate*—one of the key factors research has shown to produce enhanced levels of resilience on top of everything else you do. That's the whole idea of this model.

Now I'll introduce you to the model, and what we're going to do, and how we're going to do it. My resilience project was inspired by a book I read called *The Resilience Factor,* by Karen Reivich and Andrew Shatte. It was around 2002 that I read it and said, "This is the key. This resilience stuff is what I know and am able to do as a person, yet most of my clients and the people around me don't have a clue about resilience. This is what they're going to have to do, because of what's coming." I've been predicting what's going to happen as a result of globalization since 2000, and the things from my early predictions are now happening. It's not that I'm a future seer, it's just making sense of X and Z, X and Y.

My point is that I know resilience training is coming, just like we know leadership training is coming. You can't grow the world as we're growing it without leaders, so we have to train people to be leaders. We're also going to have to train people to be resilient — and to be resilient leaders. How do you do that? That's been my quest for the last five years.

Resilience is required in at least four domains.

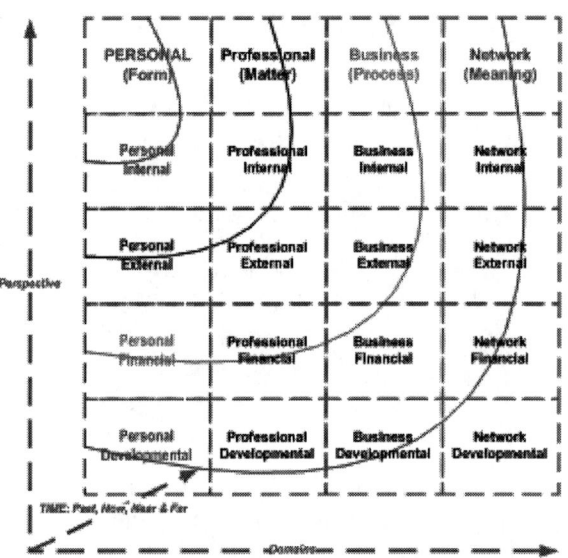

Also, I realized that resilience in the personal domain is more about happiness than anything else. If you're resilient in the personal domain, it really doesn't matter what happens to you in the success domains: professional + business + network. The success domain is broader than the happiness domain, because the success domain interfaces with the real environment. What I decided to do was create a resilience model in each domain noted in the graphic. I started with the biggest domain, the network resilience model, because I thought that if you could be resilient in a network, you could be resilient as a person. That's true, although you can't always be happy.

Then I went back to the success and happiness equation and said, "Wait a minute, success is not happiness. Essentially, happiness is an emergent property. It's derived from an equation based on alignment with what we do every day to enhance flow experiences over time being in alignment with our motivational sensitivity." People call it different things such as flow state, pleasure, whatever. What I did with the personal resilience model was focus on happiness and the question, "Can you be happy and then successful?" Can you be happy first, because happiness leads to success, at least most of the time it does.

It's like the old Porter-Lawler Motivation Theory where they found a causal relationship between *performance* and *satisfaction*. People perform because they're satisfied and are satisfied because they perform; it's a circular relationship. Same thing with success and happiness, though not altogether, because I've seen people who are not successful and could not be successful, but who are very happy. In being happy, they reach a level of success, but not necessarily success as defined in the world, especially in *The Secret* world (where if you think or feel something hard enough, you can manifest it) that most of us are exposed to everyday.

As I mentioned, I wrote the personal resilience model first (CPR *for the Soul: Coaching Personal Resilience by Design*). Then, I knew that there was a certain set of professional requirements because I've worked with professionals extensively over the past twenty years. What I found was that there was a set of things that kept coming up which were always making problems. Yet when professionals existed at an optimal level—a level that is not the maximum, but is higher than the minimum—at that optimal level, no problems were necessarily made, no matter what happened. In other words, even when complexity went into exponential growth—knowledge these days is doubling every ten to twelve months—people I observed who operated like the model I've developed *remained* resilient, almost always, no matter what happened.

Let's say you've gone back a few years, and you're a futurist. Well, it's been pretty easy to predict the future, because the future is nothing more than an emergent property of the past and the present. So people are building linear-state lines and saying, you know, if we have a car that will do 20 miles per gallon today, we should have a car that will do 30 miles per gallon by year X. But what happens when complexity starts to go exponential? We can't tell anymore what's going to happen because complexity is now nonlinear. So what do you do about resilience?

So we go back to resilience, and we begin to understand what are its central components. I looked at that in a professional frame, or domain. When I call it a professional frame, I'm basically talking about the self-employed quadrant of Robert Kiyosaki's cashflow quadrant, which was popularized in his book by that name and also in his book *Rich Dad, Poor Dad*.

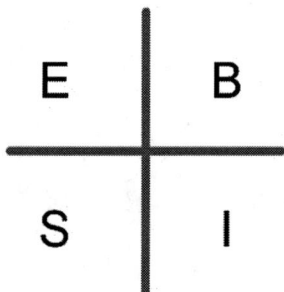

The upper left quadrant in Kiyosaki's model has an E for employee. You work for somebody. The lower left quadrant has an S for self-employed. You're working for yourself, usually as an entrepreneur, having a hallucination or as a professional of some sort. The upper right has a B for business. You own a business and can walk away from daily operations, and the business does fine. The lower right has I for investor. You don't own anything, you invest in things. The E quadrant is covered by the personal resilience happiness model. What is central to employees is being happy. We found that in the Sears profit chain (*http://hbswk.hbs.edu/archive/801.html*) and other research that we've done. If you make employees happy, the customers are happy, and the business does well. That's the model of happiness.

The self-employed quadrant is a bit of a stickler. This is the entrepreneurial quadrant. Most entrepreneurs are really employees who are having hallucinations about business ownership. They have not learned how to be a business owner, but they don't want to be an employee, so they end up *creating a bad job for themselves.* That's called being self-employed. That is what I call the professional quadrant. The professional quadrant is the one where you have to formalize a relationship, because you're doing business directly with somebody else from a position of expertise, whether you're licensed or otherwise. You're a doctor. You're a lawyer. You're a plumber, coach, consultant, accountant, insurance person, or whatever job you can think of that has a professional domain.

I asked, "What does it take to be resilient in this professional domain?" So many of my clients are in this domain. In fact, my first client was in the medical domain, and we went through a lot figuring out what was required to be successful, to be happy, to be resilient. Over the years, I've continued to refine, refine, refine. Then in 1996, I ran into *Spiral Dynamics* by Don Beck and Christopher Cowen. I read the book two or three times and still didn't understand it. In 2001, I began a dialogue with the authors and went to a Spiral Dynamics Integral (SDi) training program. My life has been different since then, and I count founder Don Beck as a revered friend and colleague. Whether you believe in the system or not, what understanding Spiral Dynamics Integral (*spiraldynamics.net*) allows you to do is to look at multiple levels of existence—or existential levels of differing life conditions, or as Maslow said, "hierarchies of need"—and the values systems they attract.

When you look at different levels of existence, you really begin to press yourself in terms of resilience. For instance, for most of you reading this right now, if you had your choice of an environment, you'd pick one that you're resilient in. In CPR *for the Soul* I explain this as *event-based resilience.* You're in alignment with your favorite environment. Things in that environment come to you easily and well. You have strengths; you're strong there. You have free energy. Stuff comes along and tries to knock you off track, and you can handle it just fine.

Now let's take you out of those life conditions and put you in a situation where you're not strong and where you have some weakness or limitations. What happens is this: Your coping system that worked so well in the level of existence that you chose doesn't work very well anymore. All of a sudden, you begin to have all kinds of issues and *all kinds of problems left at the end of the money.* I used to tell my mom that when I was in college. I said, "Mom, I still have some month left, but I'm out of money." She would send me some money so I could make it through the month.

My point is that most of us have problems left at the end of our coping system in those levels of existence that don't match well with our motivation and with our strengths, which are directly related to our motivational sensitivity. (Motivational sensitivity can be identified and measured by the Reiss Profile of Motivational Sensitivity at *reissdesireprofile. com.*)

Strengths come out of our motivation because we do things over and over, acquiring knowledge and skills in our emerging *talent* areas. The more we do them, the better we get. The more activity in our brain in the same place, the greater density it develops, and the easier the activity becomes.

So when we're moved out of the life conditions that we dearly love, we're not very resilient. We begin to produce suboptimal results, and we need help. Yet most of us don't know anything about how this works.

Remember self-employed people and why we have this entrepreneurial hallucination? We don't want to work for anybody. We want to call our own shots. At least we want to feel like we're doing that, but we're actually not. Our customers are telling us what to do. So we have a different boss—multiple bosses, actually, rather than one we don't like.

In the self-employed quadrant, there are things you have to do to be prepared for shifts in life conditions. Since complexity in our world has now gone exponential, we no longer have any clue what the future holds. It's been suggested that 70 percent of the jobs that will be available in 2012, have not yet been invented. We don't even know what the jobs are that people need to prepare for. Fifteen years ago, webmasters didn't exist; five years ago, pod casters didn't exist. How can we prepare to be resilient when we have an unknown future?

That takes us back to the prime elements. The *first prime element* is that you're going to always be resilient in those areas where you're motivated. Again, we call that event-based resilience.

Path resilience is where you look at the requirements of your life conditions over a broad span of levels of existence, and you look for those prime elements that will allow you to cope with whatever comes up and at least give you an opportunity to be resilient. What I've done is go through all the levels of existence noted in Spiral Dynamics Integral and identify the key attributes of resilience elements at each level. If you know my personal resilience model, the reason this looks different is due to the self-employed point of view. In the self-employed quadrant, you are the one responsible for your resilience. In the employee (personal) quadrant, you are only responsible for your happiness. *Your employer* is responsible for your resilience.

Now, in the self-employed quadrant, you're going to be making decisions and solving problems over a variety of levels of existence for, "Complexity is because complexity does." (That's our Forest Gumpism for today.) That means you're going to be thrown a lot of curves, or variables. There will be lots of *delays* in cause and effect, which will challenge your understanding of cause and effect, which is why things are complex.

The other thing to understand in the self-employed quadrant is that you will never be using resilience in the same way as a business owner. The self-employed person is wearing two hats. You're *self*-employed, which means you are the employee and the boss. Your two faces mean you're schizophrenic—business-wise.

What this resilience model does as the *second prime element* is take into consideration that you'll never be truly resilient as a professional unless you can make what's called the B-I Leap. That's where you go to the business or investor quadrant, and you no longer have anything to do with the operations of the business. In the professional domain, on one hand, you're attached to the business; on the other hand, you're detached from it. We have to allow you to stand on that fence, with one foot in the S quadrant and one foot in the B quadrant for you to be a successful professional. You still don't give up the nature of your work because you still love your work.

172

It's like me. I love professional coaching and training. It's where I feel that I can make the greatest contribution. But when I finish a session and have to go back to the "S-detail" things on my to-do list, I feel like I've gone from the flow state back to reality. That's the feeling you get when you're self-employed. You get to do cool things that you love doing, that you're prepared to do, that you're motivated to do, and at the same time you have to do business stuff too. You don't have a staff because you don't want the burden of a staff. You're stubborn enough to think that you can do everything. That's the self-employed quadrant.

We have to take in the attributes of the business quadrant. When you're a business owner, you can walk away from the business for two years and come back, and the business is as good or better as when you left it. That's how you know you're a business owner and not self-employed, for those of you wanting to make that leap.

What I've done in this professional resilience model is take the combinatorial effects of being a self-employed person—a professional who works on their own on a business of some sort—and a business owner. We do have a resilience model for a business too, but that model is entirely based on business systems and not any longer on an I-ness or Me-ness or We-ness or You-ness. The professional resilience system in this book is based on I, We, Us and Them.

As you go through this model, what you want to do is actually take the survey. You can do this by taking the dust jacket off your book and looking inside the flap for an eight-digit number. Then go to *uppingthedownside.com/amember/survey*, enter that code, and you will get a free assessment. It will automatically do the calculations for you and you can discuss them with your coach or resilience consultant.

Instructions for Taking the Survey:

The first element in the survey is: "I have established an emergency fund that is liquid and secure." You will give a score between one and ten based on the amount of frequency of this element you currently demonstrate.

You may say, "I already have an emergency fund." Then rate your capability on that. If you already have an emergency fund, is it at the level that you determined it should be? It's typically considered that an emergency fund should be in the neighborhood of six to eighteen months of normal expenses. As a rule, however, the more complexity we have, the more uncertainty we have, and you should raise that number. I think there will be times coming when you will have to be without income, real income, other than just pickup income, for anywhere from twenty-four to thirty-six months. The reason is that you can pretty well reeducate or recalibrate yourself in three years, or you can take a sabbatical if you want.

So if you want to have a real emergency fund for your business, it should be conservative, because what you're likely to do is use a best-case scenario that says you need $2,000 or $3,000 a month to keep alive, when what happens in a bad situation is that might double. So you probably need a longer fund than most people think. Let's say at a minimum you should have between six and eighteen months of your current expenses in your emergency fund; but if for whatever reason you can no longer earn money the way you have been, you're going to need more like sixteen to eighteen months at a minimum to recalibrate. That's how you become resilient.

Okay, so I've gotten into the substance of the first element in the survey to illustrate how it works. Note that if you're uncertain of what the model means now, that's alright because of the way I've created the survey in the book. After this Introduction, each chapter will go into depth as to what the "means/memes" at each level mean in general. Then you decide what your score should be.

In Today's World

What's happening today is that people are in a system, and their employers are saying, "We're going to downsize you, outsize you, right size you, get rid of you, or . . . redirect your career path," which is the politically correct way to say it now. The only thing is that you don't have a choice in that. If that happens to you, you'll be without money within three months. If you're like 67 percent of Americans, you can't go more than one month.

More than 25 percent — or it may be closer to 30 percent now — function within a two-week margin. That's all a person can go without being essentially bankrupt. Because you're living week to week, if you lose your paycheck, you're done. You don't have any emergency backup. You're on government support. That's it.

Everything you have worked for may suddenly change with a disruptive or discontinuous event. And those events are going to become more common as complexity escalates along the hockey stick where it reaches a singularity around 2030, according to futurists. At this point, almost all bets are off on the future, because the future is happening faster than we have the means to predict — a real conundrum.

About 67 percent of people in the United States live month to month. It's only about the top third that can go a bit longer than that. That's because they have credit cards that are not maxed. They can live awhile on credit. We've run into many people like that in coaching, even people who think they're going to quit their jobs and go into coaching. They find out it's not so easy. In six months, twelve months, they're back getting a job again. They were not resilient enough to be able to stick it through to become masterful enough that people were attracted to them.

If you stop reading now, the one thing to do is to keep in your mind what I'm saying about an emergency fund.

In each of the next eight chapters, we're going to cover one of each of the eight categories of professional resilience in the survey. Within each category, we're going cover all eight levels of existence as depicted by Spiral Dynamics Integral (SDI). I was just using the emergency fund as an example to get you started in the survey.

The best approach actually is to begin by doing a pre-survey. I've embedded the survey questions within each of the chapters for you to use for that purpose. What's the benefit in that? The reason is that you're going to answer the pre-survey based on how you think you are. Then, as you go through the program chapter by chapter, you're going to realize that how you think you are is not how you really are. As you do the actual survey online, you can correct what you originally thought. This two-part process will help you become dis-embedded from the illusion that is causing you to feel you'll be resilient if your life conditions suddenly shift.

There are some scenarios of the future where we could see life conditions shift out of our current levels of existence—characterized mainly by the search for purpose and the pursuit of advancement and progress (the blue and orange levels in SDi)—back to the levels more typical of tribal periods and the struggle to meet basic survival needs (beige, red, and purple levels in SDi).

That would lay out 99 percent of the people in the United States, because virtually none of us have hunter-gatherer skills any more, nor are we in a tribe—or self-powerful enough to go out and just take things from other people to survive. That's the level of existence we could be thrust into with a few possible and some probable events headed our way. Not for a very long time probably, but it could be for a long enough period that it would harm you financially for a long time to come. What I'm trying to do here is make you resilient enough to survive professionally if we got thrown into that kind of a situation.

Here's an example of how the survey works in the context of a resilience design. It shows the first statement of resilience that we've already explored a bit for illustrative purposes—the idea of an emergency fund.

Requirements – (Capability) x Importance = Priority Score

Score each element on a scale of 1–10; 1=low, 10=high	Requirements	Capability	Importance	Priority Score
I have established an emergency fund that is liquid and secure.				

First we'll see what your capability is in your current reality. Then you'll mark how important the element is to you. That's how you get your priority score for this element. And when you've worked through all sixty-four elements in the eight different categories of resilience, you'll have your priority list. If you work with a coach in using this system, the things that receive high priority scores will be the ones that we bring to design first — in other words, we work on those with the highest scores first.

For instance, if you do not have an emergency fund, you can start that today by signing up to have the bank do a regular payroll withdrawal. Or you could take some of the money you receive and put it away or give it to your wife or husband (though sometimes that may *not* be a good idea!). You can literally start that fund immediately. That would be something that you could do to begin creating resilience.

In order to stay resilient, which means you can last through a downturn without giving up assets, you have to have certain things in place. We're sitting here in the early part of the 21st century, and we're looking at some pretty interesting things coming over the next few years that we're going to have to deal with. If you listen to some experts, you'll be scared out of your pants, as I am, that things will not always be like they are right now. But the point is, with this survey, you will have to decide right now: What is the most important thing for you to solve first?

Here's a caveat. What's important and has leverage may have to do with your ability in lower-level life conditions than where you are now. The more capability you have in your current reality, the greater range of resilience you have to work with, and that in and of itself can buy you some time. Those who show lower capability in the lower levels of life conditions may have to start with the basics. It's just that simple.

Remember, this survey is a process that you can do with a coach or on your own. If you're working with a coach, you and your coach will start by going through the items you've selected as important. Once you have your list of priorities, your coach will help you differentiate what is important from what is really, really important. That's the first thing you start paying attention to. What will be important will be the things that have leverage. Because people are in different kinds of businesses and situations, some people will find leverage in certain of the elements, and others will find it in other elements.

The idea is to go for the things that have a lot of leverage, because leverage means this: If I do this one time, it pays me five times. But something with even more leverage would be: If I do this one time, it pays me ten times. So we're looking for the highest possible leverage. We're also going to use the IMULL model by looking for what is *important*, what is *motivating* to you so you'll do it, what is *urgent* to get done, what has *leverage*, and then, what is the *low-hanging fruit*. There will always be some low-hanging fruit—things we can do for quick success, a quick win.

If you can, do a couple items that are quick wins, that allow you to say, "This makes me feel better. I can do this. I have my emergency fund. I have this going. I have that going." And what does that do? It builds self-efficacy. That means the belief I have that I can do what I need to do. Some people are born with that, although that doesn't mean they will always be good at it or successful. It just means that they believe they can do it. The rest of us have to build self-efficacy through low-hanging fruit.

That's what *The Secret* model tries to put in use. *The Secret* says, if you can get people to feel they have high self-efficacy, they will be able to do whatever they set out to do. That's true to a point. The problem is that having self-efficacy as a natural trait and developing it are two different things.

What the early research in resilience showed was that people who have self-efficacy *make* better leaders. They also make better plumbers and better this and that. Self-efficacy means you can steer through ambiguity. You can see your way clear no matter what happens. You can bounce back from your setbacks. The people who bounce back from setbacks are the ones who say, "No matter what happens; I can do this." That's what self-efficacy really means.

We're not going to go directly *at* self-efficacy here, because it is another one of the emergent properties that is natural in some people. It is already in some people's cake. What we are going to do is create the circumstances where if self-efficacy can emerge, it will.

Starting with low-hanging fruit gives us the sense of can-do-ness, of self-efficacy. That's the *third prime element*: working with people and their talents towards self-efficacy. Because it's natural to but a few people, and it's not easy for most to learn, nor is it easy to emerge, in a controlled environment you can nonetheless help people feel more efficacious over time. That's one reason why people use coaches, especially athletes. The athlete stumbles and falls or the athlete can't run one-tenth faster, and what does the coach say? "You can do it. All you have to do is this. All you have to do is that. You're almost already there."

A coach can do all kinds of things to begin to create an emergent property out of a collaborative system. That's why resilience is important and why reaching out and coaching works so well. What does the person who begins to feel that they can do it rely on? The *other person's belief in them* is where it begins!

What does that do to the internal belief system? It begins to erode it. So you have to be careful with this. Most people will not develop self-efficacy except over time, and even then they have to be in alignment with what are clearly their talents. All of us are self-efficacious in the areas of our motivational strengths and talents. We can do stuff there, and we know we can. The thing is that we're not always allowed to be in that place, and that's what lowers resilience.

So we want to trade event-based resilience, which is in alignment with who we are in specific circumstances, for path-driven resilience, which is the help that we get from other people by using design. That, then, produces the one thing that has been found to be missing in the resilience literature until just lately, which is the ability to reach out — the *fourth prime element*. People who are more resilient, it has been shown, are the ones who reach out. Of course, in a complex environment, that is all the more important. If you keep trying to do it all on your own, you're going to stay in your self-hugging and self-sealing loops. You're not going to be able to add the resources you need to overcome what complexity is producing in advanced life conditions.

In other words, as you solve problems, you create problems. The problems you create can't be solved with the problems that you can cope with. They need help at a different level. You have to reach out. Most of us will have to reach out. Some people will be able to develop on their own because they're on a steeper, innate developmental trajectory that allows them to do that. But most people are not on steep developmental trajectories, so they cannot help themselves. Most of us are going to have to collaborate with other people to get help and to become resilient. To the extent that we're not reaching out, our levels of resilience are truncated to that self-sealing, self-hugging system. We'll be resilient within that system as long as it matches up with our life conditions. But as soon as we get into a mismatch, as soon as we get out of alignment, we are no longer in a resilient position.

What I'm saying with this model is, let's look at what we've discovered through eight levels of existential conditions. Each one of those levels requires something from us in order to overcome uncertainty, ambiguity, and turbulence at that level of complexity. What I have put together here is a kind of shortcut, a map to be able to do that.

Would you want to substitute other things for some of the elements I've chosen? Sure. What I've given here in this model is a basic beginning. Are there other elements that can be included? Absolutely. Once you reach one level of resilience, some of you will want to reach another level. What we'll look at is the baseline resilience level where you are right now — how you're going to be resilient by doing, having, being and becoming. Then we'll look at the next level that you want to achieve. And finally, we'll look at what kind of design you need to put in place in order to accomplish that level.

Chapter 14

Wellth Discipline
by Mike Jay

With this chapter we take up the first category of professional resilience: *wellth discipline*. Wellth is a word I coined to demonstrate survivability in terms of physical and monetary well-being.

As you will see, there are eight categories in developing professional resilience in the survey: wellth discipline, mastermind, engagement, customer relationship management, business development, robustness, generativity, and integroism (another made-up word). Each category becomes more sophisticated in its approach within it's own process, as well as across all other processes, making the complexity here—*spiral on spiral*—spiral its way into and through each other process. Wellth discipline is the starting point. But it is also important to understand this particular category along a course of action over time. Most of the time, I refer to these eight processes as categories. Yet if you understand that they are processes, it may help you over time when we talk about "density" of the category.

Wellth stands for well + wealth. A lot of people think I misspelled it. The reason I wanted to have the extra "l" and no "a" is that if you've got your health, but you don't have financial security, then you can't have your cake and eat it too. If you've got financial security and not your health, there's still a misalignment.

My idea is that you should have robustness built in at the wellth level, which means you look continually at well-being. That takes some of the pressure off the wealth, which some people think is the only path to resilience. I know many people who don't have much money at all, but who have adequate financial resources and are rich in other sources of resilience and therefore are quite *wellthy*.

In fact, I was raised my first couple years by my grandparents, who were amazing in their resilience. They always told me that this dated from the Great Depression when my grandfather purchased a refrigerator on credit, but then they were unable to make the payment. One day the company came and repossessed it. That was such a miserable experience for my grandparents; they decided never to buy anything again unless they could pay cash. I'm not saying that's always the best strategy, but for them it brought tremendous resilience. Once they bought something, they owned it, and nobody could take it from them. That's part of a whole culture that we don't have much in our country anymore. There are not many people left who went through the Depression and are actively living and teaching these means that we all really need to consider as complexity accelerates.

In this book we're working toward wellth to *up the downside.*

So with this chapter we begin the process of understanding and working through the resilience survey. We are not trying to surface anything new in this model. What we are doing is presenting the elements of practice that we have found to be consistent with each of the eight categories of professional resilience as *deliberate practice.*

An admonition with the survey: Some of the elements—the actions or practices listed under each category—may *not* be on your radar screen or that of your client if you are a coach. The survey is built to test a range of manifestations within each individual's *memescape,* in other words, the person's preferred ways of doing things. If a statement is not meaningful to you, just skip it. It's actually better to skip it than give it a priority score, because if you don't clearly understand a statement or feel it is something that doesn't matter in your professional practice, it's best left to another time and place.

Unlike surveys that are psychometrically verified, this survey is not intended to be a measure of your standard resilience. It's a tool to allow you to understand the requirements you set for your professional life, your capability as it relates to those requirements, and the importance of each aspect of resilience in your professional work.

There is no standard for resilience as each of us has special gifts and requirements. Note, however, that if you should score high for capability in all things, it does not necessarily mean you are more resilient. *Resilience depends on what you are actually willing to do in the face of changing life conditions when they occur.* Each of us has priorities for what we will do. The other caveat is that needs or requirements will vary according to different professions and therefore that the importance of certain elements will differ across professions.

The survey is not designed to give you a resilience score, although it can and it will. It's designed to be a tool you can employ to *improve* your resilience, as well as your success and happiness in general in your life, work, and relationships through *deliberate practice.*

What we're interested in are four basic things:

1. What actions and practices are consistent with each category of your professional resilience covered in the model?

2. What is your current level of capability right now in each of these eight categories?

3. How important are the various elements—the actions and practices—to you personally and in your profession?

4. What does your scoring indicate about your individual priorities for further attention and development in your *deliberate practices*?

A quick reality check before proceeding: Normally, when a person sees a model like this they think, "Okay, I want to fix everything at once." Then they quickly realize that they do not have enough personal or professional resources to do that, and they become overwhelmed and paralyzed.

With this survey I urge you to take a realistic, one-step-at-a-time approach. First go through the survey to assess your requirements for, current capability in, and importance of each element listed under the eight categories of professional resilience. Next calculate your priority score using the simple formula given. Now you can make decisions about how to order the actions you take in terms of priority over a period of time. And finally, budget and allocate funds and take steps accordingly.

Central to the coaching process implicit in this book is to *choose just one thing and start working on it*. That's the key. Your ability to do this yourself or to coach others depends on finding one thing to get started on that is low-hanging fruit. In other words, it's doable and you can immediately get going on it. Our aim with this survey is to help you *map the territory of your professional resilience*—where you are in terms of the roads that need to be built, the bridges that need to be fixed, the steps that need to be taken, and what the overall cost is going to be. Then we ask, can we find ways to accelerate your taking action and reduce the cost through better strategies and innovation?

If you would prefer to have a coach to guide you through this program, please visit *www.upthedownside.com/coach*, where we list a cadre of coaches trained in both professional resilience and developmental coaching.

In identifying the elements of professional resilience, from my experience over the past twenty years of working with professionals, the original version of this model was not robust enough because it was not spirally informed. It didn't account for the levels of existence in Spiral Dynamics Integral (SDi). That means a person's resilience might have scored lower than it should have because the elements did not provide enough range. Without enough scalability and scope, the tendency is to build a model based on who you are as a consultant or as a person having an experience, rather than what people using the survey who are at different levels of existence will most likely encounter.

To remedy that I melded parts of my earlier works, starting with a book I published in 2000, *The 101 Things to Do to Avoid a Recession*, which you can receive for free at: *www.upping-the-downside.com*. Then, as I began to see that the skills required at one level of existence are different from those required at other levels, I began to use a *spiral-on-spiral* approach, which means that as a system becomes more dense, it develops horizontally more so than it develops vertically, because horizontal development is easier to build density in than is vertical development.

I've therefore oriented the elements within wellth discipline to the fitness or survival level of the professional in an *integrally informed* manner. I want to make sure that the *means* people develop for their *deliberate professional practices* will have sufficient density in all the levels of the spiral they will encounter among others over time. Otherwise, we leave people in professional practice open to blind spots that decrease their effectiveness and thus their own professional resilience. This overarching part of *deliberate practice* is called *recursion*, meaning it allows me to show you both horizontal and vertical development within the same system and go back into lower-level systems to emerge higher-level system leverage. I'll point this out further as we go through the survey.

For wellth discipline, which is what I call the basic or survival level of professional fitness, many of the elements relate to the professional person rather than the professional system. This changes as we go deeper into the system and work across the categories, for each subsequent category has a higher level of sophistication to match the level of existence that one is able to function in.

Another caveat is that each of you taking the survey will find that you have capability and specific skills in all eight areas; in other words, you won't just go several levels and not have any skills beyond that. Your *memescape*—the landscape of means that maps all of your ways of doing things, including but not limited to the rules, principles, agents, and conditionals in your personal and professional practices—will be salt and peppered all the way through the survey. That's how *means and memes* develop. Means don't develop in a linear fashion; they generally develop in a network fashion—through power-law distribution, just as power becomes connected across domains by many different ideas and methods, as the graphic below illustrates.

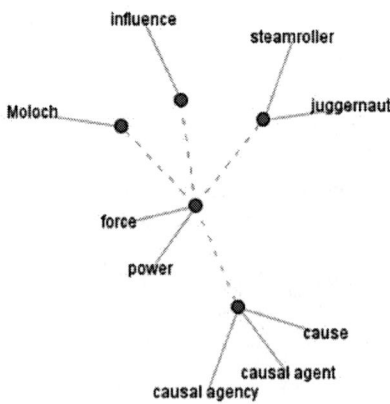

Using a set of deliberate practices guided by the completion of the survey, you'll have at least minimal coverage in all eight areas to prevent getting blind-sided by a discontinuous or disruptive event that no one predicts. The key is to have sufficient coverage across the categories to ensure the resilience you will need to confront a future in which life conditions become more complex. That's the short story here, and that's the key.

So now, let's work through each of the elements of wellth discipline.

[Note that there is a scoring table in the text following each statement and its explanation, so if you wish, you may score the survey as we work through the book. For those who wish to do the survey professionally, there is also an online survey located at www.upthedownside.com/amember/survey.]

"I have established an emergency fund that is liquid and secure."

We begin with a general statement that can encompass many types of specifics. The point here is, you're trying to store value, to create an emergency fund that will provide a buffer for you and your business should a geopolitical event or some other disruption occur that interrupts your income (e.g., an extreme storm or fire, a virus that disrupts ATMs, identity theft, or hacking of your bank account).

An emergency fund that is liquid and secure may include everything from retaining gold or precious metals, to storing at least three days of fresh drinking water and MREs (meals ready to eat), to keeping your gas tank full in the event of an evacuation. It relates to meeting your needs at a basic level of existence, so you will not have to sell or exchange assets that have taken a long time to accumulate.

If your business is a day-to-day operation and you depend on today's receipts to pay today's bills, you cannot disrupt that, and therefore you need a higher level of resilience. It's only when you can go through long periods of time without income—a week or a month without customers—that you can dispense with the deliberation on an emergency fund.

We lost a million jobs within a month after the 9/11 terrorist attacks in 2001. We lost two million more within six months. Think of the disruption after Hurricane Katrina, the aftermath of which continues today. Half of the people who left New Orleans have not yet come back! A great many of the people affected lost everything because they weren't resilient and had no resilient plans. In the Midwest, people lose power for ten days at a time during unexpected storms.

An emergency fund might include creating robustness in your office by cross-training employees to know the basics of other jobs in your operation. And there's the obvious area of technological security and backup necessary for most businesses to be resilient. You should begin by determining how much capability you need in which areas and how stiff your requirements are before you invest any money in a plan.

There's nothing to be gained by getting any of these elements to a score of ten, if you only need level-five resilience due to your circumstances. In fact, it's a poor use of resources to accumulate them where they are going to sit around and do nothing. First identify your requirements, and then close the gap between where you are and where you need to be for resilience.

Now try scoring this first element: I *have established an emergency fund that is liquid and secure.* Using a scale of one to ten in which *one is low* and *ten is high*, rate your requirements for this element, your current capability, how important it is, and finally, do the simple math to get your priority score.

Using a scale of 1–10 for each, calculate Requirements – (Capability) x Importance = Priority Score

Score each element on a scale of 1–10; 1=low, 10=high	Req	Cap	Imp	PS
I have established an emergency fund that is liquid and secure.				

The higher the priority score, the greater the attention you should give this element in your deliberative practice of allocating resources to make it more robustly resilient.

Now some people will say, "I don't need to do that because I have X, Y and Z." Okay, then this element is not going to be that important, so we don't put it at the top of your priority list. But one thing I've found that resilient people have is an emergency fund. They simply have rainy day funds.

How about millionaires, do you know what kind of funds they have? If you haven't read *The Millionaire Next Door* by Thomas Stanley and William Danko, you might want to take a quick look at it or at least read some of the principles. Millionaires have another fund—actually it's another name for an emergency fund, depending on the millionaire's level of existence. They have a "go to hell" fund, which means I have enough money that I don't have to do anything you tell me to do. In other words, no matter what happens, I have enough money that I'm going to make it. That's what really drives the millionaires. Every one of them had a "go to hell" fund.

Wayne Dyer was quoted as saying that Abraham Maslow stated that a precursor to self-actualization was being "independent of the goodwill of others." That applies here.

That's why I adopted the emergency fund scenario into the system. After studying people who are successful, these millionaires are not the kind of people you think they are. They are not the kind who are gurus and give seminars. They are just regular folks. But what these people have figured out is how to become rich by doing just a few things every day. I have paid attention to them a good bit, and I know a few of them. When you know them you'll be surprised they are millionaires because they don't act like it, contrasted with people who are trying to act like a millionaire. You can spot the differences right away.

The point is that the whole idea of a "go to hell" fund or an emergency fund allows you to do what? An emergency is an emergency for one reason—because it's an emergency. You have to go do something *now*. That's why we call it an emergency. So if you don't have something to take care of it, you'd have to be going and finding a job or finding the money or selling assets, and that is not resilience. Can you manage, for example, if you lose your best employee? That can happen in an emergency situation, because these employees are in demand everywhere, and they'll go to where they know it's safe for them and their families. So you have to consider a wide range of conditions in order to up the downside.

Lawrence Kohlberg used emergencies such as depicted in the Heinz dilemma to explain the development of moral reasoning (*http://en.wikipedia.org/wiki/Heinz_dilemma*):

> A woman was near death from a special kind of cancer. There was one drug that the doctors thought might save her. It was a form of radium that a druggist in the same town had recently discovered. The drug was expensive to make, but the druggist was charging ten times what the drug cost him to produce. He paid $200 for the radium and charged $2,000 for a small dose of the drug. The sick woman's husband, Heinz, went to everyone he knew to borrow the money, but he could only get together about $1,000, which is half of what it cost. He told the druggist that his wife was dying and asked him to sell it cheaper or let him pay later. But the druggist said, "No, I discovered the drug and I'm going to make money from it." So Heinz got desperate and broke into the man's store to steal the drug for his wife.
>
> Should Heinz have broken into the laboratory to steal the drug for his wife? Why or why not?

In my view, this is not about your moral reasoning (although in the end, that matters). It's about why Heinz got himself into the problem in the first place. He can't function with any choice at this level, except the one he chooses because of his own needs.

This is why we're going to produce resilience as an emergent property. In other words, we're each going to bake a cake. And what kind of cake will that be?

Number one, it's going to be a cake that you want to eat. It's going to have lots of layers in it and lots of flavor. It will probably have lots of colors in it too and lots of hidden benefits. It's kind of like digging into a cake and finding the keys to a new car. What's going to produce that?

We're going to look at the elements that produce the cake. Just like we would get out the eggs and flour and milk and baking powder, what I've done is create a ready mix in a box. You still have to take it and put it in a bowl, mix it up, and add a few ingredients to it, but you're buying a cake mix. That's what *upping the downside* is—a cake mix.

We move on, now, to the next element.

"I have friends and supporters I can count on in a moment's notice."

This element stems from tribal functions. A tribe functions by sharing things, by members being able to depend on one another. In our modern world, most of us can depend somewhat on our families, but beyond that, we're all over the place and disconnected. It would be difficult to summon help at times, even in a small town like I live in, because most of my friends and supporters are *virtual*. I do have a couple of neighbors I could probably depend on for a while. My point is, this is something that you have to think about. If you have a virtual business, and the people you know are scattered around the world, you don't have local robustness, which can be a real concern.

This is one of the things that I'm thinking about for the future with a concept I call *turquoise-tribes.com*. As I get older and need more help, I would like to create a community around me of people I can lend help to and who can lend me a hand. In this survey we're looking at your professional requirements. For instance, if your profession requires you to consistently seek help from friends and supporters; you will have a higher requirement here than some of us who may need help only in an emergency. Or, some people may not want or feel motivated to be interdependent, and then there's a motivational issue that can be addressed in part by design.

Using a scale of 1–10 for each, calculate Requirements – (Capability) x Importance = Priority Score

Score each element on a scale of 1–10; 1=low, 10=high	Req	Cap	Imp	PS
I have friends and supporters I can count on in a moment's notice.				

"I am currently enhancing my nutrition to optimal levels."

This is a difficult one. I don't think you necessarily have to be totally focused on physical exercise and fitness, although it's not a bad idea in order to be more robust. You do, however, need to focus on nutrition. If I'm high in physical exercise, I'm naturally going to be motivated to stay fit. If I'm not highly motivated to physical exercise, I'm not naturally motivated to stay fit. Even then there are some things that I can do to produce fitness at optimal levels.

> [Note that throughout this book, you will see references to motivation, motivational sensitivity, motivational profile, etc. If you're curious about what this means, there is information and an online profile you can purchase to provide you with this personal information at www.reissdesireprofile.com. Or, you will automatically receive this as part of your professional portfolio of assessments if you engage an upping-the-downside coach.]

Some people will see this as a higher requirement for their current needs and motivation, for instance, people working in a medical environment who are constantly exposed to viruses and bacteria. To me, these people have a higher requirement for good nutrition, because their immune systems are getting attacked all the time. I sit by myself most of the time and do not have many people coming in, which means I'm not exposed to colds and different kinds of viruses to which I'm not already immune. So in cases like mine, this element is a little easier.

Because I do a lot of sitting, though, I have to worry about what I can do to help myself. One way I enhanced my nutrition was that I had a genetic test done. The test showed that I have genes that research suggests are inclined toward heart problems. So I started a protocol specifically aimed at enhancing the nutrition needed to fend off heart problems. So far it's worked very well in lowering blood pressure and resting pulse, even though I'm overweight. [A genetic test can be purchased at *www. upthedownside.com/genelink.*]

The one thing I know for sure is that it doesn't do any good to pretend you're going to exercise if you're not. Better to admit it and start working in other areas to compensate through design. I find, for example, I'm more likely to exercise if I employ my motivation for curiosity and my strength in listening to audios. So I use an MP3 player and walk at times to capture motivational energy. There are many other ways to design in activities that can support some level of exercise without having it be like going to a dentist!

Using a scale of 1–10 for each, calculate Requirements – (Capability) x Importance = Priority Score

Score each element on a scale of 1–10; 1=low, 10=high	Req	Cap	Imp	PS
I am currently enhancing my nutrition to optimal levels.				

"I manage stress and rejuvenate through deliberate practice."

For those who come into the world with a need for emotional calm or high tranquility, stress is an issue. Cortisol will be constantly in your system, because it doesn't take much to cause a hormonal response in your system that releases Cortisol. The questions for those people are: Do you know that? Do you have a specific system in place to reduce that stress? Do you find ways to naturally de-stress? Do you take walks? Do you meditate? Do you spend a little time alone? Do you work on your systems that are creating stress and anxiety and try to reduce those? Of course, all of us need rejuvenation.

What it takes to rejuvenate you may be different than what it takes to rejuvenate me. In my case, I have a huge battery, so I can run for long periods of time without rejuvenation. Another person might require rejuvenation once, twice, three times, even four or five times a day. Do you know what your energy level is, and can you manage it? These are things that are important to scope and scale in this particular element.

Using a scale of 1–10 for each, calculate Requirements – (Capability) x Importance = Priority Score

Score each element on a scale of 1–10; 1=low, 10=high	Req	Cap	Imp	PS
I manage stress and rejuvenate through deliberate practice				

"I have eliminated all bad personal and business debt ."

This element is kind of hedging your bet, and the *bet* is that you have a plan. At this level, having a plan is the most important thing to put in your consciousness, or should I say *unconsciousness*, since our unconscious is very powerful in bringing about emergent change over time with the right kinds of cues.

You may or may not be able to eliminate all your personal and business debt. In fact, it may take years to do that, because you might have had a business failing or a divorce or a costly illness or death in the family or a combination of things. There are lots of good reasons why you could have high personal and business debt.

The key would be is it "bad" debt? In other words, if I borrow money to invest in a business that is yielding me $1.05 for every $1.00 I put in, that's good debt—as long as what the business produces in terms of environmental and social costs is included. If I borrow money on credit cards to buy something that doesn't return anything to me except my own pleasure, and I'm paying 12 to 20 percent, that's probably not good debt.

I'm not against debt by any means, but I do assert that there needs to be a plan in place to eliminate all of your *bad* debt. This could take anywhere from two to ten years. Of course, what'll you'll be doing as you eliminate bad debt is enhancing your resilience day by day. The key is in having a plan—*having a plan*, not just having the notion or knowing that's what you're supposed to do.

You have a plan.

You cannot mark yourself with high capability on this element unless you have a written plan with specific metrics. Have you established a procedure for paying X amount of dollars per day, per week, per month, whatever you need to do to reduce this bad debt? The plan allows you, when money comes in and goes out, to exercise some degree of decision making. That's the first step at this level, even if you cannot at the moment do anything more.

Now, if you do not have any bad debt, obviously you're going to be much more robust and resilient. Should life conditions shift dramatically and your income drop, you have the option to engage in all sorts of alternative solutions.

Using a scale of 1–10 for each, calculate Requirements – (Capability) x Importance = Priority Score

Score each element on a scale of 1–10; 1=low, 10=high	Req	Cap	Imp	PS
I have eliminated all bad personal and business debt.				

"I manage toxicity within and across my environments."

Begin by identifying what for you are the toxins in your environment, as they can be pretty wide-ranging and mean different things to different people. To me, the telephone is toxic because it's disruptive and rings at the most inopportune times. As a creative person, any disruption can be a toxin. Many people will have chemical toxins in their environment. For some, the lack of organic growth creates a sterile, toxic environment.

My advice is to understand how you are wired together. Understand your talents and what makes those talents generate the kinds of returns for your time, energy, efforts, and well-being. Then begin to remove the disruptive elements in your life, work, relationships, and community.

This can often be difficult, because sometimes people are served by things that are toxic for them—think of the artist using drugs or alcohol, for example—and they will find it difficult to remove the toxic element. That's where design can work well, especially in reaching out to others to help them understand what's good for you. Most of the time resilience will improve with support from others, and it's critical that you seek that support.

A word of warning is that people functioning in this way may sometimes turn inward, and turning inward becomes part of a toxic environment of adaptation. The very nature of professional resilience often depends on our ability to seek and receive feedback from others, including on ways we may be making them toxic.

Using a scale of 1–10 for each, calculate Requirements − (Capability) x Importance = Priority Score

Score each element on a scale of 1–10; 1=low, 10=high	Req	Cap	Imp	PS
I manage toxicity within and across my environments				

"I actively interweave my pursuits of life and work."

Each new element, in succession, is developmentally scaled to be increasingly complex, both vertically and horizontally. You've got a lot more conceptual space to manage with this element, even though the sentence is short. The assumption here is that we understand our pursuit as basically living our lives—and we come to the knowledge that life can be pursued in different ways. Choice is a higher level of sophistication than awareness. So when a client puts a score here, I'll ask them to reveal to me what life pursuits they have. This discloses their reasoning, or meaning-making.

One of the things I do every year is demonstrate to others my different life pursuits. By working on them, showing them, taking comments on them, getting help with them, I enable people to help me interweave my life pursuits together.

It pays to do this in a wellth discipline. If you're not knowledgeable about and actively interweaving your life pursuits, it's difficult to align success and happiness. Resilience cannot evolve if you're oblivious to yourself and your life and what's happening around you and how you're orchestrating that whole process.

Now, some people will say, "Well this is just not that important to me. There are other things that are much more important to me right now. I have low capability. Since this has low importance for me, it's not that big a deal." My point is that we've got a total of sixty-four attributes in this survey. This is just *one* of them, and there are usually many paths up the mountain.

So it's for you to decide how sophisticated you want to be in your approach at this point and time in your life. Some people, based on their motivational profile, will value interweaving their life pursuits at a much higher level of importance than, say, establishing an emergency fund. Some people would say, "I'm just going to leave it to the cosmos to decide whether or not things work out or not." I'm fine with that. It's just that you will not have the same range of choices as you would if you had some kind of emergency fund for continuity. But then, again, that may not matter, for at some level things usually work out in the end.

There's an old proverb that says something to the effect of, "If things haven't worked out yet, you haven't reached the end."

Using a scale of 1–10 for each, calculate Requirements – (Capability) x Importance = Priority Score

Score each element on a scale of 1–10; 1=low, 10=high	Req	Cap	Imp	PS
I actively interweave my pursuits of life and work				

"What I do makes a difference to people everywhere."

In the progression of elements so far, we've gone from the "I-ness" at the beginning of my being okay to the same "I-ness" being looked at through a different lens. I don't believe that you can be wellthy until what you do makes a difference to other people. Even if it's just their saying it makes a difference or even if it's just you saying what you're doing is making a difference. You cannot feel truly wellthy and be truly resilient if you are holed up in your own little cave, without regard to the impact of your actions on the whole. Even if you don't believe in making a difference (power motivation), you make a difference every day with your actions around recycling, energy use, and sustainability.

I always try to keep the wholeness effects of what I do in the back of my mind. Like Buckminster Fuller was reputed to have said: "When you flush a toilet, it goes somewhere."

So as we go through this book, and as you enhance the attributes of resilience over time, what will begin to emerge are the properties of generic resilience. If you look at wellth discipline, some of the qualities that are consistent with generic resilience are the *ability to steer through barriers, to bounce back, to navigate uncertainty, and to reach out*. Each element offers a way to cause that to happen.

Let's look at this one in depth: *What I do makes a difference to people everywhere.*

The first thing this statement does is cause you to be reflective on what it is you do. The second thing it does is cause you to consider whether what you do actually makes a difference to someone else. To do this requires you to involve yourself with someone else's perspective.

Then when we add "everywhere," it means you have to take an even broader perspective. To even answer this, you have to reach out, and that's the key. If I can get you to reach out, I can help you produce higher levels of resilience simply by adopting a perspective that is broader and deeper and more far-ranging than a single, inwardly focused perspective. Even though the wellth discipline is basically an "I discipline," this broader perspective enhances your ability to steer through, navigate, bounce back, and of course, reach out—in other words, to increase your resilience.

The difference between this resilience system and others is that I don't believe that you can be resilient in just one part of your life. Take a look at professional reality, for example, and its demands on us. Professional reality says that we should be dependable. We should be credible. We should be trustworthy. We should be legal, ethical, moral. In the wellth discipline we're trying to develop a professional who is resilient in those areas and has the professional skills needed to be resilient at all levels of existence or under all life conditions.

Using a scale of 1–10 for each, calculate Requirements – (Capability) x Importance = Priority Score

Score each element on a scale of 1–10; 1=low, 10=high	Req	Cap	Imp	PS
What I do makes a difference to people everywhere.				

Now you can tally all your wellth discipline scores:

Wellth Discipline	Req	Cap	Imp	PS
I have established an emergency fund that is liquid and secure.				
I have friends and supporters I can count on in a moment's notice.				
I am currently enhancing my nutrition to optimal levels.				
I manage stress and rejuvenate through deliberate practice				

Wellth Discipline	Req	Cap	Imp	PS
I have eliminated all bad personal and business debt.				
I manage toxicity within and across my environments				
I actively interweave my pursuits of life and work				
What I do makes a difference to people everywhere.				
Total				

If you need help, we offer monthly tele-development training in this system, as well as qualified coaches to support your resilience journey in upping the downside. Register or log in at *www.upping-the-downside.com* for more information.

Chapter 15

Mastermind

by Mike Jay

The key to resilience is the allocation and availability of resources at the right time. Resilience is lacking when the resources are missing or are not sufficiently robust to meet the specific needs of changed life circumstances. Resilient resources create choices.

This means that we have to begin thinking a whole lot differently. What happens to us over time is that as we become resilient, the demand on us to become still more resilient increases. Each level of resilience requires an increasing level of overall resilience to take our own *density* of resilience to the next level. That is what we're doing in this model. If we can become resilient at the wellth discipline level, we then look to add another layer of resilience at the *mastermind* level.

Woven into this level, too, is a spiral-on-spiral system. This is created from an oscillating model forged by Dr. Don Beck, Spiral Dynamics Integral founder, which swings between a focus on "I or me" and a focus on "we or us." The "we" focus emerges more obviously in later levels and layers. At the mastermind level, although we're still working on "I," we're oscillating the construction and accumulation of resilience density between our "I" system and an emerging "we" system. The focus oscillates from agency (self-expression) to collaboration (sacrifice of self) and back to agency (self) as we attain resilience through the system. Even though it is depicted simply in a linear survey, resilience is a constant tug-of-war between the tensions of self and other.

The oscillation model, which Dr. Beck perfected, is probably the greatest gift his mentor, Clare Graves, gave us in his primary research (*www.clarewgraves.com*):

Through decades of research, Dr. Graves built "the emergent, cyclical, double-helix model of adult biopsychosocial systems development." (When asked about the ponderous title once during a conference, he responded with, "Well, dammit, that's what it is" and a wink.) He used pairs of letters to designate the interaction of conditions-without and latent systems-within.

Oscillation helps us begin to understand answers to these essential questions:

Are we in a frame where we are sacrificing ourselves?

Are we in a frame where we are expressing ourselves?

Graves found four systems in research he conducted in the 1950s and 1960s:

1. Express self to get now, to exploit, to have your way, to force to get whatever you want.

2. Express self calculatedly to avoid stirring up the bad feelings that you might stir up if you were just acting for yourself.

3. Sacrifice self to get later.

4. Sacrifice self to get now.

These systems were found to oscillate over time swinging back and forth as development took place from agency to advocacy.

Picking up with the model, once you have some basic resilience in the wellth discipline, it's time to get started in the mastermind level. In his 1960 book *Think and Grow Rich*, Napoleon Hill defined the Master Mind Principle as "coordination of knowledge and effort, in a spirit of harmony, between two or more people, for the attainment of a definite purpose." He identified two characteristics of the principle: economic and psychic. Economic advantages may be created, Hill wrote, by any person who surrounds himself with the advice, counsel, and personal cooperation of a group of people who are willing to lend wholehearted aid in a spirit of perfect harmony. On the psychic phase he made reference to spiritual forces: "No two minds ever come together without, thereby, creating a third, invisible, intangible force which may be likened to a third mind." He saw the human mind as a form of energy, part of which is spiritual in nature. When the minds of two people are coordinated in a spirit of harmony, the spiritual units of energy of each mind form an affinity, and this constitutes the psychic phase of the Master Mind.

To be resilient you are going to need more than yourself. In a collective you are not limited by your own individual capacity. You are limited only by the capacity of the most advanced person. Therefore, you always want to be in a collective where you are a weak weakest link. If you are the most advanced link, then you've got some work to do. This leads us to the first element of the mastermind.

"I choose my relationships deliberately."

Most of the time people are chosen. We don't really choose our relationships. Something in our chemistry, our unconscious, our desires, something chooses the relationships that we have, even if it's just passing through time. At this level you begin to understand how to deliberately choose your relationships.

When was the last time you went up a really smart person, way smarter than you, and said, "I'd like to take you to lunch" or "I'd like to pick your brain. Would that be possible?" I've found most people who have greater capacity than you almost always allow you to do that.

Choose your relationships deliberately. This is one thing you can do without a lot of resources. You can begin to choose your relationships differently. Then, of course, people have to choose you back.

Using a scale of 1–10 for each, calculate Requirements – (Capability) x Importance = Priority Score

Score each element on a scale of 1–10; 1=low, 10=high	Req	Cap	Imp	PS
I choose my relationships deliberately.				

"I have a council of wise people I meet with regularly."

How do we do this in today's world? Let's imagine some of the ways.

My own approach is to interview people. I keep reaching out to people around the world and saying, "Can I talk to you?" It takes some investment on your part to do this with logistics and preparation. I'm required to deal with all kinds of personality differences and issues. But it's amazing how many people I've talked to and how smart they are and how developed they are in their particular area. I recently reached out to a person from Egypt. Now we're forming a relationship whereby I'll go there and get a chance to look at the culture and meet some of the wise people in Egypt. The easiest way for me to meet with a council of wise people is to keep interviewing these smart people.

The other thing I do is, I have an attorney, an accountant, an insurance person, and most other types of professions in the Yellow Pages. I ask them for help. I tell them what I'm doing and ask, could I do better? Do I need to change the way I do business? Do I need some different kind of insurance?

Some people have a personal board of directors. Don't limit yourself to these ideas. Find a way that works for you. It's important that you do this over time, that is, if you're interested in resilience.

Using a scale of 1–10 for each, calculate Requirements – (Capability) x Importance = Priority Score

Score each element on a scale of 1–10; 1=low, 10=high	Req	Cap	Imp	PS
I have a council of wise people I meet with regularly.				

"Through others I lower risks of cost inflation and price deflation."

This element is *agentic* even though *power* is emergent *through others*. It's something you have to do yourself. Most people are not going to come up to you and say, "Can I help you with your business?" You'd ask, "What is the catch?" and they'd say, "There is no catch. I just want to help you." Most of us are not going to find people like that.

Very seldom do costs go down in a complex system. Though some key costs may go down, overall it becomes increasingly costly to do business as a professional in the modern age, if only because of the hidden cost of learning and the exponential rise in complexity. For instance, even though it looks like the cost of technology is going down, and it's increasing your productivity, you are likely to pay more for technology when you consider the learning costs involved. The reason is the learning curve. If you're not able to adopt a technology on your same curve, you'll have to do it through others.

I'm controlling cost inflation by having some work done at a very low cost to us. Yet the people we're paying are enjoying a high standard of living in their own country. It works because these workers have a different currency and are on a different developmental curve. And I feel wonderful because we're lifting people up by offering them wages that people here won't work for.

Are you suffering higher and higher costs and yet competing for lower and lower prices? In other words, are your products and services becoming commoditized? The math adds up to a lower standard of living. Recently, I wanted some additional bookkeeping done. So I went to *elance. com*, my favorite place for hiring global labor. When I got the bids back, I saw they ranged from $20 to $2000. While I believe you get what you pay for, the stark contrast in the global or overseas bids was something to cause you to think.

In 1999, I wrote an article that was later published in *Consulting Today* called "Being a Skilled Professional is Not Enough!" In it I stated that the world we were living in was not going to be the world we were going to work in as professionals. Things are changing fast, and every professional in the developed world had better reassess their resilience and their future in light of globalization.

The key in masterminding at this particular level is the engagement of others. This is an engagement issue of programmatically reaching out.

Using a scale of 1–10 for each, calculate Requirements – (Capability) x Importance = Priority Score

Score each element on a scale of 1–10; 1=low, 10=high	Req	Cap	Imp	PS
Through others I lower risks of cost inflation and price deflation.				

"Involving others improves the execution of my business."

You will have be the one to involve and enroll others in discovering how you can improve the execution of your business. Execution is a difficult concept. I few years ago, I took an assessment. One of the things I learned that shocked me was, I don't do well in execution. I start far more than I finish. This, of course, was no surprise to anyone who really knew me, but for some reason, I had never understood how much resilient density I lacked around execution, as I had always been able to achieve almost everything I wanted. Since then I've become more effective at involving people in the execution of my business. I actually *have* become more resilient in this respect.

In the mastermind process, we're not yet talking about the ability to improve your execution. We're talking about a simple thing: Have you asked anybody lately to take a look at what you're doing? Have you sought feedback on it? Have you done a customer survey? There are all kinds of ways that you can actualize this element.

Using a scale of 1–10 for each, calculate Requirements – (Capability) x Importance = Priority Score

Score each element on a scale of 1–10; 1=low, 10=high	Req	Cap	Imp	PS
Involving others improves the execution of my business.				

"I explore specific strategies to innovate around service delivery."

This element is a bit different from the previous one about cost inflation and price deflation. Let's assume that we're not producing a commodity. Are there ways we can talk to others about how we deliver our services so we can improve our success and happiness? What are the components of service delivery?

One answer you almost certainly will not think of is the personal costs to your own life—your personal mental, emotional, physical, and spiritual costs of service delivery. What are the costs of service delivery to your peace of mind, time spent with your kids, your quality of life, your standard of living? How much time do you spend in front of the computer, tied to your cell phone, behind the wheel, or in the air? How much weighs on your mind on a daily basis? How big is your to-do list? Lowering costs here will yield tremendous resilience.

We get caught up in the professional life because we've created this job for ourselves. Then often we suffer the consequences. Through masterminding you can explore with others how to innovate around service delivery. Not only do we depend on technology, but we can depend on other people's ideas, money, effort, time, attention, and energy to lower costs.

Here's an example from my life. After coaching for fifteen years with people one-on-one, I became less enamored with the coaching business. So I wrote my first book in 1999, and after that I began training people in coaching. Soon after that I realized that training people was not as much fun as innovating around coaching, so I switched back to innovating around the past models I had used. I reinvigorated my coaching career with executives by using a system called the *www.coachcertified.com* system I had developed in the late eighties. Once I put a millennial spin on the system, I found I could get my life back and enjoy my clients again.

Innovating service delivery to improve consumption of your products and services may provide an entirely new business line. How many of you have bought something you haven't consumed? Or purchased a program on the web that you never read or fully used? Or never fully operationalized a new practice? How about the people on the receiving end of *your* professional services? Most people think that closing the sale is the end of the story. But how might you have innovated around your service delivery for your clients? Can you reduce those hidden costs and lost opportunities by supporting clients after you've closed the sale, by helping them understand and properly consume what they've purchased from you? How can you innovate to lower the costs to others of your service delivery and provide more valuable service?

Using a scale of 1–10 for each, calculate Requirements – (Capability) x Importance = Priority Score

Score each element on a scale of 1–10; 1=low, 10=high	Req	Cap	Imp	PS
I explore specific strategies to innovate around service delivery.				

"I frequently find ways to share my life and work vision."

At this point, we're not talking about *just* the "I." We're talking about the "we." We are beginning to blend the two together in sharing. One of the things that makes you more resilient as a person is letting people know how they can help you. But how do they know that? When you share with others things that you need, things that you're doing, and things that you're trying to accomplish, people want to help you.

This type of sharing isn't just telling other people about your dreams, but about the things you are trying to do. You never know, people may just step up and say, "I've been wanting to do something like that too. Is there some way that I can help?" You attract support.

Harvard professor Kurt Fischer, who specializes in cognitive and emotional development and learning, found that when you are in a supportive environment, you can work at a higher level of complexity. This means your limitations are fewer than when you are working by yourself. You're more resilient, because you have more resources to work with. You work with more intention. You work with more encouragement. You work with more support.

The formality of gathering a mastermind group for this type of sharing can be especially helpful. When was the last time you sat down with a group of people to tell them who you want to be, what you want to become, what you like and don't like, or what you really want in life? I'll bet it's close to never.

Using a scale of 1–10 for each, calculate Requirements – (Capability) x Importance = Priority Score

Score each element on a scale of 1–10; 1=low, 10=high	Req	Cap	Imp	PS
I frequently find ways to share my life and work vision.				

"I include others as I integrate deliberate learning practices."

The thing that most people criticize in this model is that you start out with a fairly basic concept, then all of a sudden it becomes so complex, it's almost hard to understand. When I first created this model a number of years ago, I told people, "Just work on the first three or four elements of the process in each category. Don't worry about the more advanced ones." You can see that the more advanced elements require more connection. If I'm including others as I integrate streams of experience, reflection, conceptualization, and experimentation, that's much more sophisticated and complex by its very nature.

We draw here on David Kolb's work on learning styles. I'm including others as I learn. Most people do not do this, because they're unconsciously projecting their own learning style, which is most likely incomplete; it leaves out part of the cycle of learning, which requires others in order for it to be practiced.

One key at this level is to step back with some perspective of your own, enlightened by the perspectives of others. It's not easy to ask for feedback, let alone not take it personally when it's given, but that's precisely what you must do to build these more complex layers of resilience into the overall density of your deliberate practices.

One example might be that you ask people to join your "developmental" team. You ask them for feedback on specific issues of your behavior and design, not overloading them with a lot of detail — they're busy too — but allowing them to participate and share perspectives they have from "their" learning style.

Using a scale of 1–10 for each, calculate Requirements – (Capability) x Importance = Priority Score

Score each element on a scale of 1–10; 1=low, 10=high	Req	Cap	Imp	PS
I include others as I integrate deliberate learning practices.				

"Whole-making is an approach considered in professional life."

I acknowledge that this one is difficult. Why include such difficult things here? It's because we're trying to produce layers of resilience. We want to produce significant density so we can bend, but not break, when surprises occur. We don't know what future life conditions will look like. Obviously, if life conditions become extremely difficult, and you're in survival mode, you will not be thinking about energizing a whole-making approach to your professional life!

Almost every person I talk to, every person I consult with, and every person I coach is a professional. You know what they're doing every day? They're getting up and fighting fires every day. They're not asking: "How can I make myself more whole in this day? How can I engage more of who I am? How can I feel the energy of what it's like to use all of my gifts and share that with other people? How can I put this at the top of my list today?"

This is a complex level of resilience construction and requires design to make it work—a mastermind. At the same time, it's there for people who want to *deliberately* practice in this way. This is not some airy approach that is abstract. This is clearly a way for you to be who you are in the trappings of everyday life.

Some people, for instance, have a lot of the elements of the mastermind process well in hand. What is next for them? In order to produce an additional layer of resilience, what you end up doing is finding a way to look at all of these concepts together: "I choose my relationships deliberately. I'm getting better at that. I have a council of wise people I meet with pretty regularly. Through others, I'm lowering my exposure. I involve others in discovering. I'm doing it at a fairly high level. I explore with others specific strategies to lower my costs. I do that pretty often. I frequently discuss with others aspects of sharing my life. I do that a lot, and probably some of you are tired of it by now. I'm including others as I integrate streams of experience, reflection, conceptualization, and experimentation. Yes, I'm personally trying to do that more and more every day, and perhaps you are as well. It teaches me about me. It teaches me about others. I do that through my teaching and sharing."

Now, the key is for me to not get lost in all of that and to think that by *doing* all the time that I am *becoming*. Certainly, doing is related to becoming, but becoming should be something that is elevated to a level of energy where you think about it and feel through it once in a while.

We don't normally sit around and ask, "What am I becoming as a person? Am I making myself whole, or do I depend on others to make me whole? What would whole-making look like for me? Does my current professional practice share with people who I really am?"

Each of us would have different ways of doing that. How high is it on your priority list?

Most people reading this book haven't even gotten this on their radar yet. But we're starting to approach a time when some people have resolved their existential issues, and they're looking for what masterminding would be like at a high level of deliberate practice.

Well, masterminding would look like a group of people with whole-making at the top of their list getting together once in a while to talk, share, and learn from one another.

Would you become more resilient over time if you were able to do that? My sense is, yes. It goes back to my philosophy of when we work in support, we work beyond our individual limitations to an extent.

Because this model is built on recursion, one of the things that you can do with this eighth mastermind element is apply it to all the previous seven. Or you could apply it to the other sixty-three elements in the entire model. You could recurse each element on everything else. That's the leverage in this model.

Each layer of the onion of our life can be peeled *around and down*. That is recursion to *up the downside*. Or we can build it from the inside out, or outside in, whichever way you prefer. Those are things that you can think about in this mastermind category. When we talk about mastermind, we're talking about the principle of moving beyond our own limitations. That's the key in mastermind.

Most of the work you will do—that people ask you to do and the things you think about doing—you'll try to do on your own. If you do not have a formal mastermind group where you are consistently contributing and sharing and asking for help, you will almost always have a lower level of resilience. You can trace the mastermind principle all the way back since recorded time. There are eight principles here, but I guarantee, if you focus on making yourself whole first every day, then everyone around you—your business, your customers, your employees, your clients—*all will get better.* They will all get better, *when* you do.

Using a scale of 1–10 for each, calculate Requirements – (Capability) x Importance = Priority Score

Score each element on a scale of 1–10; 1=low, 10=high	Req	Cap	Imp	PS
Whole-making is an approach considered in professional life.				

Now you can tally all your mastermind scores:

MasterMind				
I choose my relationships deliberately.				
I have a council of wise people I meet with regularly.				
Through others I lower risks of cost inflation and price deflation.				
Involving others improves the execution of my business.				
I explore specific strategies to innovate around service delivery.				
I frequently find ways to share my life and work vision.				
I include others as I integrate deliberate learning practices.				
Whole-making is an approach considered in professional life.				
Total				

Remember, if you need help, we offer monthly tele-development training in this system, as well as qualified coaches to support your resilience journey in upping the downside. Register or log in at *www. upping-the-downside.com* for more information.

Chapter 16

Engagement
by Mike Jay

We move now to the third level, category, or process of the professional resilience model: *engagement*. Here we bring in power. A lot of the time professionals work with power indirectly. I call them Yellow Page professionals. These are the people who go to school, take professional training, and often are either apprenticed in or taught for long periods of time to master a particular craft or discipline or way of doing things. Their power is almost always indirect—or referent—power. It's power earned through prestige or status given by the social group.

If you are in the Yellow Pages, you are most likely to be found by people looking for some kind of professional service. They're looking for someone to solve a type of problem that occurs over and over and over again in the lives of many people, and there are people who have become masterful in solving these types of problems. A florist makes bouquets and sends flowers to people. A plumber, an insurance agent, even my spa repairman or folks at my spa store are professionals because they cater to people who are interested in hot tubs, spas, steam baths. They have a specific area of expertise. There is a tremendous amount of referent power involved in the professional system.

For the most part, though, these professionals do not understand how to bring up their own *personal power*. They rely on credibility, on references, and on referrals. They rely on someone else saying this is the person you should go to. They oftentimes find themselves with low power densities—or few developed and mastered ways of doing things that create clients directly.

One of the things we want to do is be clear with the professional that there is a parallel stream in which we can build meme density in using power for engagement. We can build algorithmic density, or specific solutions that determine what you do in a specific case. We can build skill density in areas of potentially significant risk. We can employ a range of power to increase resilience. That's what we call *upping the downside.*

For the most part, you do not find professionals who have the density in a professional system to approach people directly like a sales entrepreneur or a Steve Jobs or Bill Gates, who have their own system they are trying to sell and influence people with. That's why so many professionals on the cool side of life—people who choose to "ask for permission, rather than forgiveness," people on the sacrifice-yourself side of life—prefer the professional way, because they don't have to get into that agentic role.

This third category—engagement—is agentic and "I" related. As a professional, although you may not share this particular area with your clients or peers, you may want to think about it, because this is density around the "I."

In our politically correct society, at least in the United States in 2008, there is a tremendous de-emphasis or rejection of the "I." In fact, self-promotion or self-*anything* in today's society is frowned upon. You can be shunned directly by showing any kind of reference to self, which is why U.S. society at this time is almost completely in a sacrifice-of-self mode, at least on the surface. Underneath that political correctness, to me, is a huge shadow and an underlying yearning for agency. What I am trying to do is to bring light onto the shadow for the professional through this process category.

Essentially, there are some downside issues to being a professional. There are downside issues to relying on your referent power—the power that you get from others or what we call social-proof or social power. So, part of what we talk about in the eight elements of the process of engagement are some things that we do to take care of the "I" part of the profession. By doing these in a parallel or simultaneous design, even in what may need to be more of a covert process at first, you do not risk feeling that as a professional you are becoming self-aggrandizing or self-promoting.

This category of resilience, then, is centered on people who are working on the cool side of sacrifice of self, where *other* is more important. Its purpose is to build more "self" density. We're going to *up the downside* so that if life conditions or levels of existence shift and you're forced to change the sacrifice-of-self structure—the structural coupling between who you are as a person and what the requirements are in your world—you will have developed some of the skills and increased the density of algorithms you will need to rely on under these existential conditions.

What happens is that when life conditions hiccup or levels of existence hiccup, the *requirements*—those specific things you must do to maintain your standard of living—shift dramatically. They require you to draw on a different kind of power. Life conditions continue to ratchet down, ratchet down, and ratchet down until they reach a level you can satisfy in order to stop them from cascading still further down—this is the definition of downside. The downside is where your professional level of capability will finally stop you from sinking any further when life conditions regress dramatically and suddenly.

Requirements get more severe, for instance, in recessions, which most of us have not encountered in our recent past, so we're not able to evoke, having recently adjusted to the dangers in lingering memes that might come to the surface in these discontinuous or disruptive circumstances, such as wildly oscillating stock markets and runaway commodities prices.

At the time of this writing, in early 2008, we have a real estate bubble in the United States that if it hasn't popped, has a big hole in it and is seriously leaking air. You might picture one of those blown-up balloons that when you let it go, sputters all over the place chaotically. That's what the real estate industry is starting to do only in a more controlled fashion. Homeowners are starting to get scared. They see the value of their homes dropping and the length of time houses are on the market extending dramatically. Other related issues are starting to pop up as this thing flies around letting out air. Professionals in this industry are scared. They're taking home a lot less money than they were before. How do they manage in a situation of a serious downturn in the real estate market, in real estate requirements?

The requirements have shifted dramatically. It used to be if you had a license and you could go out and find some listings, you could make money in real estate. Now all of a sudden, the only people making money are the ones with sufficient algorithmic capacity to be able to match the new requirements, namely, that there are a whole lot of people competing to sell a lot of houses to a few buyers. All kinds of new dynamics are going on. This is a perfect example of the need to up the downside as a real estate professional.

Now if you had been going to resilience training and had been looking at some of the eight elements below, you would immediately rise from the pack and go right to the top. You would be able to pick up power and skill in an area that says the only way to differentiate yourself is to power up when current conditions change the professional business model.

And so we begin examining the elements of engagement.

"My instincts and goals are crystal clear for my professional life."

Let's use "uncertainty" as the context for engagement.

This first statement seems simple, but actually is profound. There are two things that undergird agency in the statement: "My." It's an "I" statement and it's an "are."

What does that mean?

It means we have specific, innate, inborn, wired-in ways of doing things that are instinctual for us. They are not instincts for everyone. These include inborn talent, strength, weakness, opportunity, or thin-slicing (see *Blink* by Malcolm Gladwell). In other words, when the real estate market begins to go down, what do I do *instinctually* in real estate if I'm a real estate agent? I have specific things that I do naturally. Am I clear on those? Can I understand when and how those are triggered?

The second thing I need to understand is what my goals are (my intention towards requirements) and how the world works. What are the requirements I need to be constantly weighing and prioritizing? What happens, for instance, if my goal is to sell a million dollars worth of real estate in a month, and all of a sudden what it takes to sell a million dollars is doubled or tripled? What then?

Do I understand what I need to do as a person to continue to reach my professional goals? What is it going to take from me? Am I going to need some additional support, some additional encouragement? Do I have to contact three or four times as many people as before when I was working in the old market? Do I understand that? Do I understand how the things around me work? These are the kinds of things this first statement gets at.

If you can't answer questions like these for your profession, and you don't understand your instincts and goals, and you can't understand your goals relative to the environment that you're in, then you probably need to do some work on the elements in this category if you're going to *up the downside* when life conditions change.

Using a scale of 1–10 for each, calculate Requirements – (Capability) x Importance = Priority Score

Score each element on a scale of 1–10; 1=low, 10=high	Req	Cap	Imp	PS
My instincts and goals are crystal clear for my professional life.				

One caveat before we move on that I need to make clear. As a professional, you have a fiduciary responsibility to rise beyond your own "self" needs and get your professional domain's questions and answers clarified. Yet, most of you are going to be working in a single-person, professional role. How are you going to keep "you" from suboptimizing your professional practice? This is most likely the most difficult situation you will ever be in when existential conditions tank or are disrupted for a period of time.

In other words, what *you* want and need, will conflict with your professional wants and needs, and if you're unclear about where the "I" begins and ends, you're most likely headed for difficulties . . . in other words, your downside is a *lot* lower than for someone who is clear on these two domains and what's required in each case. A word to the wise: Do the work necessary to resolve element one in engagement before moving on.

"I seek out people smarter and more experienced than I am."

This is a difficult one, because it seems counterintuitive to the powering up of "I." What this one does is recognize that if you depend only on yourself, you have limitations in terms of your professional power.

On the other hand, if you depend on your own appropriate instincts and then seek the rest of what you need from the outside, you have no limitations. What we're talking about here is that if you have enough ego strength to seek out other people who have more experience and are smarter than you, you will be more professionally resilient.

If you're selling a million a month in real estate, but you're constantly taking people to lunch who sell ten million a month in real estate, that's a pretty good way to create resilience, provided you can learn from them. That's a good way for you to *up the downside*.

Or, if you're working with a certain group of people, and you notice that there are a couple of them who always seem to solve problems easier and faster than the others, and their solutions seem to come with more elegance, perhaps those are the people you want to seek out.

Note that this level of the model doesn't necessarily say that you *align* with people who are smarter and more experienced than you are, but that you notice those people who are out there and begin to reach out to them over time.

How can we keep things that we don't know are going to happen from narrowing our prospects? How can we keep the future from coming at us so fast that it takes away our standard of living? Resilience comes from being able to reach out beyond your present paradigm, which can be limiting in the downside. *That* is upping the downside.

If you are constantly paying attention to people who are smarter and more experienced than you, even if you do not know them, you will notice when things happen a lot sooner, because the smart and more experienced people have most of the time already seen it coming or have already been through it. "I" has better radar as a result.

If you pay attention to your neighbors, and not just any neighbors but the ones who are probably leading and managing things a bit differently, that's part of powering up your indirect downside in this particular area of density.

It's also a challenge to your ego.

One thing that's going to happen to your ego position in this program is you'll find that upping the downside involves being less embedded in your own ego. This element is one particular way to achieve that. Some people cannot work directly on ego issues because they are constantly comparing themselves with others. Part of the process here is to relieve the direct pressure on ego and still allow you to go through the same set of mechanics that working on your ego would. We are dis-embedding your ego by giving you the tactics without so much of the strategy. Okay?

Using a scale of 1–10 for each, calculate Requirements – (Capability) x Importance = Priority Score

Score each element on a scale of 1–10; 1=low, 10=high	Req	Cap	Imp	PS
I seek out people smarter and more experienced than I am.				

"I know the leading indicators of success in my profession."

This is one of the biggest problems I see with people today who get caught unaware and are blindsided by change. They don't see what is happening though other people are starting to see it, because they don't have a clear idea of what the professional scoreboard in their industry is, says, and does. If you can begin to understand this, if you will spend time with a coach or someone else who can guide you in understanding the leading indicators of success and failures in your profession, rather than being caught off-guard by change, you'll anticipate it.

In my case, for instance, I have a lot of different areas of success to understand because of the range of my work. I have to compete with internet marketers, because I am choosing to stay and build online. I have to compete with other coaches, because I am in the coaching industry. I have to compete with trainers who are continually offering people choices for learning things that I also offer. I have to compete with people who are politically correct. I have to understand how my own lack of political correctness sometimes creates issues. There are a lot of indicators of my professional success that I have to be aware of across a pretty broad spectrum. I continually look at them and try to understand whether or not the indicators can give me any idea of how to be successful over time with lower costs.

Do you know what the critical success factors are for your profession? If not, there is a good chance you're not practicing them, and they will come back to haunt you. This means that your downside is a *lot* lower than someone who understands what those leading indicators are and can shift or adapt as needed to become more resilient. The big part of the process in this element is the knowing part. Do you have the knowing part down? That is the key here.

Using a scale of 1–10 for each, calculate Requirements – (Capability) x Importance = Priority Score

Score each element on a scale of 1–10; 1=low, 10=high	Req	Cap	Imp	PS
I know the leading indicators of success in my profession.				

"I am currently optimizing the use of my energy."

Your energy equation is how much you are spending to get what you're getting, or how much you are investing to do what it is you're doing. Any time you face a challenge, any time you get into a situation that puts pressure on your business, the more optimal your relationship to *energy and information*, the more resilient you will be.

There are several reasons to look at resilience as an equilibrium of energy and information. If you are in a position of strength and are optimizing energy, you're spinning off what I call free energy, which means you have the energy available for adaptation. If you are not doing that, if you are not working mostly in and through your limitations, you have no energy for adaptation. You are stuck at the current level of performance, because you're using all of your energy to deal with whatever is happening now. You are most likely in a struggle of trying to close a gap, which uses all of your available energy.

Now imagine what happens when change comes in the form of a cascading series of requirements that dramatically shift your industry or your marketplace. Imagine what that does to a non-optimal use of energy and information. It makes it a lot worse. You have no additional energy to apply to doing things that are necessary to meet new requirements. You will cascade down as far as your own equation takes you. That can be way, *way* down, which means you have a lot more range over which you have to manage your energy and information than someone who has an optimal energy and information situation and can spin off some free energy while continuing to work some in their talent or strength areas. Even when working through your strengths is net negative on others around you, *you* are still spinning off free energy—something to keep in mind.

Let's imagine a real estate professional who is optimizing energy. It's fairly easy to make twenty contacts in one day and show three houses a day. All of a sudden with a shift in the market, a sub-prime meltdown, I need to show six houses a day. But I've had a little bit of time available; I've got my system down; I'm pretty optimal; I wasn't using all of my day. I can easily add three more appointments a day. I'm resilient now when the requirements have gone up, because I was optimizing my time before and had some free energy available. Therefore my standard of living remains the same because I was *optimal* coming into this period of change.

Part of the process of optimizing the use of your energy is having clear knowledge of what energy you have to use and what energy is required in the environment, per the three previous elements. So it's very important that you're optimizing. You also *have* to understand where your free energy comes from. One thing that I found over time is *very* helpful in understanding where the well of free energy is the strengthsfinding paradigm created by the people at Gallup. If you do *nothing* else as a result of this book, buy the book *Strengthsfinder* 2.0 and take the online assessment included in the book. When you identify those top five talent areas, at least you'll know where the areas are that generate free energy for you!

Note how the spiral-on-spiral system works as an example here with our realtor. We're looking at a sacrifice-of-self system in this element in the engagement process category. In addition, I'm currently optimizing the use of my energy, which is actually an avoidant system, in other words, *sacrifice self now to get later*, as Spiral Dynamics would say. This means I have free energy, because I'm avoiding working to the full extent of my limits, and I'm taking advantage of my talents to create strengths.

Using an avoidant approach at this level of power density means you have more robustness in the system, because you understand the use of the "I" in this relationship with energy and information. You also understand that because you have saved some for later, you have some additional free energy to spend, even though you created that relationship with personal power.

It's like having a bank account that you're continually making deposits in, only the deposits are made with agency. When you're working in an optimal way, you are continually, each day, each minute of your life, making deposits into your bank account for the use of energy and information. This means you are not overtiring yourself. You are getting enough sleep. You're not overexerting yourself. You have enough time to continue your physical regimen and are getting or keeping yourself in shape. You have time to eat right. You have time to manage yourself. All those things are occurring as requirements, depending on your own particular self-knowledge.

Guess what this is doing?

It's creating a store of resilience that you then can draw on when you get into situations that are less optimal. If, therefore, you have no store of resilience, you are using energy and information poorly, there is no low-hanging fruit for you to pluck.

You're getting buried, because in your normal situation you have never gotten yourself to a place where you take care of yourself, where you manage your energy well, where you are creating a store of resilience—where you really understand your unique gifts and challenges. Robustness emerges from optimal being, having, doing, and becoming, not from over-stretching your system on a continual basis.

Optimization is essentially an issue of the accountability or avoidant system. You become accountable to your instincts, your goals, *your* requirements, to other people who serve as the canary in the coal mine, to the smart people, the experienced people who have been there and done that.

The indicators of your professional success are in the forefront of your design, and all of a sudden you have an accountability system that actually has a reserve built up. The reserve keeps you from cascading past the point of the downside. You don't end up losing your standard of living. You don't end up crashing your whole system and having to reboot the whole thing. You are resilient enough to take a hit or two or three or four. You have some stored up resilience.

This goes with families too. If you are not taking care of your family, investing in your family, and you hit a downturn and need to ask your family for support, there is nothing for them to give you. You have no reserve of energy to draw from, no store of resilience. When we talk about energy, we're talking about everything that is powered by energy and information.

Using a scale of 1–10 for each, calculate Requirements – (Capability) x Importance = Priority Score

Score each element on a scale of 1–10; 1=low, 10=high	Req	Cap	Imp	PS
I am currently optimizing the use of my energy.				

"I know and am leveraging my talents optimally."

From Gallup's StrengthFinders Assessment, we know that "talent + (skills and knowledge) = strength." This element in the survey is basically the achievement equivalent of the power level, which means that I *know* and I *do*. Not just I know, but I know, I do, and I do it optimally. This builds enterprising density.

If you're working through this survey and you're the cool, self-sacrificing type of professional, you may be asking, how can I build my offside or agentic density? How can I become more enterprising, more able to develop and achieve? That is a key point with this element. (Note that the odd-numbered elements under this category of engagement are for the sacrificing-self people to build offside density. The self-oriented people who want to be kinder, gentler, and more considerate should focus on the even-numbered elements to develop offside sacrifice-of-self density.) Both are required in sufficient amounts under existential requirements in different circumstances. In other words, you could be the efficient person in either side, but because you're not robust enough in both sides, your downside is a lot lower than someone who is moving towards an optimal understanding of all the requirements. As I made the case in my earlier book, CPR *for the* SOUL, you don't have to change, but you do have to have the conversation, and change will emerge from that conversation.

This book is *not* about changing yourself. It's about awareness of who you are and who you are not, and developing the capability to get help optimally.

When I say work on these elements, I don't mean that you have to change. I mean that you have to bring them about, to emerge them (algorithms = solution sets). Some of you will say, "I'll never be able to do this." Then you need to get some help, to reach out to others with strengths in those areas.

Most of us hallucinate about our ability to change. We refuse to change but *pretend* that we will. At the surface, we may modify our behavior to a certain extent, but we only do that when we're motivated. Since many requirements of reality are often not aligned with our motivation—our talents—because we really can't change our motivation, which may be high in one case but low in another area, we don't do whatever it is that reality says must be done with enough frequency in our professional practices. So our success rate goes down. If our success rate starts going down, we end up becoming less resilient. Of course that is hard on you, and it's hard on everybody else. So, do yourself a favor and don't pretend that you are going to change. To resolve these things, reach out to people for support.

I *know and am leveraging my talents optimally* means I understand what my talents are. I want to spend more time there. But I also understand that as a professional I need to emerge a system that takes care of *all* the requirements, not just those requirements for me in my talent areas.

Remember, though, that you may have a talent that develops because of "conditioned" skill and knowledge into a strength. It doesn't mean that the strength beyond the range in which it's actually considered to be a strength is going to be optimal. Often our strengths are the seeds of our greatest limitations—keep that in mind.

Using a scale of 1–10 for each, calculate Requirements – (Capability) x Importance = Priority Score

Score each element on a scale of 1–10; 1=low, 10=high	Req	Cap	Imp	PS
I know and am leveraging my talents optimally.				

"I consider how I relate to others."

Notice that this doesn't say I change the way I relate to others. It doesn't say that I relate to others well. It says I consider how I relate to others.

This is a low level of engagement that says if we can just get people to begin to *consider* how they relate to others instead of saying you have to change the way you relate to others, we're already farther down the road without raising barriers driven by unconscious fears. These emotional intelligence tests that are in vogue tell you you're low in empathy. Now, as a result of taking the test, you have to change the way you relate to others. The first thing you get is an increase in fear; the second is resistance. If you want to drive out fear and resistance, you don't go at these things directly.

First of all, let's *consider* it. Have you just considered how others relate to you? Have you just considered how you relate to other people? Have you considered that? The first-stage person who has no awareness will say, I hadn't thought about it that way. When is the last time you got real feedback from someone about how you consider others?

Earlier in my life, most people were telling me I had to change, but I really never questioned it. I just kept working on trying to change, to put myself in other people's shoes. When you hear a person say that who has no empathy, trust me, they have no concept of what that experience means.

Listen. The very fact that you don't have empathy means you *can't* do that. Why would you pretend that you can? Why would somebody else try to teach you what that is like when in fact the way in which you have to do that is all driven through a natural wiring system — having emotional radar that helps you look out for other people, having ideas about what it's like to actually feel like somebody else must feel? (Which comes naturally to people who have high empathy talents.)

Those of us who have no empathy can't even do that. Why would we pretend that we can? How can we pretend we have a theory of mind that doesn't exist? Remember, *strength* requires more than skills and knowledge, it also requires *talent*. You can have a lot of skills and knowledge, and that will help. But if you are missing the talent—and consideration of others, empathy, has certainly been identified as a talent—then you have unmotivated skill and knowledge working at a much different level of efficacy than when combined with talent.

I'm constantly amazed at this dance between those low in this natural area of empathy and those who teach it, who are high. The same dance occurs when people who have logic talents try to teach logic to the illogical. Will we ever really learn the dynamics of what is occurring here?

People who work in blank-slate theory—meaning there are no inherent limits to how society can shape human psychology, versus the opposing view that human nature is primarily influenced by epigenetics—pretend that we can grow our strengths through skills and knowledge.

Yet it's become reasonably clear that innate *talent* is a necessary addition to achieve levels that are both competent and frequent enough to satisfy demand requirements—for emotional intelligence or other high-performance indicators.

Again, the idea of considering how you relate to others is the first step of awareness and dis-embedding or moving the ego position not totally out of the way, but just enough to the side that you can say, "I don't plan on changing, but I could consider how I relate to other people." Fine. Let's let that do whatever work it can, because whatever self-awareness is there will improve if you consider that and if you ask people about that.

This week did you consider how you relate to other people? Well, yeah, I did. I found myself a couple of times wondering about that. That is the first stage. Again, not going at it directly. Purpose and competence emerge later on if they can. If they don't, then get help, reach out, and bring in "talent" to create more resilient levels of consideration. So again, this is cool-side density we're considering in a warm-side process. I know, it may sound confusing, but it will prepare you with greater resilience density if you work with a system that opens the doors both ways.

Using a scale of 1–10 for each, calculate Requirements – (Capability) x Importance = Priority Score

Score each element on a scale of 1–10; 1=low, 10=high	Req	Cap	Imp	PS
I consider how I relate to others.				

"I differentiate how I engage with different people and activities."

Basically, what this element is saying is some form of: I treat people the way they want to be treated. The reason it is written this way is to give an indication of whether a person understands the *conceptual* range of this algorithm. It's an indication of whether they are at this particular level of sophistication. If somebody can articulate to me several different ways they engage different people differently, I know they are able to range conceptually in a different area than someone who gets stuck in the language.

To illustrate this element, if a person is motivated to high vengeance and feels the need to be vindicated, you engage that person significantly differently than you do a person who is low vengeance and has no need for vindication. Not only that, we know which one is going to avoid conflict; therefore, can you differentiate how you engage those two different people?

Whether you use one model or another, at this level you are going to have a model that you can articulate regarding how you differentiate your engagement with different people. You are going to be able to articulate the algorithms in the model, or you are not going to function resiliently at this level of the process. That's all there is to it.

The process of discovery tells us something. Do you need to function at this level? How do you know? What are the requirements of your business, where functioning at this level is optimal? What would it take to up the downside? There's no use wasting energy and resources in an area where you're not going to need to function, because there are no requirements.

In this particular case, obviously a professional would need to know how they engage people. Therefore, you are probably going to want to work at this level, at least on design to remove the gaps, if nothing else.

Quick example: A pediatrician with no bedside manner. We can do several things: We can try to change the doctor and send him or her to bedside-manner training school, or we can make sure the doctor is always accompanied by a nurse who has great bedside skills and can lead. Over time, this design will support the increased conditioning of the doctor if there is any hope at all. If there isn't, then the "design" would redirect the career path of the doctor to an area where their talents allow them the greatest opportunity for success.

Using a scale of 1–10 for each, calculate Requirements – (Capability) x Importance = Priority Score

Score each element on a scale of 1–10; 1=low, 10=high	Req	Cap	Imp	PS
I differentiate how I engage with different people and activities.				

"I engage people outside of my circle of concern."

This last level of engagement is purposely counterintuitive. But if you're going to be more resilient, if you're going to up the downside, you need to understand people outside of your circle of concern and engage them. This means that you need to read things in other people's industries.

I love going to the shops of different professionals. I get a massage every now and then. I go to the barbershop. They always have different kinds of magazines than what I read. I spend a little time looking at them. What is it like to be in a women's industry? What is it like to read *Family Circle* magazine? What is it like to read *Sports and Field*? What kinds of things are going on in those magazines? What's going on in the legal world or the accounting world or the insurance business? Engaging people outside your circle of concern is a key pathway (energy and information) of having other people bring insights or knowledge into your circle of concern.

If you look at how you are structurally coupled right now, you have a circle of concern or a circle of interest or a circle of friends or whatever your circle is called, depending on how wide it is. Do you function outside of that very much? If you are going to improve resilience at this level of sophistication, you are going to have to engage people outside that circle, because one of the ways to stay resilient in a downturn or to just stay competitive is to be able to move beyond the requirements of your profession.

For instance, a public relations agency called in a phone person, because calls were backing up on the selection of the American Idol. "Could this affect voting on American Idol, because everybody is calling in and punching those buttons?" they asked. The phone man knew nothing about American Idol or its voting system. But he knew all about business phone systems and interactive voice response systems and those kinds of things. So he could establish that at certain times people were calling in and getting busy signals, and some of those people were abandoning their calls and not even voting. It could be that the voting itself was skewed.

This man knew a lot about phones and nothing about reality shows. Was that job able to make him more resilient? Yes because as soon as they quoted him in a magazine, he got all kinds of calls for phone information consulting and, I assume, follow-up business because his name had gotten out in a completely different industry. This is a simple example of how this element functions to create engagement indirectly, in this case, at the level of global action.

How far are you reaching out in quality and in quantity? When you engage people outside of your circle of concern, you open yourself up to the universe. That is a key in upping the downside, because if you have friends in different industries that are not going down, they can open up new ideas, new possibilities. That is how you *up the downside* and build resilience at this level of sophistication. It involves *glocal*—both global and local—engagement.

Using a scale of 1–10 for each, calculate Requirements – (Capability) x Importance = Priority Score

Score each element on a scale of 1–10; 1=low, 10=high	Req	Cap	Imp	PS
I engage people outside of my circle of concern.				

Now you can tally all your engagement scores:

Engagement				
My instincts and goals are crystal clear for my professional life.				
I seek out people smarter and more experienced than I am.				
I know the leading indicators of success in my profession.				
I am currently optimizing the use of my energy.				
I know and am leveraging my talents optimally.				
I consider how I relate to others.				
I differentiate how I engage with different people and activities.				
I engage people outside of my circle of concern.				
Total				

Remember, if you need help, we offer monthly tele-development training in this system, as well as qualified coaches to support your resilience journey in upping the downside. Register or log in at *www. upping-the-downside.com* for more information.

Chapter 17

Customer Relationship Management

by Mike Jay

This particular category of adaptation has become much more important in recent times: *customer* or *client relationship management.*

We have an opportunity just now to prepare our professional businesses for what are probably going to be some pretty disruptive circumstances and shifts in the way professionals execute their crafts over the next few years.

Consider, for example, one possible scenario from Harry S. Dent's Investment letter of October 2007 (*http://www.hsdent.com/download/dow*20000. *pdf*):

> Taking all of the fundamentals and cycles into account, the most dangerous times for the stock market will likely be, in order:
>
> (1) late 2009 to late 2010;
>
> (2) mid-2012 to mid- to late 2014;
>
> (3) late 2017 into late 2018; and
>
> (4) late 2019 into mid- to late 2022.
>
> Real estate is likely to lag the stock market by a year or so; hence, home prices are likely to start weakening seriously from late 2010 onward, especially from late 2012 into early 2015 when unemployment levels and bank failures are likely to be the highest (like early 1932 to 1934 in the Great Depression).

Even if only parts of the "Dent" scenario came true, there would be a large global recession or depression, and you don't want to be sitting on either side of that. You want to be sitting in the middle of resilience. So if we're in the eye of the hurricane now, there is a window of opportunity of perhaps eighteen to twenty-four months on average to build in resilience.

We can't predict what's going to happen, but you want to prepare yourself for a future discontinuity. Something people seldom ask because most of us operate in a narrow time frame is, "How do I build resilience when I can?" The worst time to build resilience is when life conditions are deteriorating rapidly, because then you're in the midst of the psychological turmoil that is leading the downturn. We need to build resilience now, not then. That's the goal of *upping the downside*. It's not a crisis system. By taking this approach, you will solidify the current opportunities you have in this window of opportunity.

As we near the halfway mark in this process model, it's a perfect time to focus on customer relationship management (CRM). This element will give you the opportunity to create a system that will hold you in resilience longer than those who are responding to life conditions without mitigating elements.

Part of the process of upping the downside is giving you the time to create a more *relational* resilience, which then allows you different kinds of choices during a downside caused by events or unexpected conditions.

A turning point for me in my work was to create, over a period of time, a CRM system. The interesting thing about this system is that I use it more *ineffectively* than anybody I know, but it still produces significant levels of resilience. I don't know anyone who with any kind of concentration or focus at all would not be able to do a better job than I do, but just because I *have* one, it's actually creating resilience.

So I'm hoping this is encouraging to you, because you do not have to do a great job with a CRM, you just have to have one. The most frequent thing I see is that everybody "has one" but it is so small, they don't think of it as a CRM system. They don't think of it as a referral engine. They don't think of it as any sort of social-organizing engine at all.

Therefore, as soon as you just "turn on the thought" that you are going to have a customer relationship management system and begin to operate even in rudimentary ways, you will be able to increase your resilience as a professional dramatically. This is where the first three levels we've talked about—wellth discipline, mastermind, and engagement—really begin to pay off. Together, the first four set you up for the level of resilience that we're going to talk about next, which is business development.

I think this is a psychological toolset wired into our systems, but most people don't think too far ahead, because if you do it will scare you with ambiguity. We can nonetheless create a significant amount of resilience if we just take some very simple actions in the present. And so we turn to the first element in customer relationship management.

"My referral engine produces significant revenues."

If you threw out all the other seven pieces that follow, if you just had this first piece, it would tell you a lot about your customer relationship engine, because the key thing about a referral engine is leverage. When you consider all the things that CRM does if you have a referral *engine*—one that you can put fuel in—the key is . . . *having one.*

Most people have friends, they have clients, they have associates, but they don't really understand how to create a referral engine out of those relationships. A referral engine is something that when you turn it on, when you work with it, when you excite it, you create leverage.

Leverage is as leverage does, as Forest Gump would say. Maybe I don't have friends who are going to purchase from me, but maybe they know somebody who knows somebody who knows somebody who can purchase from me, or do business with me, or even do business with other people I know.

How many of us, every day, send a referral to someone we know from someone or about something that we've read that would be good for them? That's a key question to ask. Because if you're not doing that every day, then you're not back-flowing your own referral engine by helping other people get referrals. Too many people think, "My referral engine is just about other people referring things to me."

No, my referral engine is an engine that works in all directions, and therefore I'm constantly on the lookout in things that I read and hear for things people are asking for, to make referrals to other people I know. You build a wider network of referrals by continually referring others to people who will form a good relationship with them. That way you create a *win-win-win engine*.

Going back to the mastermind principle, one of the things you're trying to accomplish at the beginning in setting up a mastermind is the rudiments of a referral engine. You have people you can refer others to, because they are not in competition with you.

So with the formalization of the customer relationship management engine, we want it to produce a significant portion of your revenues. And what constitutes significant? If, in the beginning, you're not using a referral engine or a CRM system, then a significant portion of your revenues would be "any portion of your revenues not currently being produced by this means." Then, over time, you continue to build that up.

Ideally, you would want to not have to ever market or promote your services because you're getting so much referral business you have to pass some of it on to someone else. Why? Because the time you spend marketing and promoting could be resourced into providing services or producing leverage in other activities—activities that motivate you to be a professional in the first place. So you want to *do* yourself out of marketing and promotion by creating a referral engine. And getting started is simple: Just ask people with whom you are doing business to refer others to you. Of course, we know that most of you reading this are not agentic, and therefore you can create agency with an "engine" like that, can you?

Another way is to tell other people you know that you're looking for referrals. You can send out a note and say, "I don't know if you know that I have these products and services available, but I do. I would appreciate if you run across anyone who would like these products and services, or would like me to introduce them to the products and services, that you would pass this on to them."

Another approach is a joint venture with people whereby they endorse your products and services. We simply do not ask people enough for this kind of support.

And then, you need to make it easy for people to refer to you, to inform others about what it is you do. This means having a list of your products and services and making sure you have a system that operates easily for the referral source.

Finally, be sure that your system provides adequate administrative support. It will weigh down your success and cut into your happiness if you trade delivery for administrative support. Ideally you can automate and build some kind of virtuality in the system for a self-service type of customer relationship. Otherwise you may find yourself serving your clients in areas of *administrivia*, rather than in areas where you're most likely to have high levels of motivational satisfaction, flow experience, and joy.

Using a scale of 1–10 for each, calculate Requirements – (Capability) x Importance = Priority Score

Score each element on a scale of 1–10; 1=low, 10=high	Req	Cap	Imp	PS
My referral engine produces significant revenues.				

"Customer loyalty and repurchase is increasing."

One of the things we know about professional systems is that customer loyalty is essential. I actually call this "customer productivity." In other words, how productive are our customers? For the resources that they are using or that are allocated to them, how productive are those resources, and how productive are my customers? Are they repurchasing anything? Are they moving through the process? Are they continuing to look at how I can serve them in better and more efficient and productive ways? Are they telling me what they want? Am I giving them the opportunity to give me feedback? These are things you to begin to look at here.

In any professional business, you can track loyalty by the number of times that a person has used or consumed your services. Most of us are not doing that because it requires some record keeping and bookkeeping. That's why I recommend a CRM system that is automated. You can easily track a customer's name, their loyalty, whether they are doing any repurchasing, or whether you need to re-mail them and let them know that there's something else going on with your business and how they can get involved.

Using a scale of 1–10 for each, calculate Requirements – (Capability) x Importance = Priority Score

Score each element on a scale of 1–10; 1=low, 10=high	Req	Cap	Imp	PS
Customer loyalty and repurchase is increasing.				

"Details of my business are handled in a proactive manner."

This is a tricky one, because in the professional world, people become professionals because they want to do the particular work that they are interested in. One of the major drawbacks, however, is that in doing this work, there are unintended effects of the demands for support, of service, and of detailed administrivia that are a function of the fiduciary responsibilities of a professional business. How do you handle those details, and have you figured out a way to handle them in a proactive manner versus a reactive one?

This has been a difficult process for me, because I have no depth orientation and very little patience, and I'm not good at sequencing or processes or procedures or any of those kinds of details for managing my business. One of the ways I've dealt with this—and I'm not necessarily advocating this, but just giving it as an example—is to off-load as much as I can to other people to handle. That design works in reducing bottlenecks, although I do at times end up with management issues as a result.

Take McDonald's, for example. One of the things McDonald's is known for is its ability to off-load service to its customers. You place an order; you pick up your food; you choose the condiments, napkins, straws, salt, and everything you need to consume the food; you eat the food; and then you dispose of the garbage. As much of the detail as possible is off-loaded to the consumer.

This is something we can learn to do in our professional businesses. If there are details that are hard for you to manage, or you don't manage very well, you can off-load them by hiring help or through automation. Perhaps you can put some details into the hands of the consumer.

Many professionals have assistants and administrative people, but in general, I find that details are not handled very well. This is especially the case in customer relationship management—in asking people for referrals, in keying people into the system to produce additional revenue with the "combo-meal." At McDonald's they'll always ask, "Do you want fries with that?" In our professional businesses there are ways we can add to the revenue of a customer visit or call or procedure by merely asking the customer if they want additional services.

These are details of the business that generally do not get handled well, and therefore the revenue and profit sides of the business are always lower than if you are proactively handling these small details, these up-sells, cross-sells, even just making additional choices available for your consumers or your professional service environment.

Using a scale of 1–10 for each, calculate Requirements – (Capability) x Importance = Priority Score

Score each element on a scale of 1–10; 1=low, 10=high	Req	Cap	Imp	PS
Details of my business are handled in a proactive manner.				

"We employ automated systems wherever possible."

The automation of system is always going to produce an effect on the first three elements we've already discussed, as well as on the next four still to come.

Automation can be an effective way of helping people understand how to manage their own relationship with you. It can be done in an enormous number of ways. Something I did just recently, for example, was to have a person who is helping us automate our customer relationship services incorporate the sending of cards via *changing-lives-one-card-at-a-time.com*.

We knew we weren't doing enough of that activity and wanted to increase it, but couldn't manage all the logistics ourselves without automation. This is something that will expand significantly our ability to manage the details and the relationships of the business.

Automation of systems is something we can expect to see increasing over time. You can often be much more effective in an automated format than in-person processes that you don't have time for and therefore don't do.

There isn't anyone I know in a professional business who has a significant amount of time, unless it's a start-up with no clients. Yes, people want synchronous attention. Yes, people need to have that. But much of the time you can automate the systems around you and get increased levels of leverage.

Using a scale of 1–10 for each, calculate Requirements – (Capability) x Importance = Priority Score

Score each element on a scale of 1–10; 1=low, 10=high	Req	Cap	Imp	PS
We employ automated systems wherever possible.				

"Clients get access to additional products and services."

One of the things that is so difficult to do, in order to create opportunity, is to create a developmental path for people. As customers learn, grow, and are satisfied or consume your products and services, they are at a different level than those who have not yet entered your system. So for those who are consuming your products and services and are having good experiences, you need to have strategies in place—beyond becoming raving fans who are referring new clients—for them to be able to consume at the next level. Providing access to additional products and services can be done in a number of ways.

Something that's easy to neglect is to offer additional products and services we already have that people might want to consume. We don't mention them, we don't offer them, we don't *even* have a system in place whereby we ask, how did it go?

Quick example: I have chronic back pain associated with the work I do, and so while traveling recently, I went to a major resort and spa for a massage. While I was there and they had me as a captive audience, presumably satisfied, they didn't ask if I wanted to come back, if I wanted to schedule another appointment. They didn't offer any additional services. They just took my money with a "thank you very much," and off I went.

Part of what we're failing to do, not only as professionals, but as people in charge of designing systems; is to provide increasing access to products and services through automated systems that handle events in a proactive manner. Establishing these processes actually saves you from having to market and promote and sell, because there are specific windows of opportunity that are wide open at particular times when people are consuming your products and services and are satisfied and will, given the chance, take additional products and services if you have them to offer.

In his excellent book *Think Two Products Ahead*, Ben Mack writes that you should always try to think where a customer is going to be when they consume a particular product and then what additional products and services are going to be a perfect fit for that consumption path (see *leadu.com/think2*).

Of course, my thought has always been to try to create a *developmental* path for people who want additional quantity and quality of what they consume. This means not only do they consume your products and services, but as they *consume* them, they mature in ways that they can leverage your products and services to accomplish more things in their lives, or have more joy in their lives, or really get a return on their motivational sensitivity.

Such a system needs to be thought out in strategic ways, for you're putting in place some pieces that may not yield significant returns in the short term, but will do so over a longer period of time. We call this idea a memeplex, with a *meme* being a cultural unit of instruction, and a *plex* being the interactive medium.

So the earlier element — *My referral engine produces significant revenues* — is nothing more than an algorithm that we call a meme because it has some instruction in it that causes you to take some kind of action, or do some kind of thinking, or have some kind of feeling. Well, the memeplex that we are discussing in this particular process of CRM is one that says, "Do *what you have to do right now*, even if that costs some money, time, energy, attention, and motivation, *so that later you will get benefits."*

This particular CRM memeplex is important for enhanced resilience, because in resilience, much of the time you *can* "have your cake and eat it too." So it's not only sacrificing yourself to get later, as that doesn't describe all of resilience. But to sacrifice now in order to put yourself in a position for later almost always has significant amounts of leverage. Many people call this memeplex delayed gratification. I call it a *developmental path*.

The systems we're talking about here in customer relationship management actually keep you from having to prospect. The point is, what are you doing now to make sure you have the opportunity to compete at a later time when competitive pressures may be higher and you'll need every bit of leverage that you have? Or, alternatively, are you picking the low-hanging fruit today, which stems from having served this customer before, satisfied them, and being able to give them increasing access to your products and services? Resilience in this memeplex would be, "We're building up an account, a customer account, that we can withdraw funds from at a later point in time." That, of course, is customer relationship management.

Using a scale of 1–10 for each, calculate Requirements – (Capability) x Importance = Priority Score

Score each element on a scale of 1–10; 1=low, 10=high	Req	Cap	Imp	PS
Clients get access to additional products and services.				

"We're incrementally becoming more glocal."

There are a couple of things that are important in the memeplex or algorithm of this element of the CRM process. The idea is that you don't have to *be* global to be global. You can begin to think outside your own particular niche formed around your business or professional practice.

You can understand that your customers have needs for additional products and services that you may or may not want to provide.

As you reach out to the people around you to provide additional products and services that you know your customers will want and consume over a period of time, you're actually beginning to think incrementally in more global in terms. The idea is to think globally and then to re-localize things in your area, so that you begin to produce offerings that are available to people, not just in your locale, but are offerings that could be produced in other locations.

Ask yourself, "What is a more global approach? What is an approach that I would not normally think of?"

Many professionals will immediately think that there's no way they can become incrementally more global, because the customer has to come to their office to receive the service.

Yet through innovation, through thinking differently, proactively, globally, through feeling your way around your business, you can come up with ways you never realized of making your business more global in terms of the products and services offered.

But most of us don't think about the global. We fence ourselves into thinking that the only way we can offer and deliver services is when someone steps through the door. And yet, there are many more ways in which you can provide service in any particular business, even if it's making referrals to others. Having a referral engine in place allows you to start playing at a much different level than you ever would have thought you could play. Now you're referring customers to other people you know, and that same reciprocation exists for people to refer customers back to you.

Using a scale of 1–10 for each, calculate Requirements – (Capability) x Importance = Priority Score

Score each element on a scale of 1–10; 1=low, 10=high	Req	Cap	Imp	PS
We're incrementally becoming more glocal.				

"We continually differentiate the needs of our customers."

Continually is the key here to differentiating the needs of our customers. People think in a professional business that they are coming to you for X. Well, obviously, people have needs for X, Y, and Z. Therefore if you're continually differentiating the needs of those customers, you can get a feeling for the kinds of needs they have. You discover that you have ways of helping them meet their needs in a more efficient, effective, and sustainable way just by understanding what the needs of those customers are.

It's like my experience at the spa. If they could have understood what I was looking for, they could have helped me, perhaps, by giving some additional information. But they haven't been instructed to think beyond their local professional delivery of services. Consequently, they didn't refer me to other parts of the property or locations in the area that would help the entire system do a better job. If they had referred me to others in an interconnected system, they may have had others referring people back to their area.

Continually differentiating the needs of our customers is something most of us do not do well. We don't collaborate well. We don't differentiate well. We don't work on this incrementally. If we did just one tiny little thing this month and one tiny little thing next month, the next thing you know, you're doing twelve things in a year, and in three years you're doing thirty-six things.

These are things that can be done very simply over a period of time, and they are small things, but yet people don't think of them, and consequently resilience goes down. For when life conditions shift, the more ways you can move through the barriers to success that life conditions present, the more resilient you're going to be.

Resilience is coming up with additional ways to solve problems when you're presented with barriers. The key thing is to have additional ways to identify algorithms that will work when the algorithms you're using no longer solve problems well.

To be able to innovate and incrementally make your system more robust, more redundant, you need to have more opportunities to actually serve people in many different ways.

I'm convinced—and I hope I'm wrong, but I know I'm not wrong—that competitive pressures in the professional realm are going to increase dramatically in the United States. About 90 percent of everything we do is in some form or another connected to a professional service that is subject to dislocation under global pressures.

As competitive pressures increase, for instance, in the coaching profession, we will not only be competing with other coaches for clients, but we'll be competing for the discretionary income that a client has to spread over a number of services. We'll be competing with chiropractors, therapists, beauticians, spas, even with movies, theaters, or anything else that a person can spend a discretionary dollar on. And it will be more complex still in that we'll be competing against any kind of activity where someone has limited discretionary income to spread over what would give them the greatest return to their motivational sensitivity or their current life conditions.

That's why I see things changing rapidly at not too far off a point in time. We're still in a window in which the old ways are being projected forward, but over the next five years, we could begin to see the writing on the wall in terms of the amounts of services that are actually being provided and sought.

Another factor will be significant professional encroachment. Not only will we be competing with the coach from Wisconsin or the coach from California or Nebraska, we'll be competing with the coach from India, or Korea, or Hungary, or Romania. Globalization is going to rewrite all competitive pathways that we now see.

If you could spend $10 on one thing versus spending $50 on the same thing, and the quality of the $50 is only 20 percent greater than the quality of the $10, which one are you going to opt for when you're under pressure to leverage your discretionary income?

We haven't seen anything yet compared to what is going to take place in the next five years in globalization and people coming in to fish in our pond. This will be facilitated by broadband video, broadband audio, literally time-warped, time-shifted, and time-irrelevant synchronous activities that can be done in different ways from other countries.

When we talk about customer relationship management, therefore, we're talking about customer loyalty. We're talking about share of the customer and of the discretionary dollar, about all these kinds of things. And the way in which it has been proven that you can be more effective is to begin to understand the eighth element in this category, which is to reach out universally.

Using a scale of 1–10 for each, calculate Requirements – (Capability) x Importance = Priority Score

Score each element on a scale of 1–10; 1=low, 10=high	Req	Cap	Imp	PS
We continually differentiate the needs of our customers.				

"We experience our reach universally as it feels appropriate."

This means understanding the competitive market. Understanding resilience means understanding the number of different ways that you can get a share of that discretionary income on a regular basis and serve clients in a way that is going to have them referring people to you and have them coming back for more and more and more because it is part of the *experience*.

For instance, what if we provided services to people we do not currently serve in a market that would allow us to offer services at a lower cost? Could we do that? Well, of course we could, we're doing that right now in many different forms. We need to understand that perhaps we are not just a professional service provider, but rather can become a professional access point, where people could access different kinds of services.

For instance, we used to think that a doctor, a lawyer, a chiropractor, a plumber, an insurance agent, they did just one thing because they were experts in that business. But what if you've been able to differentiate the needs of your customers, and you can understand that instead of their leaving your business for other services, they could actually be served by some additional affiliations, because the customers trust you, and you have a service provider network that you trust. You could begin to create combo-meals. It's all driven through a customer relationship management system or architecture.

So, to begin we want to understand this idea of differentiating the needs of our customers, understanding how to create automated systems, understanding how to create access points for our services, understanding what the definition of a professional practice actually means.

When I started out in the coaching business, I began in medicine. One of the things I found when I studied physicians was that inside that room, physicians were talking with their patients about a lot more than what was ailing them. They talked about life, about illness and wellness, about insurance, about children and parents. There was a doctor giving people advice on many different things, because the doctor was a trusted source. This is something we have not begun to explore in terms of universal services.

To give an example, when you join a frequent flyer program, think about the messages you receive with notices about when you can fly. One of the most valuable things airlines have is not their ability to fly people around, but rather having people read their message every week to see what's up. An assured contact with one of their customers each week is a *profound* amount of capital that is basically not being used.

When we think what customer relationship management really is, we realize the relationship with the customer is far more valuable than any particular services we provide or can recommend over time. The fact is that there is a degree of trust, a degree of satisfaction, that we can create a dialogue with that customer, an intimate dialogue, where over a period of time they reveal to us the different things they are wanting, learning, doing, and how they're growing. We have an opportunity, through that relationship, to offer access points to services on a *programmed basis*, rather than the basis that we do now, which is mainly through happenstance.

Of course there are privacy issues and boundaries, but in these *trusted networks*, we have high levels of closeness and between-ness where we can serve the client in a much different way over time and create significant amounts of resilience for both ourselves and the client experience.

If you reach out universally whenever it feels appropriate, you form a relationship that is a trusted bond, a relationship that you protect, grow, and nurture. And you see it as an opportunity for two-way flows of information—not just you marketing, promoting, and selling, but the client telling you what it is they want, what they need, what is going on in their lives, and how you can help them experience greater satisfaction. This becomes a powerful point of leverage and, of course, an increasingly advanced form of resilience.

So, *upping the downside*, creating relationships with customers that are deep and trusted and that you begin to hold as an opportunity for leverage over time—by differentiating, referring in, referring out, looking out, reaching out—those kinds of things are going to be very powerful in creating experiences that really matter.

Using a scale of 1–10 for each, calculate Requirements – (Capability) x Importance = Priority Score

Score each element on a scale of 1–10; 1=low, 10=high	Req	Cap	Imp	PS
We experience our reach universally as it feels appropriate.				

Now you can tally all your CRM Scores:

C RM				
My referral engine produces significant revenues.				
Customer loyalty and repurchase is increasing.				
Details of my business are handled in a proactive manner.				
We employ automated systems wherever possible.				
Clients get access to additional products and services.				
We're incrementally becoming more glocal.				
We continually differentiate the needs of our customers.				
We experience our reach universally as it feels appropriate.				
Total				

Remember, if you need help, we offer monthly tele-development training in this system, as well as qualified coaches to support your resilience journey in upping the downside. Register or log in at *www.upping-the-downside.com* for more information.

Chapter 18

Business Development

by Mike Jay

We now turn to one of the most important parts of what a resilient professional does: participating in *business development*.

Returning to Kiyosaki's cashflow quadrant, I find this to be a simple and powerful metaphor. When you look at the roles of employee, self-employed person, business owner, and investor, those are hugely different roles. Yet lots of times people assume they're in one quadrant but behave as if they're in another. Understanding this model is key to *upping the downside* in business development. You want to be clear about what it is you're doing and where you're doing it.

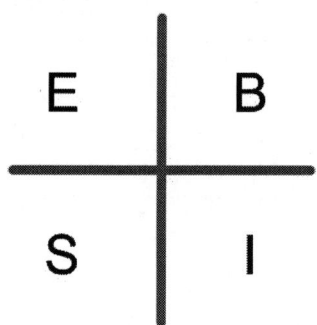

A refresher:

E = employee; S = self-employed; B = business owner; I = investor. Each of these is a mindset that is key to an understanding of the reality of that position. Making a B-I leap means moving out of the mindset of the self-employed professional and moving into the mindset of the more resilient business-owning professional.

A few years ago I created the RightAction™ concept: *right people, doing right things, in right ways, at right times, in right spaces, for right reasons—to get right results*™.

Out of this model I then created *Right Performance*, which teaches what it means to perform rightly. It was influenced by Eastern religions, which I was studying in the late eighties and early nineties, because rightness is important in the idea of enlightenment.

I felt that indirectly influencing people towards spirituality would be better than talking about Eastern religions and some of the more esoteric ideas. And, of course, Eastern religions don't talk much about business development. I thought I would combine the two and begin to help people understand how to create resilience more holistically by understanding this idea of right action.

I started out with "the right people doing the right things in the right ways at the right time for the right reasons to get the right results." But over time I realized that the idea of space was a more important part of our lives than most people understand. You have to understand space for business development, because you have to assume multiple roles. You'll notice that more recently I've dropped "the" from the model and have realized there are many rights, rather than "the" one right.

So, looking at the cashflow quadrant system, space in the employee area means that there are certain things that you've been assigned to do that have to get done for resilience to emerge. If you're not going to do them, you'd better *find* someone to do them, perhaps a self-employed professional who has a body of knowledge to disseminate.

People mostly get trapped because they can't make the B-I Leap—the move from the left-hand, employed/self-employed side to business owner on the right side. The definition I like to use of business owner is that you can walk away from your business for two years and come back and it's still there, better than when you left. That means that you have management in place. You have leadership in place. You have standards and operations in place. You have execution going on. You understand how customers are treated. You have employee loyalty, customer loyalty, all of that going on. That's difficult because most people don't ever take their businesses seriously enough to get themselves out of the self-employed mode, which means they continue to suboptimize business development.

The investor part means that you're in a meta position where you are *about* the business. As an investor, you don't care about the business operation itself. You're looking at whether or not the business can provide a return on the capital you have invested. Or, as I say in the ITEAM model, a return on the information, time, energy, action, and motivation that you have invested.

The key thing to understand as we grow to a still higher level of complexity in this new category of business development is that we have come out of customer relationship management where we have created a tactical system. Now it's a matter of beginning to *develop the system strategically.*

The reason they are not in reverse order is that good marketing and development can ruin a bad CRM system. You want to build the CRM system first. That's why in Spiral Dynamics Integral, the blue avoidance or accountability system precedes the ability to be existentially okay in the orange system where *enterprising* takes place. At this particular level we have built the car, and it has an engine. Now we're going to put some fuel in it and begin to drive it. That's where we are with business development.

We start by looking at the "I" or agentic position with the first element:

"I view my professional practice from all directions."

Remember that the model of resilience we're working with in this survey is keyed toward the self-employed quadrant, and it's preparation for making the B-I leap. It's keyed toward having you as a self-employed person holding a degree of expertise that you sell or barter or trade for value. Here, though, we're trying to get you to make the B-I Leap or at least think about it at this level. *Upping the downside* from the business standpoint is all about making the B-I Leap. The key is to understand how to position yourself to make the leap over that fence without the pain of ending up with one foot on one side and the other foot on the other side of a rather pointed fence, if you catch my metaphor here.

The first thing to do is begin to view your professional practice from all directions. That means viewing it not only from the inside, but also the outside; not only as an individual, but also in a collective form. I like to use the I-We-Us-Them system of the integralists rather Buber's I-We-It, because I don't agree with Buber that anything is an It. Everything viewed from a *perspective* will be a part of us—as defined by the perceiver. Otherwise it doesn't exist. I recognize, though, you may view this differently as we work through multiple perspectives here.

I-We-Us-Them works pretty well for viewing yourself and for understanding what's happening outside the system, as well as inside. Too many professionals have too narrow a viewpoint; they've spent so much time learning their stuff, they're a mile deep and an inch wide. In business development you begin to reverse that and understand what it looks like to hold a wider perspective. You take in more breadth; you increase your viewpoint conceptually; you look at your professional practice from all directions. Most of the time you will not be able to do this by yourself. If you try to do it on your own, you're likely to thin-slice reality, as Malcolm Gladwell suggests in Blink.

The first thing you'll want to do is some kind of survey. I like to do surveys. They're easy and inexpensive. They contain a specific amount of data that you can go back and recheck over time. You can create fairly significant volumes of verifiable data using surveys. I often use a system called InfoTool-Online.com. (Call my friend Stan there and tell him you heard about him from me and that you'd like to buy him a Bombay sapphire martini with four giant blue-cheese stuffed olives for a real discount on your project.) I have also built some systems in Zoomerang and Survey Monkey. You want to begin to get verifiable data that several people can look at it and say, yes, we agree that's the data. When you say, "I view my professional practice from all directions," you want to make sure that you're basing that on verifiable data and not on a thin slice coming out of your perspective, which will limit your ability to develop business.

Using a scale of 1–10 for each, calculate Requirements – (Capability) x Importance = Priority Score

Score each element on a scale of 1–10; 1=low, 10=high	Req	Cap	Imp	PS
I view my professional practice from all directions.				

"We weave opportunity into my current business offerings."

This means that you begin to see your system as a system. To use a quick metaphor, you begin to "think two products ahead," as Ben Mack advocates. If someone comes into your office to get their teeth x-rayed, they might as well get them cleaned too, or receive some instruction on how to take care of their teeth, or schedule follow-up visits. You might as well sell them a dental product or even some nutrition if you're looking at dentistry holistically.

Four years ago I gave up sodas, both diet and regular, because of the low pH. They destroy your system in different ways, especially your teeth. I've noticed a big change in my health since I stopped putting low-pH beverages into my system. The reason I bring that up is, I didn't learn that from a dentist. Why shouldn't I have? Why shouldn't my dentist have helped me understand nutrition—and that there are things I could do that are more powerful than brushing my teeth, that I'm destroying my teeth from the inside out, not from the outside in?

For the life of me I don't understand why more chiropractors don't have alliances with massage therapists. What the massage therapist helped me do is *not* go to the chiropractor. Now look what happened to the chiropractor's business. I used to enjoy going to the chiropractor on a regular basis, but then I found a different way. I liked massage so much that I started my own website *realmassagetips.com*. Now when my coaching clients complain of having aches and pains, I can offer them the tips I had someone create for me on massage as an additional service. Getting the picture? My massage therapist gets referrals from me, an executive coach. Do you think they like getting that kind of client referral?

Again, having additional opportunities to weave into your professional business broadens your ability to build a business. The same is true with a coach. If you're a coach, then you're a consultant in some area of expertise. You might even be able to be a mentor—someone whose been there, done that in several ways. There are additional things you can weave into your current business offerings that you're not thinking about right now. That's one of the first things you can do to build your business. You build that through your mastermind, your alliances, your affiliation, your association, and your *combinatorial* effects.

Using a scale of 1–10 for each, calculate Requirements – (Capability) x Importance = Priority Score

Score each element on a scale of 1–10; 1=low, 10=high	Req	Cap	Imp	PS
We weave opportunity into my current business offerings.				

"I actively pursue networks with my target customers."

For these first three elements of business development, the words are important on an individual basis: I *view*, I *weave*, I *pursue*.

Most professionals reject the notion of selling anything to anybody. They think you should represent your profession and your expertise in a way that does not involve selling. That's why most professional people do not do well at business development. So with this element we change the wording a bit and thereby the memeplex, so professionals will not reject this critical part of business development: to *pursue a network with your target customers.*

Robert Collier, a famous copywriter, is credited with saying something to the effect that if you want to influence people, you show up in a conversation that they're already in, rather than trying to create a new one.

Most professionals today who are not Yellow Page professionals are trying to create new conversations. Coaches are trying to create new conversations. Consultants are trying to create new conversations. It's important to understand that your target customer group is already in some kind of conversation. What you want to do is pursue the network of that conversation (or conversations), *not* create a new network from scratch.

So, for instance, coaches would never think of affiliating with a spa operator, because they don't think that's where coaches can coach. Yet what kinds of people show up at spas? Usually it's people with lots of discretionary income who have businesses, and they're coming to the spa to rejuvenate. Imagine the conversation you could enter with the spa owner; you could offer services to customers that they don't provide without cutting into their business. Then you could give the spa a cut, and they could actually provide a better experience. That's actively pursuing networks with your target customers.

Asia is, of course, very different from the United States, and they're much more open about these kinds of things. When you go to a massage house in Asia, you'll probably find fifty to one hundred therapists working. There are people being massaged right next to you like you'd find with customers in a hair salon or barbershop in the United States. Guess what you end up doing? You start conversations with the people next to you, just like you might start up a conversation with somebody next to you on an airplane. You find out where they're from and what they do. You realize you have something in common. You might never expect to find your target customers there, yet I've gotten good leads and good customers from exactly those kinds of situations. It happened while I was doing what I needed to do to take care of myself—I found a conversation my target customers were already in.

We need to think about where our customers are and about our customers' conversations. Then we can actively pursue those kinds of networks.

This element according to spiral on spiral is part a power memeplex in the business development process: a direct-power, exploitive type of memeplex. Most people as professionals are working on the other side of the spectrum, which is an absorption or indirect, "cool" type of system. This *actively pursuing* is scary, especially when it comes to customers. To some people it sounds almost *illegal*. Many professionals will choose to not start a conversation and not actively pursue networks in venues like these.

It's important to understand that this is meme density you have to create from design, not yourself. This set of business-development algorithms some of you will not do. *Just make sure that somebody or something does them.* Relax, you don't have to do them, but just make sure they're done. Don't let your *own* worldview suboptimize your ability to live in it!

Somebody in your professional practice or business should be actively pursuing networks with your target customers and getting leads and moving those leads into conversation of some form or another. Or, you should put in place systems that do this for you.

Using a scale of 1–10 for each, calculate Requirements – (Capability) x Importance = Priority Score

Score each element on a scale of 1–10; 1=low, 10=high	Req	Cap	Imp	PS
I actively pursue networks with my target customers.				

"We have a plan for survival during disruption or discontinuity."

With this element we drop back into the avoidance side of the spectrum. I can't tell you how important this is, and I can't tell you how many times I've been caught by this myself over time. I'm getting better as we move along, but most professionals have no contingency plan at all for a disruption of any kind. Over the next five to ten years, you're going to need do this if you want to remain resilient.

You're going to need to have a contingency plan—to understand how much money your business needs. You're going to need to have funds set aside, or at least understand what happens if you have a bomb threat, or your neighbor has a bomb threat, because you're going to be affected. Or what happens if the drinking water gets poisoned, or you lose your electricity.

We haven't had much disruption in the United States, but as I travel around the world, it reminds me of how things could be here. One time I was speaking to a group in New Delhi. The room was entirely full—not even standing room left—with some five hundred human relations people and students. I was giving a talk on coaching. The lights and power went off five times during my ninety-minute presentation. So much for PowerPoint slides. So much for audio. So much for video. So much for anything predictable. So much for sitting there in the dark and continuing to present to people who are expecting you to keep going because they understand interruptions and discontinuities. They're woven into these people's everyday existence.

We have no concept of this in the developed world. We pretend that everything will continue to function the way it's supposed to. I live in the American West, and we do have lightning storms and power outages, sometimes for half a day. So we have contingency plans built. We pay for two forms of internet access, so if one goes down, the other one comes up. We have portable power. We have the ability to stay in business, because our business is about being connected. We have phone lines that work without plugging in, so you can stay connected. Do you ever think about these kinds of things?

Most of us don't think about them, so there is no survival plan. If your business is out of function for a period of time, what are you going to do? If you're a restaurateur, what happens if you have an outbreak of something? How do you handle the press? How do you use the media? How do you shut your restaurant down? How do you make sure things are safe? I've seen many businesses wrecked. I used to do consulting with food-service professionals, and I watched people ruin their businesses with situations like that.

These kinds of things matter to us. What if your best employee hops ship and goes somewhere else and carries with them all the history of the organization and all the customers that really liked them?

I orchestrated something like this earlier on in my career as a strategic plan. In some ways I'm proud of it, and looking back now, in some ways I'm not. I destroyed a medical practice, because I helped the best doctor. The best doctor was being mistreated. We took the best people along with the best doctor. They had friends, and we took all the best clients. Within two years the place he left was gone. Why? There was no plan, no contingency in place. No real thought about the future. Everybody pretended—or assumed—that everything would stay the same. This could be any business anyplace in the world. You need to understand what could cause a major disruption or discontinuity in your life or your practice and have some kind of plan in place or an idea of what you will do.

This is an avoidance system, but it's very important in terms of your business development. It would not do much good for you to do a lot of business development, build up your business nicely, and then lose it in a flash because of some kind of interruption or disruption.

Something like that happened to me as an independent professional in 2001. I lost a couple of big clients when the Trade Centers collapsed. Our other clients pulled back. People don't spend money on their credit cards when they're scared. Is your business entirely a credit-card business? Is it an internet-based business? Is it a local business? What would happen if a tornado came through like it did in Eagle Pass, Texas, or Greensburg, Kansas?

I'm not saying that you should obsess about these kinds of possibilities. I'm not saying you need to spend a lot of money. But you do need to think them through strategically with the enterprise in mind.

Using a scale of 1–10 for each, calculate Requirements – (Capability) x Importance = Priority Score

Score each element on a scale of 1–10; 1=low, 10=high	Req	Cap	Imp	PS
We have a plan for survival during disruption or discontinuity.				

"I systemize sales through bundling, financing, and referral."

The easiest way to tell you about this element is with a simple metaphor from McDonald's. It's called "Do you want fries with that?" At any McDonald's restaurant that is well run, you'll always be asked that question. If you order a hamburger, they'll ask if you want a combo meal. If you want a combo meal, they'll ask you if you want to super-size it. What they're doing strategically is systemizing sales through people who are not themselves all that capable. They have scripts that they teach their employees, to bundle offerings and help us get what we want and help the business become more profitable and develop itself.

One of the best things we ever did in our business was start financing our training program. People are often in situations where they cannot come up with thousands of dollars at one time. By financing, especially in other countries where currency exchange is an issue, we find that people will continue to train and use other services we offer.

Do you offer financing? Do you know how to offer it? Do you know how to create referrals through the process that you're using? If you've established a customer relationship management system, you'll be able to do that easily and automatically by asking people for referrals, by bundling products and services to create new opportunities, by offering financing and creating pay plans. Do you do that? Do you do it strategically?

So here's the secret. You need to have a developmental path for your clients. Economist and software entrepreneur Paul Zane Pilzer talks about the ability of people to want additional quantity and quality. When people have sufficient quantity, they will want more quality. When they have sufficient quality, they will want more quantity.

Do you understand how to create a developmental path for your customers, your clients? If they're satisfied and if they're enjoying themselves and they're getting what they want and they're prospering as a result of what you're doing, why not have a next step for them? Why not have an additional thing that they can take part in, because most of them will want to engage at the next level.

Are you doing that strategically? Do you understand how your system works? Or do you sit like my dentist and my barber and everybody else I try to coach every time I go in, trying to help them understand how to reach out to people, as they complain about fewer clients? These Yellow Page businesses don't understand business development at all. They don't understand that we really need and want their services, but we're not going to trade out something for their services if they don't ask us to, because we have so many choices. Of course, when people have a lot of choices, you're going to constantly have to ask them to forego one choice over another. You have to make a case for why, strategically, it's a good idea for them to do so.

Don't become part of the noise, become part of the solution.

Using a scale of 1–10 for each, calculate Requirements – (Capability) x Importance = Priority Score

Score each element on a scale of 1–10; 1=low, 10=high	Req	Cap	Imp	PS
I systemize sales through bundling, financing, and referral.				

"We have and nurture an affiliate sales system."

Moving now to the next level of complexity and building still more robustness into the resilience of your system, if you're selling strategically, if you're systemizing sales through bundling, financing, and referral, then the next thing to do is set it up so other people will do it for you. You don't want to keep doing that yourself.

If you nurture your affiliates—people who receive a commission when they refer others to you—they will sell *you* strategically. They will systemize their approach to clients. They will refer people and show them how to get bundles and financing. You're much less effective at this if you're doing it alone.

Now I want to admit to you, I don't do this all that well myself, so I'm not trying to hold myself up as a model of reality. But I can tell you one thing, I'm working on it.

I'm telling you this so you won't think you have to be perfect at each of these things to get some benefit for you and your customers. You don't have to have a fancy affiliate system; you can have a simple one for people, for example, by using an asynchronous system such as *ecomincs.com*. It has a built-in affiliate module. You have people sign up at the site, and they can send your link around to other people. Believe me, it pays off.

This element pulls us back into the communal side of business development. When you systematize your affiliate approach and begin to reach out, collaborate, create a communal system like this, and nurture people, results begin to accrue fast. Affiliates need to be nurtured, and you may literally have to change your design to make sure this is happening.

A lot of professionals are analytical and technical in nature, and they don't nurture anything, let alone their affiliates. Consequently, they don't have a good affiliate system, even if the CRM system is functioning technically. Part of this process can be built through design. Hire somebody to do this for you, and you can make a lot of progress in this area.

Using a scale of 1–10 for each, calculate Requirements – (Capability) x Importance = Priority Score

Score each element on a scale of 1–10; 1=low, 10=high	Req	Cap	Imp	PS
We have and nurture an affiliate sales system.				

"I improve sales results by differentiating my approaches."

The first system that you create—and the first system you want to create—is a car-wash type of system. Everybody who comes in goes through the same thing. That's the easiest way to build a system and scale it fast. You create standards, which are operating events that can be replicated with improved quality over time.

You standardize the system when you make a car-wash system, and it will begin to produce benefits for you. Once you've got that one system working, you can proceed to build multiple options. That's what we're saying here with this element: *We're going to improve sales results through differentiating our approaches.* This means for some people my approach needs to be X. For other kinds of customers my approach needs to be Y. We see this as required in the developed world because people have so many choices.

A book I recommend to anyone is *The Long Tail*, written by the editor of *Wired* magazine, Chris Anderson. He talks about the functioning of the power-law distribution, a concept that graphically resembles a long tail instead of the regular bell-curve distribution. It has a few nodes with a tremendous number of connections and activity, and then it trails off from there.

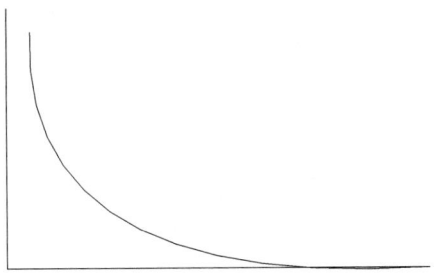

Once you're on the tail, only a few transactions occur, but those transactions are very differentiated. What we're seeing, in other words, is micro-fragmentation. I suggest this fragmentation—which we can differentiate—will continue to happen, as long as we don't have a major disruption and regression back into lower levels of cultural potential. Assuming things continue to move in the direction they're currently moving, the long tail will grow, which means that more and more people will fragment into micro niches. Therefore, your business might be one that works—differentiated—among those micro niches.

If, for instance, I take my coaching business to the spa business—if I talk to massage therapists about adding coaching and assessments to their offerings—that's a micro niche. Why? There's a target market there. Are there going to be a lot of customers there? No, but I can nonetheless add onto my business by differentiating my approach and making my services available in areas I previously was unable to penetrate or never considered as opportunities.

Using a scale of 1–10 for each, calculate Requirements – (Capability) x Importance = Priority Score

Score each element on a scale of 1–10; 1=low, 10=high	Req	Cap	Imp	PS
I improve sales results by differentiating my approaches.				

"A universal approach is considered for development."

In this last element of business development we're looking at universality, a very complex notion. *Consider.* Note the changed language here. *Considered.* It doesn't say I implemented, or I'm applying. It says consider. At this level of complexity, the only thing you can really do is to consider a universal approach when developing your business.

What is a universal approach? Essentially, a universal approach would be structured around how anyone and everyone is and becomes part of my business in an ecology. How would my business fit in the context of *everything*? When you consider this, when you open your mind and open up the thin slice that you're making right now in developing your business, you begin to come up with these different kinds of ideas that I've been sharing with you. Sustainability will also emerge as part of the equation.

The idea is that my business is not me, and I am not what I do. My business is a part of everything. Therefore, when I look at this universally, how would people in India or China or Bulgaria or Mexico or Canada or Nebraska look at what I do in developing my business? How can I find ways to do business that would be universally applicable to all of those systems? In terms of business development, we need to have this kind of conversation.

Where can you have these kinds of conversations? They're not going to be easy to find. You can, however, orchestrate the design that produces them. You could invite your customers to talk with you on a regular basis. You could have a customer appreciation event or get-together. You could invite your customers in and show them your business. You could show them your new dentistry system. You could show them your new chiropractic machine. You could show them the new way you can change the plumbing.

In fact, when I was in Home Depot I learned that people use more water rinsing off their dishes to put them in the dishwasher than if they just took them off the table and stuck them in the dishwasher. You could save 62 gallons a week. That's a lot of water. I never realized that. How did I learn that? I went to one of those demonstrations about dishwashers for customers because my wife wanted a dishwasher. How would I have known that otherwise?

Give people the opportunity to learn about things you do in your business. Yes, because I'm high-curious I might attend something like that. Yes, because my wife has been wanting a dishwasher, but I didn't want to get one because they use extra power—supposedly. You have to put in a new water heater in—supposedly. What I found out is that you don't need to do any of those things.

Again, a universal approach. Learning more about what your business does, how it works, how it carries on. My plumber knows more about things than I thought he did. The people who supply things to me know more things than I thought they did. I never thought of asking. We can learn about these things when we understand the synergy that exists when people around us know a lot about what it is they do.

In our world today, people are so specialized in professional work, they are a mile deep and an inch wide. It's helpful for us to reach out to a lot of different people in order to develop our own business. Of course, I then get the opportunity to tell them what I do when I buy my dishwasher. Business development—you're always talking about what it is you do and what it is you provide and the benefits that people get from what you provide in your professional practice. This opportunity exists at every turn.

You never know when your next "great" client is going to show up, and you never know where your next "great" client is going to come from. Therefore, you want to consider this universal approach. You want to understand how to develop your business wherever you are, whatever it is you're doing, rather than saying, "I'm in a casino in Mesquite, Nevada. I'm out of my element here."

Little do I know that there are people there who could use some coaching. Like the time I'm at a buffet, and I ask the people about the rest of the place, and they don't know anything about it. Could they use some coaching? Sure. You want the buffet people to refer customers to the theater and outside to the golf course. If they're in their own little silo, and yet they're working all together out in the middle of nowhere—literally, if you've ever been to Mesquite, you know it's in the middle of the desert—you want people to be able to share.

A universal approach to understanding what's going on in that system could yield that larger enterprise significantly better results than they're getting right now with a local, thin-sliced approach. Look up, look out, look around, look inside. That's what we're talking about here. Those are things you can do.

Using a scale of 1–10 for each, calculate Requirements – (Capability) x Importance = Priority Score

Score each element on a scale of 1–10; 1=low, 10=high	Req	Cap	Imp	PS
A universal approach is considered for development.				

Now you can tally all your business development scores:

Business Development				
I view my professional practice from all directions.				
We weave opportunity into my current business offerings.				
I actively pursue networks with my target customers.				
We have a plan for survival during disruption or discontinuity.				
I systemize sales through bundling, financing, and referral.				
We have and nurture an affiliate sales system.				
I improve sales results by differentiating my approaches.				
A universal approach is considered for development.				
Total				

Remember, if you need help, we offer monthly tele-development training in this system, as well as qualified coaches to support your resilience journey in upping the downside. Register or log in at *www. upping-the-downside.com* for more information.

Chapter 19

Robustness

by Mike Jay

We're moving deeper into the professional resilience system. More layers are now exposed, and we're metaphorically peeling an onion around and down to get to places where most of what is done will not be very conscious in terms of bandwidth.

This can be difficult for people to do in a system that's developmentally scaled, meaning the further you get into it, the more complex are the things you're asked to think about. As this happens, much of the literal nature or certainty begins to evaporate, if it hasn't already. We can't always expect the same level of concreteness or performance that we had at earlier stages, where things were smaller and easier to do and manage. We're ready now to talk about *robustness*.

Robustness as used here is a concept that comes from computer science. They talk about it in regard to how a system scales and whether or not it can handle the scalability that people are trying to manage it with. If, for instance, you go from ten hits on an audio to sixteen hundred hits, the robustness of your system will show up quickly with that level of demand on your server to stream the audio to sixteen hundred requests.

As long as your server was getting a few requests at a time, there wasn't any problem. But as soon as it reaches a point where the density of requests stretches the limits of the capability of the system to respond, failure occurs and the system must be regressed, limited, or slowed down to limit requests—or it can't scale.

Most of us have not had these kinds of problems yet, because we haven't had high volumes of people hitting our servers at one time. They literally will crash the servers when a lot of people hit at once. So the level of scalability, the level of robustness or resilience in the system, is directly related to how well it can match up to those complex demands all at once. That's a good metaphor for what we're talking about in *upping the downside.*

It's one thing to have things working well. It's another thing to have things work well over time, in time, under a lot of pressure. So robustness is one of the things that we want to build into our professional practice as we look at upping the downside in these last three categories of the survey.

In other words, while the metaphor is about servers, we're now speaking to all the elements and processes we've considered previously, as well as those we have not. In relation to complex demands on our professional practice, it's people and it's clients.

Is the system robust enough that it can scale more than one level of existence? The ideal thing would be to create a professional practice that can maintain resilience as you go through different levels of existence and encounter different kinds of life conditions and additional complex demands. Of course, that's what this model is designed to help you do.

The model is itself pretty robust because it creates a lot of connections—a lot more algorithms or codes—ways of doing things—for achieving high levels of robustness. When one thing stops working, another way is open, because this redundant set of pathways allows the system to be plastic and mold to its demand. One of the things I see in resilience is plasticity. If you can create a system that is reasonably plastic when it encounters significant threats or hits from tension and pressure, the system has a tendency to stay up and running.

As we move into more complex conditions with discontinuities likely over the next three to five years, unless you're prepared to give up your standard of living, you will need to increase robustness to keep your business running, income coming in, demand sufficient, client population high, and to maintain customer loyalty and service.

Discontinuities are nothing more than unexpected disruptions in the way the world works from our perspective. Complexity can be defined as the number of interacting variables in a system plus the dislocation between the cause and effect in those variables.

It's difficult to understand what is happening to you when you have a lot of variables; and it's difficult to understand cause and effect in a noisy system. That's because as human beings we thin-slice based on who we are and what we belief about how the world works. This worldview protects us naturally under normal conditions. But it also forces us into using rather limiting solutions, when we may need to have many more types of solutions ready as demands or requirements shift.

Part of what we will discuss now in talking about robustness — and later in the last two categories, generativity and integroism — is how the overall system can be plastic, adjustable, and adaptive in the face of changing life conditions or disruptive activity. Some people call this contingency planning, and that is a good thing to do as well. Robustness, however, also leads to your ability to manage contingencies and thus remain resilient over time.

And so we turn to the first element of robustness.

"Key ingredients of professional survival are crystal clear."

The only way for this to happen is for you to understand what the key issues in your professional survival are. So I'll give you a secret tip. All sixty-four elements in this survey are key issues.

How could you have sixty-four key issues, you ask. Well, almost all of these will generate what is called KPI: key performance indicators. So essentially, you could use all sixty-four. Some of them, however, may be less meaningful to you because they are more complex than you have ways of managing or access to resources. But if you have gone through the survey and identified through priority scoring those elements that are important to you, then you can take those important ones as the key issues — or most likely the leading indicators of success and failure for your system right now.

The only thing is, those can and will change as you map them to shifting existential requirements. Most of what you mark as important are what you need right now, not what you may need in the face of changing life conditions. So you want to be aware of how narrow, or thin-sliced, your important scores are. Many people will go through the survey with a narrow time perspective and mark elements as low importance, when the elements may be very important in terms of key issues.

A lot of the elements are high-leverage issues. For instance, if you look back at business development, it says I *pursue networks with my target customers*. A lot of people may not score this element very high, but it's actually one of the huge issues of leverage when we talk about building robustness. It will keep you out of trouble, because you can switch clients if you need to. Or you can switch modus operandi if you need to, if you have particular elements in an industry go down.

Returning to our example of the American real estate market, if you are only in real estate, your system is not robust, and you may be having a more difficult time. However, if you've been paying attention to what your customers tell you they want, there are other options for you in terms of morphing your activities to generate revenues when real estate drops off the cliff. Of course if you were in networks with your target customers, you would have known this way before the crowd anyway, and may have adjusted ahead of time.

We're trying to create a path-driven system here, rather than an event-based system. Event-based systems are where you have natural alignments between who you are and what you do. When you are able to function in your strengths, and life conditions are calling for more of your strengths, you do pretty well. What happens, though, when life conditions shift and take you out of your strength areas? Well, you're not robust in other areas unless you've done some design work and created some flexibility or robustness.

The first survival issue at this level of robustness is your professional survival. Your downside, therefore, is limited to at least survival and no lower—failure to survive. Believe me, there will be people who trade their current standard of living during future discontinuities and disruptions headed your way. If you don't want to be in that group, then know where to turn your attention quickly in case of discontinuity or disruption. This is key whether you are doing well or not doing well. There are specific parts of the system that you will have to manage over time that will have great leverage during changing life conditions.

That is what you are trying to identify as key survival issues. Without them, you don't have the basic cash-flow requirements and profits that can drive investment after downturns, or even better, during downturns. Someone once told me that their father used to always keep $100,000 in the bank during the 1930s, because there were untold bargains to be purchased, as one after another of those people around him sold off assets to keep going.

Crystalizing your clarity around key survival or leverage issues can be done as a self-driven, self-generated system. If, however, you are trying to do this on your own and not with the help of one of our *upthedownside coaches* or someone who understands this resilience model, you are most likely working in a very thin slice. And your resilience is directly equal to the size of slice of reality you can manage. If you are thin-slicing reality, life conditions have to be in a narrow set of conditions for you to have resilience. Remember that axiom while you score the following survey statement.

Using a scale of 1–10 for each, calculate Requirements – (Capability) x Importance = Priority Score

Score each element on a scale of 1–10; 1=low, 10=high	Req	Cap	Imp	PS
Key ingredients of professional survival are crystal clear.				

"Connections are fostered with leaders."

One of the reasons that you have connections with leaders is to make sure that connections are fostered with leaders. The reason is that a leader has leverage because leaders have followers.

If you connect with a power node, which is what a leader is, that power node will have a lot of connections. If, however, you connect with a regular node, it does not have very many connections and is not going to be very robust. You'll need lots more connections with followers than you do with leaders to get the same number of connections.

If you are connected with leaders, then they can connect you with their followers. What's more, they can connect you with other leaders, or power nodes. This power node system of power-law distribution is important in creating robustness. You have to create enough connections that if you were to lose some of them, the system has enough connections left to sustain itself in discontinuity. Therefore, connections are continuously fostered with leaders.

Using a scale of 1–10 for each, calculate Requirements – (Capability) x Importance = Priority Score

Score each element on a scale of 1–10; 1=low, 10=high	Req	Cap	Imp	PS
Connections are fostered with leaders.				

"Adaptability to ongoing needs provides new resources."

The leverage here is to have two systems running. Stephen Covey, author of *The 7 Habits of Highly Effective People* and *Principle-Centered Leadership*, talks about a system in which people deliver performance in real time and also have the capacity to deliver performance over time. That's what we're talking about here — having two or three systems running in parallel, not putting all our cards into one system, but executing well enough that we don't dilute the *main thing* either.

The first is a basic system for general operations involving input, throughput, and output, with corresponding feedback into each loop. Everyone has some sort of technical expertise, whether you're a teacher, plumber, insurance person, chiropractor, doctor, lawyer, coach, or consultant. You have inputs coming in. You do something to those inputs, whether it is a request for a proposal, a patient coming in, or a new plumbing system to develop. And you field an output. Somewhere with throughput. you make your living. There's a basic technical operation system going on in the background.

As the system functions over time, however, life conditions shift or we move among levels of existence that are situational at times. An example might even be the holidays, where large-scale shifts in working hours occur. We may find ourselves in a set of life conditions that works pretty well for us in an up market. Then all of a sudden the market shifts to neutral demand or a down market, and with those new life conditions, our level of existence normally has to shift. If you don't make an appropriate shift—a nonresilient case—you begin to lose your standard of living. The idea is to be able to adapt to your ongoing wants and needs.

Things are changing rapidly now as knowledge is doubling every year or so and keeps accelerating. What you knew last year will be outdated in a year. So you have your system running, and it's attempting to remain stable over time, and yet you're also trying to adapt it as life conditions shift. New knowledge is created. New contextual complexity arises. You are going to have to shift that system in order to move to where alignment between capability and requirements creates stability.

The second idea in this element—provide new resources—is counterintuitive because you'd think that adapting to ongoing wants and needs would mean using up resources, rather than creating or providing new ones. But what is emerging out of this adaptive process is that you will be getting access to new resources, new ways of thinking and doing things.

For instance, take plumbing, which has become more complex as the demand to save water and energy has increased. As I mentioned, you can save tremendous amounts of water now that dishwashers are plumbed with a grinder in the bottom, so you don't have to rinse food off the dishes before loading them. I think plumbing will become very complex in the future as ideas of how the world can work shift more and more—adding new resources to the game plumbers are playing.

The point is, as we adapt to growing needs for resources, we're going to actually create new resources. In Europe they use a tankless water heater, which uses less energy because it only heats the water when you use it. But it uses more water, because you run the water for a little while to get the temperature you want. That is wasted water, and water may some day become more priceless than oil. What we have to understand in these more complex systems where we need robustness is the full amount of complexity that is emerging when we adapt.

Now, they do make some tankless systems with more complex plumbing that will give you instant heat. What it does is recycle the water in the system until the water reaches a certain temperature and then turns it on. So they've made an adaptation to an ongoing want and need, and that has provided the opportunity for newer resources to emerge by which we get hot water on demand without wasting another resource during the provision.

These are the kinds of things you're going to have to look at in your professional business. How is your adaptation to ongoing wants and needs providing you with new resources that you then can use for further adaptation and resilience? This is a complex concept. Many people don't think this way. In order to be professionally resilient and to up the downside, you're going to have to think in orders of consequence beyond just the order of consequence of the current behavior.

Using a scale of 1–10 for each, calculate Requirements – (Capability) x Importance = Priority Score

Score each element on a scale of 1–10; 1=low, 10=high	Req	Cap	Imp	PS
Adaptability to ongoing needs provides new resources.				

"Scenario planning just-in-case strategies informs our plan."

This is a complex statement. It begins with scenario planning. What you are looking at here, a *just-in-case strategy*, is a strategy that is not used except when it is triggered. Yet in order to have it available, you must consider it ahead of time.

A lot of times what you do, to use *management speak*, is called firefighting. It's crisis management. If you do that, most of the time you will move your system resource-wise into a dangerous area where it consumes as much as it produces. So your standard of living is liable to be discontinuous when you hit bumps in the road with disruptive activities.

In this element we're thinking about what kinds of scenarios might take place and how that informs our plan of contingency or disruption or flexibility or plasticity or adaptability. We're spending some time on the front end to think about things as if they were *not* the way they are right now. If they were not, then what kinds of *just-in-case strategies* would you have? One of the things I've done throughout this model is preload the system with scenario planning of just-in-case strategies. If you go back to the early elements of the system, most of the things we were putting into the system are just-in-case strategies.

For instance, an emergency fund is a just-in-case strategy. That allows us to say "yes" and "no" to different things if we have a disruption or discontinuity in our income. You want to have that in place so you can implement other just-in-case strategies to keep your plan moving. If you have a plan to grow your professional practice in some way over a period of five, ten, twenty years, which most professionals would want to have, you don't want that plan interrupted at particular points because of discontinuities or the failure to scale. You want to grow with the conditions.

There are particularly vulnerable points where if your professional plan is interrupted, you could lose your complete standard of living, as well as those of people around you. Therefore, you want to be careful about these vulnerable points and protect them. Professionals have a fiduciary responsibility for others in their employment to make good decisions in the present that protects the employees' future.

If, for instance, your plan calls for borrowing money and paying it back over a period of time, you want to make sure that is not interrupted. If it were to be interrupted, that might affect your credit rating, and that, in turn, might affect your ability to get capital or access to financing, leasing, and these kinds of things. By giving prior consideration through scenario planning to just-in-case strategies, you can keep yourself moving through a period of time that will cause other professionals to lose their standard of living. This is what we are talking about in *upping the downside*.

We don't know what the downside is going to be. Anybody who thinks they do is kidding themselves, in my view, or is naive. How, then, can we *up* the downside if we don't know what it will be?

One way is to think about the kinds of just-in-case strategies you need to have in place in the event of a crisis, to keep yourself moving and not become vulnerable. Vulnerability, it seems, is attractive to the universe in terms of stirring up more crisis. The more vulnerable you are, the bigger the crisis. Therefore, you want to look at vulnerability and begin to understand whether it can be mitigated over time through prior consideration and just-in-case strategies.

Many people talk about capital budgeting, which means you build a building or buy vehicles or equipment because of a return-to-investment decision you make in a capital-budgeting formula. Why can't you put in the capital-budgeting formula funding for your just-in-case strategies? Why can't you fund an emergency plan over time? Why can't you fund some type of disruption insurance or disability policy or Health Savings Account over time? You can. We're talking here about prior consideration of just-in-case strategies, things that will not necessarily come up except under certain conditions. Then if they do come up, we can manage through what could be very vulnerable points in time.

Using a scale of 1–10 for each, calculate Requirements – (Capability) x Importance = Priority Score

Score each element on a scale of 1–10; 1=low, 10=high	Req	Cap	Imp	PS
Scenario planning just-in-case strategies informs our plan.				

"Just-in-time leverage points create advantages."

Imagine a situation in which several people are doing business in the way you do business, and someone is going to retire and make the business available to you. Could that be a just-in-time leverage point for creating something to your advantage? Or a plot of land comes up for sale. Or an employee that you want but really can't afford becomes available.

Do you have any strategy built in for buying that business or land or hiring that good employee and taking care of them? Or a valuable employee or someone working with you decides to go somewhere else. Is there a way that you can match their salary and keep them for a period of time so you can adjust your system to function without them? There are many possible just-in-time leverage points. You want to look at where your value is created, where your money is made. Those are going to be your leverage points.

For those of us who are looking further out, you can begin to understand some other leverage points that we have in the United States.

For instance, in spring 2007, the price of gas hit an all time-high. If you are in a situation where the cost of fuel is a leverage point in running your business, then you're vulnerable, and a price jump of 45 or 50 cents a gallon would create some real disadvantage for you.

Is there a way that you can identify and understand these leverage points for your business?

Now, imagine that you had been thinking about shifting part of your business into a virtual format and eliminating some of your route sales. In the event of a gas-price increase, this shift would create a distinct advantage for you. You could take advantage of the increasing gas prices to make that decision, because the price increase would finance this move. For you this would be a just-in-time leverage point.

I think it was Earl Nightengale I heard quote Napoleon Hill's saying that "every failure brings with it the seed of an equivalent success." This is what we're talking about in this element. When you have difficulty because of a disruption or discontinuity, if you know how to recognize just-in-time leverage points, and you have or can get resources, there will be significant opportunities available to you.

If you have done some looking ahead to understand your business processes and how the world works in your system, you will know that if certain things happen, there will be an advantage. Say, for instance, that your business is growing, and you've been thinking about acquiring more space or a better location, but haven't been able to afford it. There may be an advantage to doing that within a window of opportunity that is beginning to swing open in the real estate market. Again, a just-in-time leverage point.

What about the real estate agent who is using our upping the downside system, connecting to leaders and a variety of other elements. They could start looking for people who are going to outgrow or who have already outgrown their businesses. Now, when the real estate market is down is the time for those people to act. There you have a just-in-time strategy that can bring your business right back on top, as long as you're willing to do a little detective work. And you won't even have to do that if you are practicing the design inherent in this resilience system, because someone will volunteer the information in your mastermind, leadership circle, or professional group!

My wife and I did some checking for where to winter for 2007–2008, and we noticed that in Las Vegas rental and ownership costs were dropping significantly, even though there are eight thousand people coming into the city a week. They've way over built, way over constructed, and are very much in a downturn in Las Vegas. Rents are going for anywhere from half to two-thirds of what they were just twelve to eighteen months ago. This is the kind of just-in-time leverage point you can take advantage of to improve your standard of living and increase the value you can give to your customers and clients.

Using a scale of 1–10 for each, calculate Requirements – (Capability) x Importance = Priority Score

Score each element on a scale of 1–10; 1=low, 10=high	Req	Cap	Imp	PS
Just-in-time leverage points create advantages.				

"Our network of connections shares what it learns."

This is a two-part element. The network of connections we're talking about can be one with employees, shareholders, stakeholders, clients, suppliers, venders, or just about any group that you are connected to.

In terms of robustness, the ability those connections give you is that not all of your eggs are in one basket. If, for instance, you had a supplier shift in a discontinuity, you might lose supply. We had some web issues recently as a result of some hacker attacks and found out that our network of connections was too narrow going forward. We had become too vulnerable to an outage, even though we were enjoying economies of scale. The upshot was that we were not robust enough to be able to take additional discontinuities that would appear in times where life conditions were shifting dramatically. We were lucky to discover this because we were able to increase our robustness and our number of connections by rebuilding the system with a totally different set of ideas, and not have to do that in a downturn. I consider that to have been lucky, even though it was quite expensive at the time.

In terms of sharing, one of the things we often don't do well as professionals is to share much of our operating knowledge, our operating resilience, with other people. We're too afraid as professionals to let anybody else help us or to appear weak or like we don't know what we're doing. We put on a huge mask and significantly pretend that everything is okay, even when it's not. And so we lose out on the ability to have sharing taking place. Sharing, to me, is where you become able to link into the systems of other people and share a discontinuity or a disruption or a situation that is not going to be easy for you to handle on your own.

I know this concern does not represent our current world, but I'm suggesting that as we move forward to where discontinuity will become more likely and unpredictable, we're going to need to learn to share, to reach out, to do some of the things we have to do to help one another through difficult times. I don't think we talk enough about that. I don't see it with my clients. I don't see it in the businesses I work with. I don't see this concern about whom we're connected to and how robust those connections are and how we are able to share in times of trouble.

Even in my own life, as I study this material and have been studying it for the past five years, I'm just now coming to the realization, which is a very early stage of resilience, that there is a lot of opportunity out there if you begin to rely on other people, if you allow other people to lead, if you provide the way for other people to share and grow and do things for you that they're good at and want to do to help you. At the same time, offer ways in which you can share with them.

This is something that I see coming, because we're starting to look at social-network analysis, and that is leading us to understand a couple topics called *betweenness* and *closeness*.

If we worked to develop this concept a bit more, we would look at our network of connections to identify robustness and ability to share in terms of how much betweenness and how much closeness we have. Betweenness has to do with people in a group knowing one another. Closeness is related to the closeness of our connection and how many times we make ourselves available to and seek availability from the other person or node. A network increases in value to the extent that there is betweenness and closeness among its members—to the extent that we have social *sharing* networks.

Using a scale of 1–10 for each, calculate Requirements – (Capability) x Importance = Priority Score

Score each element on a scale of 1–10; 1=low, 10=high	Req	Cap	Imp	PS
Our network of connections shares what it learns.				

"We are guided by new economy rules of engagement."

These rules of engagement—*networking, affiliation, asynchronicity, execution, mastermind, resilience,* and *right action*—are important here because this is a system within itself, a metsystem that begins to portray the complexity coming in the next category, or process, of resilience: generativity.

It's a system within a system, and so you would expect to see complexity at this level of developmental scaling in a robustness process at this level of complexity. We are now combining seven rules of engagement into one central, agentic idea. The idea is that we are doing the *networking*. We understand *affiliation*, and I'm not talking about affiliation as motivation, although that's important. I'm talking about using affiliates as a referral engine, getting people to refer to you.

Asynchronicity has to do with our business continuing to operate when we are not there, when we're not watching, when we're asleep. This is quite easy to identify, by the way. All you need to do is map your revenue, margins, and profits while your business is open—during its "hours"—and when it's not. Are you producing business when you're not open? That's a key idea. Are you affiliating while you are not open?

Execution is the same way. Are people able to come and go? Does your network execute twenty-four hours a day, seven days a week? Think of an ATM network, where anybody around the world can withdraw money at any odd time, even when the local stores are closed. What about electricity? Can someone come to your service and be served without you being there? That's one of the things we don't think about in terms of our professional environment, because we think about the historically classical version of professional practice of nine to four, don't we?

Masterminding we've discussed above. It's very important. *Resilience* refers to this model functioning in the whole as a system of engagement for upping the downside. And, of course, *right action* is right people, doing right things, in right ways, at right times, in right spaces, for right reasons, to get right results. In other words, we're now talking about creating robustness *among* all of the different attributes of our professional practice. Of course, for some this may not be important, or even if so, they may not be able to turn over new resources to achieve it.

This is the kind of robustness we're seeking at this level of complexity.

Using a scale of 1–10 for each, calculate Requirements – (Capability) x Importance = Priority Score

Score each element on a scale of 1–10; 1=low, 10=high	Req	Cap	Imp	PS
We are guided by new economy rules of engagement.				

"We grow and create universally, linking our experiences."

When we talk about universal linkage here, we're talking about what we could be doing in a *globalizing* world that would create for us the ability to grow and create, as much as we are concerned about the day-to-day experiences we are creating among the stakeholders. Each is an application of universality. How can that happen? How can we look at universal linkages and understand that everything is connected?

By doing this, we're actually improving our resilience. It's just like listening to debates among presidential candidates. One of the things I look for is how linked a candidate is in terms of what's going on in the world. Are they talking mainly from an I mentality of "I built this. I did this." Or are they showing that they have linkages that allow them to grow and create, so we would not have to depend so much upon their own individual ability, but their linked experiences. Do they see their individual ability as being enhanced through the contribution of others? If a presidential candidate doesn't get "we," but instead focuses on "I," then I'm concerned that they are underestimating real complexity.

We're just not seeing this much in our world right now, although maybe we shouldn't expect to be seeing it at the level of developmental complexity currently in the world.

In resilience—and more specifically, under conditions of robustness—one of the things we know is that the more nodes, the more linkages, the more connections you have, the more likely you are to be resilient. You have more resources and more relationships with resources that may appear when needed. This is especially true when you're linked with people who are looking at things universally as to how things work around the world.

I don't think many people are ready to practice at this level, but it's time to introduce this not only into our own lives and practice, but also into the commons. One of the things we study in the program *spiralnextware.com* is enterprise facilitation in what is called Array 5. It's a system of creating linkages to resources in a community. What it does is identify all of the available resources in a community that most times people do not understand are there and consequently do not access.

We're talking about understanding that linkages exist, that resources cross boundaries of what we know and don't know. For instance, many professionals link to their academic institutions for research and development, especially businesses that do training and development and related activities. This is a way to improve our sense of robustness and the number of linkages that we have in order to have *universality*. Or, the same things that we're doing in the United States people are doing in Asia or Europe or Africa. We can build linkages over time with our experiences, so that we can move resources virtually in ways of doing, being, having, and becoming that are manifest differently than we are doing them right now. This is part of the process of creating universal linkages.

The other thing that linkages provide us with is ownership. When you have a link with someone somewhere else, you have ownership of that relationship through the linkage. We'll have to begin to understand that as we look at a globalizing world with geopolitical events that affect us all, rather than being isolated in one part of our own country.

That's one reason that we in the United States have such consternation about the Middle East. We depend so much on what happens in the Middle East for our day-to-day activities. If energy supplies were to become disrupted, the world as we know it in a suburban economy would shift dramatically. It would change life completely. We are so much more vulnerable than most people in the world, because we've created a suburban economy, which means that very few people today do not have to drive to commute somewhere. The average commute time in the United States is twenty-eight minutes, and in some places it's an hour and a half or longer.

Because of the suburban nature of our economy, we depend on energy to move us around in our private automobiles, rather than through public transportation, as in Europe and other regions. This makes us particularly vulnerable to any disruption that could cause isolation.

I saw this happen when I first started coaching in the medical profession, as medical people were becoming isolated by politics or because of disruptions in the medical system their local area or region. They were actually having to change the way they did their whole practice because of political barriers preventing linkages. Now today in medicine we see private practices linking to hospitals and medical providers and MRIs and all kinds of things that we wouldn't have imagined years ago, which create linkage through the use of other people's resources.

It makes us more resilient if we can begin to link and use and share and also provide these same types of things to other people through linkage.

Using a scale of 1–10 for each, calculate Requirements – (Capability) x Importance = Priority Score

Score each element on a scale of 1–10; 1=low, 10=high	Req	Cap	Imp	PS
We grow and create universally, linking our experiences.				

Now you can tally all your robustness scores:

Robustness				
Key ingredients of professional survival are crystal clear.				
Connections are fostered with leaders.				
Adaptability to ongoing needs provides new resources.				
Scenario planning just-in-case strategies informs our plan.				
Just-in-time leverage points create advantages.				
Our network of connections shares what it learns.				
We are guided by new economy rules of engagement.				
We grow and create universally, linking our experiences.				
Total				

Remember, if you need help, we offer monthly tele-development training in this system, as well as qualified coaches to support your resilience journey in upping the downside. Register or log in at *www.upping-the-downside.com* for more information.

Chapter 20

Generativity
by Mike Jay

With this next category, we take another step into the more complex and abstract. Even so, *upping the downside* occupies a specific niche in that it's a concrete system overall. It tells you specifically what to do in each element in each process category. It may not tell you the tasks exactly, but if it says to get an emergency fund, you can identify what an emergency fund is for you and go to work on that. When we get to this level — *generativity* — there is a degree of complexity that puts us in a position to leverage everything else we have done in the prior categories of professional resilience. If each of the first six categories were processes and can be seen as a system in and unto themselves, then the seventh process, or system, is a metasystem — a system of systems.

Generativity is a concept that means a lot to me. In 1987 I came up with the term *generati* to describe the kinds of people who are, by their very actions, generative. They generate more than they use up. They "be, do, have, and become" a generator. They have a specific input, and with some kind of throughput, they put out more than what they started with. This whole area of generativity in a professional practice is important, even though some of the terms that I use may be a bit obscure.

I'll do my best to explain them, because the first element itself is not a very concrete statement:

"Aware of the agents, rules, tensions, and conditionals present."

It becomes concrete, though, when you come to understand that all of the other statements, or elements, in the model are in fact *agents*. They are acting upon or can be used to act upon conditions of reality in one form or another. They even act upon one another, and through rules, tension, and conditions become interactive, intersubjective, and interdevelopmental—making this categorical process difficult and complex.

Let's look back, for instance, at business development: I *view my professional practice from all directions*. That is agency. You are actually taking a specific view of your professional practice from as many directions as you and your team can conceptualize and create. What emerges from that view are things that we can talk about as *tensions*. For instance, when I view my personal practice from the inside out, I have a particular way of seeing how I want that to be for me.

Yet when I ask others to give me feedback about what they see looking in, oftentimes it is very different from what I see looking out. Am I aware of that? Am I aware of the kind of tension this is going to produce? Am I aware that a *conditional* is going to arise? A conditional is like an "if-then" circumstance, or "if and only if," or "and-or," or "but," or perhaps a "both-and." Those are all conditionals.

And finally, if I'm aware of what is going on in my business, the kinds of people I'm dealing with, the interactions, the types of systems I have, the types of procedural *rules* that take place both inside my practice and in society, I most likely will have more resilience.

Take the point of awareness a physician has in their practice—certain *rules* govern. If I'm a plumber or an electrician, the building codes and regulations govern my practice. So, *awareness* in this context means being aware of agents, our agency, or things that we do to create action or to act upon our realities. It means being aware of the kinds of rules that exist in that reality to govern and regulate and the tensions they increase or decrease among the conditionals that are both emergent and complex in situations as they change. This gives me choice and adaptability.

If I see my practice from an inside-out perspective, get feedback, and am fortunate enough that I am able to receive it and maybe even consider it—not everyone is!—I notice that there could be conditionals, things that matter differently under different circumstances. I could see that if I continue to do the things that I'm doing, it's likely to produce certain kinds of consequences or outcomes in view of the realities. I can try to understand whether or not those outcomes are things I want to do and see happen.

I face this daily in my own work. I face the tension of being who I am and the reality of what I am as an agent. These are the kinds of tensions that emerge as situations dictate conditional change in the rules that govern and regulate my behavior. I'm not generative all that much, but at least I am aware of some of the specifics and can decide to move into the space of generativity through my own action or through the design I create with others. This gives me the most leverage for generativity. I often face the consequences of being out of alignment either between my own internal view and a coherent view of things, or with the view that reality has looking inward from the outside. The onset of generativity comes from the ability to be aware of what is going on—to be able to both self-assess and assess what is taking place in the environment accurately.

Resilience is produced when you begin to understand the interplay of the ingredients of emergence—*agents, rules, tensions, and conditionals.* That is essentially what is happening here in this primitive statement of emergence.

I understand that I get a certain cake, for instance, every time I use a particular recipe. Now I want the cake to be different than the cake that is being created by this recipe. I'm well aware of the ingredients that I'm using, because I'm paying attention to how yeast or baking soda or eggs are agents. I recognize there are specific rules for how things combine in baking to create certain types of final outcomes. Then I can begin to fool around a bit with the recipe based on what I see emerging every time I create a cake. I can do so in a lot of possible ways that may be more efficient, effective, and sustainable with feedback over time.

If I understand those agents, rules, tensions, and conditionals of emergent reality, I see that if I continue to do things the way I'm doing them, I'll keep getting what I'm getting right now. If I want different results, why don't I tweak how I'm going about process? Of course, as soon as you begin to talk in the language of awareness of agents, rules, tensions, and conditionals, you put yourself in a different position—into a different language paradigm—and emergence is no easy process. Yet you will have changed your attribution of meaning. As soon as you change your attribution, you might remove some of the tension from changing yourself or from someone else changing. You might, for instance, decide to bring in some additional help or resources.

At this level of generativity, the process is to reach out and be aware of how things fit together and what is going on in the processes you have as results emerge. When people first started doing reengineering in the early nineties, many of them did not do process mapping. Then when they brought in Six Sigma technology, everyone started doing process mapping and modeling. Now, of course, that is widespread and commonly done. Everyone knows that you need to do process modeling and mapping to understand what is taking place within and across your systems. This allows us to be generative in making decisions by saying, "I've got these inputs. I've got these kinds of throughputs. I'm getting these kinds of outputs. The feedback I'm getting says if I keep doing the same thing over and over, I'll keep getting the same results. I don't want that."

How do you interrupt the process? You intervene by being aware of the agents, rules, tensions, and conditionals present. If you rearrange this list, you can remember them by using the acronym CART. The cart carries the system. The cart carries the baggage. The cart carries the weight of change. It's the interaction between these things that produces the emergent reality each of us has. Are you aware of what's going on in your practice? Are you aware of how things fit together? Do you understand much about anything at all?

By this stage of the model, it's best to work with an intervener—good catch some type of coach, mentor, consultant, facilitator, psychotherapist, counselor, or whatever. Can the person you've engaged to help give you ideas about how things fit together or help you get the feedback you need to be generative? Then you can begin to choose where to make interventions even though the system is self-organizing. This is how to become generative. Once you can choose where to intervene as a result of awareness, you will be more purposeful and competent going forward. That's part of the process of generativity.

Using a scale of 1–10 for each, calculate Requirements – (Capability) x Importance = Priority Score

Score each element on a scale of 1–10; 1=low, 10=high	Req	Cap	Imp	PS
Aware of the agents, rules, tensions, and conditionals present.				

"Content, context, condition, codes, and culture are differentiated."

You would *not* normally expect to work at this level of complexity, and therefore, it's not easy to put a concrete or formal label on something. What this element means is, do I make errors as a result of poor critical thinking that makes category errors? Do I make mistakes that confuse what things really are? Or do I begin to understand what is taking place and how?

In David Myers's 2002 book *Intuition*, he talks about a study in which people were meeting with a young woman. The woman was assigned by the researcher to be ornery with some people and not ornery with others. Each of them made up their minds about the young woman based on how she acted towards them. Of course what they found was exactly what you would expect. The people who experienced her as short and edgy with a wry face said she was a bad person. The people who experienced her differently said she was a good person. In fact, neither was true per se, because she was acting.

This is part of the process of stratification. Are we making fundamental category errors of attribution? Are we assuming something to be true because it's the way we think it is? Or because we've looked at the person, what they're saying and doing, the context they're doing it in, and the conditions revolving around the person? If you take anybody and squeeze them tight, you'll get a different kind of attribution than if they were in a non-stressed position. When we begin to dissect the different ideas of what is happening in our professional practices, including our own feelings, behavior, thinking, and ways of doing things, we're able to see different ways of attributing meaning and making judgments more efficiently.

You can't just push everything together in a big wad and say the reason this is happening is because it's happening, when in fact, there could be cultural issues or issues of goal-state tension. For instance, the conditions my wife was in when she was recovering from the death of her pet are entirely different from the conditions she's in now. If we look at the five items listed in this element, her *context* behavior has changed.

Codes are the ways of doing things (algorithms as we've referred to them throughout the book). When somebody comes in with a specific health problem, I give them this prescription. If somebody has that kind of problem, they need to buy that kind of insurance policy. Codes are algorithms, the ways of solving problems that we develop over time through association with our knowledge, skills, and base of experience according to a set of conditions.

Conditions are the ever-changing, situational goal-states that we have every minute of every day.

Content is the choice of language or nonverbal responses of behavior that we choose to use as a mechanism to move around in a context or execute a code or work in a condition. You might say content is the syntax of the semantics.

Then, of course, *culture* is pretty easy to understand. We have cultural norms. If you behave the same way in Mitchell, Nebraska, as you do in New York City, people will think you're odd and vice versa. Cultures in other countries have different rules and ways of doing things. Words mean different things in different contexts. Certain actions and gestures shift their meaning from here to there. You have to sort through this idea of stratifying your meaning.

Though a bit complex, this actually can be done quite easily when you begin to think in this way. It pulls you back from making attribution errors like saying that person is a jerk or this is not going to ever work here or things like that. It's impossible to do justice to this particular element, as it is to all the elements in the last two processes, but I'm introducing them to you nonetheless, so you might consider working at more complex levels, should you find yourself mastering elements in the other processes. I have produced an entire twelve-week course *just* on this element at *spiral-nextware.com* —*Array 2: Animation.*

Using the five Cs in this element, plus an epigenetic core, allows you to peel away noise and find the signal present. In a complex world, the signal is often obscured by high noise levels.

Using a scale of 1–10 for each, calculate Requirements – (Capability) x Importance = Priority Score

Score each element on a scale of 1–10; 1=low, 10=high	Req	Cap	Imp	PS
Content, context, condition, codes, and culture are differentiated.				

"My system actions are based on what really matters."

This statement is, thankfully, more concrete, because it's one that we can view both from the standpoint of espoused theory, what we say we're doing, and the theory in use or what we're actually observed doing. If we are able to incorporate the prior two elements with this one, we can identify the layers of what matters when—a critical guide for action.

Many people today are not acting on what really matters. The reason is that they're acting to serve what is inherently a motivational sensitivity, which is almost completely unknown and unconscious to them. Because they are mostly unaware of that sensitivity to want what they want and need what they need in a lot of different contexts or conditions, they behave in a way that serves that sensitivity, rather than a way that will really matter to them and the reality they're subject to or, in best cases, object with. We have to understand that resilience is an *emergent* condition or property coming out of what is happening on the ground at the time. It's almost impossible to pre-plan resilience because resilience itself is an emergent property, which means that it can't be pre-defined a priori.

There may be times when we are personally resilient and working in an area that has a lot of motivational sensitivity for us, while at the same time we may be professionally low on resilience. The reason is that when you move through the cashflow quadrant of Kiyosaki's metaphor, you start in the self-employed area of professional work. But that bleeds over into the business and investor areas, and then, in a lot of cases, professionals are employees or working with an employee mindset trying to manage situations that require different codes or culture. What you have is a very clouded rule set. Therefore, unless you are really clear, you are most likely not going to act on what really matters. What you are going to do is work to resolve whatever tension is present, as in firefighting. Some of us, for instance, are curious (high motivational sensitivity in curiosity) and would rather learn about things than *do* anything. That is just the nature of curiosity.

Now, does that really matter to us? Yes, it does. It's important for our own personal resilience to be in alignment with that curiosity. Does that actually get in the way of producing professional resilience? It can, and oftentimes it does. When we talk about acting on what really matters, *what* really matters has to be clear in terms of content, context, codes, conditions, culture, core, and the kinds of things in our professional domain.

We have to understand what really matters, and not just to us, but also in the system of systems we're working in. So when you say to me, "My system actions are based on what really matters," as a coach, I say to you, "Give me two or three pieces of evidence." Along with the evidence, tell me some of the impact of those outcomes on your life. I can begin to judge very quickly whether or not you are acting on what really matters. If something really matters, there is going to be a significant amount of evidence that it matters, so that you can judge it from mattering to *really* mattering, other than just saying it does. It's going to be *manifest* and self-organizing in your systems.

There is going to be impact or what we call leverage created from its presence. Therefore, acting on what really matters will produce a much higher level of resilience in two ways. In the personal way, you are going to understand what really matters for you. Then, if you understand and are aware of the agents, rules, tensions, and conditionals present, you will also be aware of what matters to other people. *All of that* goes into the equation of "what really matters" broadly, and so on. That is the key. Acting on what really matters becomes a way in which you can coax resilience constantly into whatever condition arises, while maintaining connection with what really matters on a number of levels.

If what really matters guides you, then whatever condition occurs, whatever future begins to emerge, you can continue to guide your own actions based on what really matters. There will most likely be real alignment and sustainability behind that. It will produce a high level of resilience, because every time the target begins to move in the environment and you're fixed on that target, you're going to move with the environment and the target. And you will produce a higher level of success while mattering, so to speak.

Of course, now, happiness gets a little tricky here. That's why when you get into these higher levels of resilience, you can't always bring happiness with you. Sometimes you get a separation of what is successful for you in a professional circumstance and what makes you happy in a personal circumstance. You begin to get some separation, possibly some misalignment, especially if you are a self-employed professional and you find your own success being limited by who you are and what resources you have readily available, which happens a lot.

Using a scale of 1–10 for each, calculate Requirements – (Capability) x Importance = Priority Score

Score each element on a scale of 1–10; 1=low, 10=high	Req	Cap	Imp	PS
My system actions are based on what really matters.				

"Professional intentions are mapped through a variety of lenses."

We've given you a number of lenses already through prior elements in this process category. But there are some additional lenses that you can pick up that I like a lot. They come from the balanced-scorecard work being done around the world, and most notably credited to Robert Kaplan and David Norton. Even Ken Wilber's quadrants are directly derived from Kaplan and Norton's ideas on Balanced Scorecard. The components of the scorecard I use are internal, external, financial, and developmental, where Kaplan and Norton use learning, growth, and innovation where I use developmental. I like *developmental* because it's the kind of work I enjoy doing. Developmental allows us to encompass learning, growth, and innovation and still look at different ideas around how development itself actually forms.

In mapping your professional intention, this is where we get into the idea of action theory, for action theory is what we *intend*. So we actually have three theories that are functioning, not just two. The first, again, is *espoused theory*—what we say we know, or say we believe, or think we know, or think we believe, or feel that we know, or feel that we believe, whichever way you want to contextualize it. Then there is the way that others observe us believing or behaving. They say, "You believe this because we see you behaving this way." That is *theory in use*. These two are explicit from the work of Chris Argyris and Donald Shön in *Theory in Practice: Increasing Professional Effectiveness*.

The third, in my view, is the theory of intention, or what I call *action theory*. Intention can be conscious, though most of the time it is unconscious. What we fully intend arises out of the unconscious soup that makes us all human. Therefore, our action theory is most of the time very ambiguous.

For instance, I'll say I intend to get the work done that I need to do this week. I intend to take good care of my patients. I intend to make twenty-four sales calls. I intend to try to find a way to contact new clients. The intention is a way, in some cases, of actually allowing ourselves to come into alignment with and stay flexible with very difficult tensions. That is who we are versus what we do based on behavioral requirements brought about by conditions, context, and culture.

We use this gray area of intention in some ways to manage what most of the time is a lack of coherence between what we say we believe and what we actually do. So the way to take that out of the gray area is to *examine intentions* or to more deliberately map them.

Remember, we're now getting into the cashflow quadrant deep enough to where your business as a professional is your responsibility. You're becoming accountable for your business, your business reality, your professional reality, as you prepare to make the B-I Leap, as Kiyosaki calls it. You can't operate out of your back pocket anymore (like an entrepreneur does) and still be as effective and resilient as you need to be, because if you do and you have employees or customers or other people depending on you, you begin to make it up as you go. Few people can follow or anticipate what you'll do next, which means they become co-dependent on you for their actions, and you begin to give up significant levels of individual creativity and innovation.

Depending on the kind of person you are and your identity, making it up as you go may be in alignment with your motivational sensitivity or values instrumentation. And if your personal reality or your business or professional reality is aligned with that motivational sensitivity, you're okay. But most of the time it is not. Most of the time, as a professional you will be functioning *out of alignment* with business reality, therefore, your professional intention needs to be clear. It needs to be mapped. You need to be able to point your finger and say this is what *we* intend to do over the next twelve to eighteen months. This is the reason I'm spending money on that building. This is the reason I'm hiring a sales person. The reason is that it fits with the intention, the clear intention between the identity of who we are and the action that we perceive to be right by realizing the intention.

While establishing clear boundaries between who you are as an individual and your professional practice design, we're looking for alignment now between your identity, your intention, and your ultimate behavior. This is not just a single-person identify, intention, and purpose any more; it's a professional system, and that's a big difference! Then, of course, there are a couple more pieces that we have to add, one being the behavioral products or outcomes of the behavior. If we behave in certain ways, what happens after that? And finally, of course, are the results that they produce.

To give a quick example, I could be dedicated to making twenty-four sales calls. My behavior would be to call up twenty-four people. *Behavioral products* would be how many of those twenty-four people responded to what I wanted them to take action on. The *results*, then, would be out of those who responded, which ones actually created a result for us in our practice or in the company.

There are different levels of looking at your behavior, behavioral products, and your results. These are things that you have to map to be generative. What happens when the sales person is dedicated and makes the twenty-four calls? What happens when they don't get the outcomes? What happens when outcomes don't produce the desired results?

How are you going to help them be generative at that point? Didn't they do what you asked? Well, you have to be clear on the intention. Is everybody clear on the intention of the call and clear on the process intention? Their intention is to make the calls, to follow a certain kind of process that you've agreed upon, that you're clear on. But at the root of it all, the entire sales design is to produce concrete results. People have to understand intention, but also be allowed to modify the process when results are not emergent. This creates the generative path.

A lot of times by not mapping the intention, by not mapping fully the process, you get into gray areas that are ambiguous, and employees break down under pressure. They don't get the results you feel they should. Surely, if they are going to make twenty-four calls, you are expecting some kind of sales results. Again, what is it that you intend? Clarifying this is a very important part of the process, and it also allows for innovation and creativity to occur within bounds of this clarity, so we don't push systems constantly into chaos.

Using a scale of 1–10 for each, calculate Requirements – (Capability) x Importance = Priority Score

Score each element on a scale of 1–10; 1=low, 10=high	Req	Cap	Imp	PS
Professional intentions are mapped through a variety of lenses.				

"Effects on others are considered, almost always, before acting."

Obviously, you can't do this always. That would mean that we were conscious 100 percent of the time, or we have a choice all of the time. Clearly, situations will present themselves in which we have to decide *now*, without considering long-terms effects at all. So, why worry about it?

The important thing is that you try to consider your effects on others. In order to be generative with other people, in order to reach a level of resilience, you have to at least *consider* the effects that you're having on other people.

Now, it might not change your behavior or it might not change the outcomes or anything else that is taking place. Nonetheless, the act of considering the effect you have on others, or what others may feel or think about what is happening to them as a result of your actions, will likely generate a serious response from you in terms of empathy or caring and people feeling paid attention to, or at least create some Hawthorne Effect.

In studies conducted in the late twenties and early thirties by Elton Mayo at Western Electric, researchers found what they called the Hawthorne Effect. They were trying to understand the effect of environment on production and the performance of workers making phones. One of the findings was that you can increase performance if you pay attention to people.

People want to be paid attention to. If you consider the effects you have on others, you're paying attention to people. It will improve the results you get if you understand that by doing X to Z, people may respond in a certain way, and you may not come out so well in the professional reality. You may want to change your approach.

What makes you more resilient? You'll become more resilient to the extent that you can consider how the actions you take in your professional practice are affecting other people.

And there's another reason. If you consider the effects you'll have on others before you act, you'll always be doing scenario planning. Creating scenarios and doing scenario planning allows you to become ready or plastic in the face of disruption or discontinuity. If you are considering effects on others, you're likely to be getting feedback from people, asking them ahead of time, using trial balloons or a "what if?" scenario. What they're going to do is tell you how much and how quickly you need to adapt.

Say we have instituted a price increase, and now our business has dropped off 50 percent. What was that about? We didn't consider the effect of the increase on our customers. Had we asked them ahead of time, "If we're forced to go up on our prices, what kind of actions do you think you'll take?" done in the right circumstance we might have received feedback that would have led to a better solution. Again, being generative to be more resilient has us considering our effects on others, almost always, before acting.

Using a scale of 1–10 for each, calculate Requirements – (Capability) x Importance = Priority Score

Score each element on a scale of 1–10; 1=low, 10=high	Req	Cap	Imp	PS
Effects on others are considered, almost always, before acting.				

"Alignments with virtues are shared."

The idea here is that somewhere between the Aristotelian vices of *defeat* or *excess* lie virtues. Virtues will almost always be determined by the actors in the system: the agents, rules, tensions, and conditionals. The idea of aligning with virtue to me has the overriding notion that we *can* act with virtue.

What is *virtue*? Virtue is moderation. Virtue is value that is seen by others and can be held up as an example. If we're acting virtuous, if we're attempting to align with virtue—remember, this is most of the time defined by the beholder—we would have to continuously do what? Reach out.

To align with virtue, we have to find out what virtue is, which means we will have to ask others—the people we work with, the people we serve—what they think is fair, what they think is a good way to behave. It's almost like in medicine.

When I started coaching in 1987, there was not such a thing as a patient's bill of rights. Within a few years, people had complained enough that leaders began to say, "Look, patients have a right to certain things." That, to them, was virtuous. Aligning with patients' rights, aligning with the privacy that people deserve, aligning with confidentiality issues, these kinds of practices are virtuous. Of course, when you do that, it produces resilience over time. The reason is that virtue remains constant, much more constant than most of the change situations that you are going to be forced to adapt to. What is virtuous in a particular culture will remain fairly consistent over time, because cultural norms resist fluctuation and change.

Honesty is always going to be virtuous, and in some cultures, dealing directly with people and being candid are virtues. It's like when we talked to the veterinarian about our cat. I said, "Tell us the truth. Tell us what you really think. Tell us as if it were your animal. What is happening?" The vet said, "This is what's going on. I wish I had better news, but you asked me to be candid." To me that was virtuous. Then we as responsible and caring pet owners knew what the situation was.

Alignment with virtue is important in many different ways in professional practice.

Using a scale of 1–10 for each, calculate Requirements – (Capability) x Importance = Priority Score

Score each element on a scale of 1–10; 1=low, 10=high	Req	Cap	Imp	PS
Alignments with virtues are shared.				

"Coaching is sought at every opportunity in the system."

This element seems fairly obvious, but few people are actually doing it. In fact, I couldn't name more than a dozen people I'm aware of who continually seek coaching to increase their performance and development.

It's not an easy thing to do. At this level of activity, people are not always able to seek continual help. If they did, we would have such a demand for coaches that we couldn't fill it in today's world with the literally millions of professionals out there. Of course, it's not that professionals are not seeking to perform and develop, but there is an idea that we get to a certain point and then we sort of stay there—we don't have to reach out anymore.

It's like certain kinds of people who get through school and just stop learning, because they're done now. To create a resilient professional practice, you have to continue to reach out and seek coaching to perform and develop yourself and the people around you and your ideas. Even if you yourself do not change, you still have to develop your ideas about what is changing and what needs to change if you want to get better results. You want your professional practice to grow, your customers to be happier, your clients to be more satisfied. You don't want to have lawsuits of any kind. What is it that needs to be done? Answers can be found most of the time through coaching, feedback, interaction with people who continually give a viewpoint, even in some cases a 360-degree viewpoint—a coach-driven assessment orchestrated to get feedback about your behavior from people who interface with you.

Oftentimes, when people tell me they're already doing this, I ask them if they have a formal developmental team. I haven't found a one yet who does. Let's say, for instance, if I'm in a professional practice, I may have a lawyer, an accountant, an insurance person, even some professional people on staff whom I can refer to and turn to for advice. And then, do I also have a *personal* developmental team—a group of people I can ask difficult questions and have them give me feedback about how I'm performing and developing, not just a strategic business team, but a strategic personal development team?

Next consider—unless you are alone in your practice, and most professionals these days are not—how are you helping your employees to perform and develop? What kinds of mechanisms do you have in place? Do you have a regular conversation with them? Are you not only seeking coaching to perform and develop yourself, but also coaching or offering coaching to them? These are the ways you can be generative.

The key in looking at generativity is the ability to *actively reach in all directions, in, as well as out, up as well as down, through as well as into, etc.*

In other words, do not rely on your own point of view without checking to see whether it is informed or is actually a narrow, thin slice of reality. Any time you can engage in some activity that causes you to check that out with the real world, to get multiple angles and perspectives, in most cases, you're going to be able to make better decisions, perform at a higher level, and develop faster.

In professional development, we have all kinds of continuing education that we're asked to do by people concerned about our professional skills.

Yet a lot of the time we don't do anything to enhance the vessel itself—the personal vessel of who we are, our own identity. We're constantly focused on *what it is we do* versus *who it is we are and are becoming.* The latter is very important to focus on when you get to this level of complexity.

Using a scale of 1–10 for each, calculate Requirements – (Capability) x Importance = Priority Score

Score each element on a scale of 1–10; 1=low, 10=high	Req	Cap	Imp	PS
Coaching is sought at every opportunity in the system.				

"Learning, growth, and innovation are hallmarks of a glocal approach."

For many professionals, building capability professionally is not a real issue, because they have a structure that causes this to take place. They're forced to do it to stay licensed or to maintain their professional credentials or designation through continuing education units.

One thing I do notice, though, is that because they are forced to do it, professionals will sometimes wait until the last minute before they seek out ways to become a little sharper in their practice.

The purpose of this element is to make sure that people slow down or stop for a little bit, to take stock and understand what is happening around them. So with this eighth and last element of generativity, I encourage you to look at the previous seven elements as a good way to sharpen the saw. Sharpening the saw means more than just going to continuing education to increase your professional capability. It means sharpening your capability as a citizen, as a leader, as an individual enjoying your life more and becoming more successful. Increasing your capability, much of the time, allows you more choice when you do get into situations that require you to adapt. As we have seen, choice is often a key to increasing resilience.

Let's look at the term *glocal* here. In as fast-moving an environment as the professional world, where knowledge is doubling at accelerating rates, we have to consider not only our local conditions, but global conditions as well. There is increasing pressure on professionals today to maintain high standards in the face of increasing global competition. As we continually shrink and flatten our world, travel to and by professionals in other countries is making the landscape increasingly glocal.

Using a scale of 1–10 for each, calculate Requirements – (Capability) x Importance = Priority Score

Score each element on a scale of 1–10; 1=low, 10=high	Req	Cap	Imp	PS
Learning, growth, and innovation are hallmarks of a glocal approach.				

Now you can tally all your generativity scores:

Generativity				
Aware of the agents, rules, tensions, and conditionals present.				
Content, context, condition, codes, and culture are differentiated.				
My system actions are based on what really matters.				
Professional intentions are mapped through a variety of lenses.				
Effects on others are considered, almost always, before acting.				
Alignments with virtues are shared.				
Coaching is sought at every opportunity in the system.				
Learning, growth, and innovation are hallmarks of a glocal approach.				
Total				

Remember, if you need help, we offer monthly tele-development training in this system, as well as qualified coaches to support your resilience journey in upping the downside. Register or log in at *www.upping-the-downside.com* for more information.

Chapter 21

Integroism
by Mike Jay

We move now to the final process category of the upping the downside model, which I have named integroism. I like to use different kinds of words to explain things that don't exist yet as a way of cataloguing the work to be done. *Integroism* has a number of different meanings for me. First, as an "ism," in the Spiral Dynamics Integral framework you would expect it to be blue, certainly cool. My sense is that like chords on a piano in which music often repeats itself at different octaves, there are things in life that repeat themselves too. "Integro," a concept that is growing in use to convey the idea of integralizing things, is the reason why we've put this category here. It is an octave of blue.

What I wanted to do with this model was to create a system that people could grow with, that was scaleable, and at the same time could be modularized. I wanted people to be able to use parts of the program on a stand-alone basis. It's not necessary to use the entire survey. If, for instance, you're working as a coach with a person who feels very much in control of their life and you want to discover if they can take a different perspective, some elements in the survey may give you ideas for how to work with them. Some statements at the integroism level are built-in *paradoxes*. To some of you they will not make any sense at all. In the survey, there are no right or wrong answers. In fact, there are times when both sides of the equation may be necessary to form any reality at all.

Take, for instance, the first element in integroism:

"Survival of my professional life is paramount, but unnecessary."

How can you ask a person to accept a statement like that? You're asking them to hold at the same time two basic truths that are in some ways opposites. That's the idea at this level.

We have to understand that in considering the survival of our professional life, which is the domain of this survey, we have to take in all the considerations of what professional life looks like. Some of us will go through life as a professional. We'll never be anything but, and we'll die as a professional. Other people will move in and out of professional life. Some people will move through a professional life and then move on to whatever it is they're going to do next. So part of the idea in integroism is to look at the survival of one's professional life.

This is both an ego issue, and it is not. Let's look, for instance, at four perspectives: internal, external, financial, and developmental. If you were to say the survival of my professional life is paramount internally, what would that mean? What kinds of issues would that raise? Or, if you were to say the survival of my professional life is paramount externally, or financially, you could begin to identify certain aspects of what you were doing and evaluate them for their importance in the survival of your professional life. On the other hand, if you say *survival of my professional life is paramount but unnecessary*, how can you hold two opposite truths as right?

What happens at this level is that you both focus in and focus out. This means we're going to take ourselves seriously enough that we concern ourselves with the things that matter in our professional life, and therefore the survival of our professional life may be paramount to keep a professional life together. On the other hand, we also realize that all of that is virtually unnecessary in other perspectives at other levels. We're therefore going to be both serious about our professional life, but also take it and ourselves less seriously. It's a way of having something and then letting it go. You can't let it go, if you don't have it, can you?

This is something that most people can't hold—a paradox. The idea of intergroism is full of paradoxes. It's the way life really is, especially ego life.

I wanted for people to be able to use this system not just as a mechanical set of constructs with which you put your professional practice together like a puzzle or Lego machine to be successful. I wanted you to understand what it means when you become successful, and you also realize that personal success itself is unnecessary in the grander scheme of things.

How can you hold these paradoxes together in your mind as valid constructs?

Most people will not do so. They'll consider this a stupid question. That's fine. People functioning in paradoxes are a different kind of folk. In fact, this is probably the last level that people would function in before moving to a level of complexity or resilience that no longer has anything to do with a "professional life."

These paradoxes may act as sort of a *transduction system*, by which we convert energy to another form. In transduction, your body feels a touch and translates that into meaning. Perhaps it's the same way here. Integroism gives us an opportunity to work with people at more complex ends. Once they have all of the other elements working in pretty good shape, then they can work all the way at the other end and look at the transition to a *glocal* resilience. This is a level of resilience that will take us into what, later on, I call network resilience.

To recap: The domains in the resilience series model are personal, professional, business, and network—or in lieu of network, perhaps ecological or universal, although those terms are not as effective in describing the *mechanisms* taking place in the network mode. *Network* describes what occurs once you move past the personal, professional, and business, because everything is connected; everything is networked. If you look at network rules, at network ideas, you're going to *be* different than if you use concepts like ecological or universal, which do not paint a picture in our mind of how things may be occurring when hooked together using power-law distribution principles, which govern network systems.

Another way to understand this is with the starfish and the spider, as explained in a book of that name by Ori Brafman and Rod Beckstom. Spiders are the old world, while starfish are the new. When you cut off one of their points, they grow a new one. There's an inherent intelligence in the starfish that causes it to be able to replace or manufacture itself again. This is called autopoiesis:

> An autopoietic organization is an autonomous and self-maintaining unity, which contains component-producing processes. The components, through their interaction, generate recursively the same network of processes which produced them. An autopoietic system is operationally closed and structurally state determined with no apparent inputs and outputs. A cell, an organism, and perhaps a corporation are examples of autopoietic systems. (http://pespmc1.vub.ac.be/Asc/AUTOPOIESIS.html)

Integroism is a way to begin transitioning from what is essentially a professional paradigm to where you have a professional life that is pretty well structured autopoetically, to a basic life, to where you're looking back at the professional life you've had. You're seeing that survival in that life was paramount, but in the end it was unnecessary.

What, then, does this bring about in terms of understanding resilience?

I'm not able to say that I've done a lot of unfolding in this area, because the area itself is merely beginning to unfold in our culture. There are few algorithms out there at this level of complex being, having, doing and becoming. Little is known about this level of resilience. So what I've tried to do, if nothing else, is give you some ideas about how you may begin to transition along with those few people who are of and in the mind to take part in this transition. Very few people will try. Fewer can succeed.

I'm thinking maybe fewer than 1 percent of people will ever consider this level. Why, then, would I put something in the program that plays to only 1 percent of the population? Well, I think that resilience itself will only play to 3 or 4 percent of the population, in any case. For the people in that population who want to begin to look at higher levels of transition, it may be important to give them opportunities to begin to create a discussion. That's what I'm doing here.

Survival of my professional life is paramount, but unnecessary. Again, I would not expect to see people with high scores on this element in terms of being able to practice it now. Nor would I expect to see people putting very high scores on this in terms of importance. In fact, when you see the final survey online, you'll see an N/A (non-applicable) button for some of these elements. I would expect to see many people mark these. If someone does mark this as important, I'm going to quickly test what it is they're marking and what they think it means. To my view, very few people are going to be able to work within this paradox, yet having it around gives us information about people.

Using a scale of 1–10 for each, calculate Requirements – (Capability) x Importance = Priority Score

Score each element on a scale of 1–10; 1=low, 10=high	Req	Cap	Imp	PS
Survival of my professional life is paramount, but unnecessary.				

"Deepening connections to my professional roots allows wisdom."

This next one is not quite so paradoxical. It might mean, for instance, that you come from a family that has been in a particular profession for a long time. We're starting to see many people in the developed world who are descended from generations of professionals of one form or another and are carrying that forward. They have deep roots. Often times, however, they don't have a deep connection. This is where we can help them reconnect with professionals earlier in their heredity, as well as people in their profession who have taught them and helped them to grow. That's the other idea of professional roots.

When we begin to look at coaching, one of the things we find is that coaching has been around a long time, some say as far back as Aristotle. I would say that coaching has been around ever since there have been two people. Most likely one person was always more knowledgeable in something than the other. That person was in a position to be asked for help or guidance or to show what it was they found out so that others could do that as well. When we look at the continuum of coaching—ranging from telling other people what to do to not telling anybody what to do—there's a huge connection to a root that may go back as far as the beginning of mankind and womankind.

Again, would a person want to spend a lot of time with this particular statement? I don't know. The key would be where the person is in terms of wisdom. In other words, if a person continues to make the same mistakes over and over, if they're not reaching out, if they're not taking the time to understand what's creating the failures, if they're not trying to use other good information, they may not be growing wise. This might be an opportunity for them to settle into this transition by deepening the connection. Where this fits is in the vein of what Richard Whiteley calls the Corporate Shaman in a book by that name. It involves trying to understand the mystical parts of the connection with the past that has woven itself through us. Why do we want to be who we are? Why is it important that we live on or not? Those are questions that to me begin to create some wisdom.

This may be typical of archetypal work that seems so valuable over time, as archetypes are woven into the psyche of the individual and the collective. Over time, we run into these archetypal icebergs and find ourselves confronted by the sheer mass of understanding that archetypes hold within their purview.

One of the things most people don't realize is that the professions more than anything else require wisdom that is passed on, including the trial and error and mistakes and failures from people who have gone before them. We have a tendency not to pick up on that wisdom or what I call *density of experience* until we've had a similar experience ourselves. That to me is a very slow way to gather wisdom.

You take your whole life to gather wisdom in from what wisdom has already been gained, and you end up reinventing the wheel because you think you're something special. I've had this in my life. I'm going through a transition now and beginning to realize that most of the things that I think about have already been thought about in one way or another. It's just finding the signal in all the noise. When you read *The Lessons of History* by Will and Ariel Durant you realize that wisdom has been around a long time, and we continue to ignore it at our peril.

We're entering an age now in which knowledge will no longer be the key, because knowledge will be ubiquitous. What, then, will be the next defining age? More than likely it will be wisdom—the density of experience—along with a person's relationship to the connection among all things that will allow them to move to a whole new plane of resilience.

Resilience at intregroism is going to look different than resilience at the other levels. I feel it is important to open this up and give us a peek into what it will look like as we move forward, as people continue to ask the quintessential question of mankind in search of the Holy Grail: "What is life and what does life mean?"

This piece for me is very mystical. It's a mystical place to find connections to the roots of wisdom. I expect to find some scores for this element, even though most people will not fully understand what it means. That's okay. It doesn't matter whether a person at a low level of complexity scores this element or not. The questions surrounding it and the journey contained in it make the statement worth it. That's not to say that someone at another level of resilience wouldn't want to begin to use this element. They could. That's why when you see this model framed; it will frame out much differently in a matrix than most models.

Using a scale of 1–10 for each, calculate Requirements – (Capability) x Importance = Priority Score

Score each element on a scale of 1–10; 1=low, 10=high	Req	Cap	Imp	PS
Deepening connections to my professional roots allows wisdom.				

"Consciously engaging others when necessary is easy."

For the most part people move from unconscious incompetence to conscious incompetence to conscious competence to unconscious competence. That's the place we're talking about at this third elemental level of integroism. Someone is moving from unconscious engagement to conscious disengagement to conscious engagement to unconscious engagement.That's the cycle. It may not be a perfect cycle, but I wanted you to see that metaphor.

Consciously engaging others when necessary is easy. If you build meme density — if you create many connections to a single node — here's what that might look like. It might be that as you're working in your discipline, something comes up inside of you that you know you need. Well, as a professional, there's a tendency to be put on a pedestal. There's a tendency to be a know-it-all and expect to have all the right answers. There's a tendency to not reach out to other people and engage them in areas of the unknown. It's almost like pulling teeth to get professionals to pull themselves out of these entrenchments, these grooves that they have in their minds, and begin to reach out to other people. It's like having a beginner's mind, you might say. It's very difficult, except that a lot of people can do it when there's a crisis.

And when you're looking at the issues of resilience, you're looking at the issues of crisis. They are always going to be associated together. Otherwise, resilience wouldn't be necessary. Resilience is always in tension with some crisis, some difficulty, challenge, or opportunity. Therefore, when we go into crisis, we have a tendency to do things that are natural for us almost unconsciously.

My idea here is that if we understand what's happening to us in our own ego, our own sense of self, our own self-knowledge, we're going to be able to consciously engage others. This will be easy for us to do, because we realize the value in setting aside our *own* ego. This is paradoxical, especially at the level that I'm introducing it, which is at a *power* level. What you're doing is in part high power and in part low power. So you have a high power–low power paradox here. To reach out to others, you have to sublimate your own ego, your own system of expertise, and realize that someone who's not functioning at anywhere near this level of resilience might see you as weak by being vulnerable. This is a true paradox, one that's not easily answered.

That's why most people will not look at what's really happening in this statement. When they take this survey you'll basically get a *read* of noise. What is it that they're interpreting? Do they see the deeper meanings? Most people will not, and that's okay.

When people we're coaching interpret something, it doesn't matter whether they interpret it one way or another. The process of interpretation gives us the answers we need to begin to work with them where they are. If a person were to score that they're doing this element frequently and that it's important to them and they want to do more of it, we might test around the ideas that they have about what this is.

In the Coach2 model I've developed (*coach2system.com*), this is a perfect place to use inquiry and *ping* a little here and *probe* a little there. What you end up doing is revealing the meaning-making of the client. This allows us to understand how we might begin to approach this piece if the client says, "Look, I'd like to work on this." Again, is this for everybody? No. But it does reveal information to us if the client is making meaning around these ideas.

The purpose of a survey, in my view, is to get information and data. But you also want to get knowledge. How can information become knowledge? That happens in a survey when you go through it with the client and use dynamic inquiry. Do a little *pinging, probing,* and *perturbing.* Give them permission to reveal some things. Give them the opportunity through inquiry to give you some of their meaning-making. This is primarily why the upping-the-downside system is at its best when used with an intervener of some kind. Although the system can be used as a self-help, self-study course, this surveying process works best in a situation where you have a facilitator, counselor, mentor, coach, consultant, relationship expert, minister, teacher, priest, rabbi, parent—whatever you may be doing by way of engaging another person's help to become more resilient.

Of course, becoming more resilient as a professional leads us back to the idea of becoming resilient as a person, even though we don't talk specifically about personal resilience here. This particular statement— *Consciously engaging others when necessary is easy*—is a direct lead-in to the personal resilience model and gives us an opportunity to begin to understand what it means to become resilient as a person, not just as a professional (see CPR *for the* Soul).

There are many resilient professionals out there who are not as resilient as persons. They have dual lives. In their professional life they are honored, obeyed, and things work great. In their personal life it's different. Part of the process we're working with here is to allow us to begin to weave together an intersubjective system of personal, professional, business, and network resilience.

Using a scale of 1–10 for each, calculate Requirements – (Capability) x Importance = Priority Score

Score each element on a scale of 1–10; 1=low, 10=high	Req	Cap	Imp	PS
Consciously engaging others when necessary is easy.				

"Systems around me support continued success."

This is a systems statement and a huge statement. What in the world does it mean? This, too, is paradoxical. The reason is because it asks you about the systems around you.

When somebody asks, "Does that mean me?" that depends on your perspective. Who is the *me*? If you realize the me is really some abstract concept of a person and not a real *you*, then you realize that what we're talking about here is everything. If you are like normal people and you interpret this as the systems around me, you'll look out into your mechanical systems, your family systems, your relationship system, your employee system, your stakeholder system, and those kinds of things. That's not so bad either. In fact, it's also a big part of a systemized approach. What we're trying to do is to give you the opportunity to set yourself up for success.

What we're really talking about here is *design*. Does *the* design support continued success? We don't talk about design per se in the survey, but that's what we're doing. All of what we're doing is *by design*.

Of course there are two ways that you can work on things. One is to work on them consciously, step by step. You can make out a checklist and work on the items mechanically in a concrete fashion. In fact, we suggest that be done. The other way is to dump them into your subconscious, which is about 99.7 percent of who you are, and let your subconscious stew the elements or gestate them for a period of time. They'll reappear at the time and point in your life when things tap you on the shoulder and say, "What about me?" Again, there are different ways to approach designing resilience into a system.

At the risk of sounding mystical, I've found that in order to increase my own personal resilience, I have a number of things that I'm working on in my conscious environment. There are things to be, do, have, and become. I also have a complete other system that has dumped and is dumping things into my subconscious and saying, "Give me an answer down the road. When I need an answer to this, I'm trusting that an answer will come to me. What I'm going to do is supply you with the questions and supply you with the resources. At some point in time, you're going to give me the answer."

There are many descriptions of this process — nothing new, of course — including prayer, meditation, projection, mysticism, and perhaps just integroism. Now, have you caught the real idea here?

For an *expedient* person to be saying this, you have to see that this requires some understanding. I'm expedient, which means I work in the present. I don't work in the future per se. So why would I be dumping things into a hopper about the future? This is the reason I've found over the past few years that *integroism* is so effective.

Some people call this intuition. I see it as something else. It's more like the morphogenic fields that Rupert Sheldrake has written about, the *seventh sense* that he calls intuition. The sixth sense is the sense that comes from the hair standing on the back of your head, the resonant sense that you have perhaps as a *sensor*, rather than an *intuitor*. They come from two different systems, one being sensory and connected to senses, the other through pattern recognition and the emergence of thoughts from direct access to a universal field or cosmic intelligence, which is more likely. That's the intelligence that we all have access to, but some people more than others, depending on Jungian preferences, most likely.

And so, the sixth sense is when you sense things in your environment. You know things. You can connect to things.

The seventh sense is closer to this huge iceberg that you have with a little tiny tip sticking above the water that some people call intuition. This huge giant subconscious mind is literally connected to everything else, including everything else that came before.

Most people are not using their subconscious minds very much, because they don't know how to use them. To begin with, they don't understand enough about themselves to know what they can say "yes" and "no" to. And then, when they do get ideas from the subconscious, they don't know how to evaluate them. Research shows that 50 *percent of the time our intuition is wrong.* We have a lot of people going around saying, "You should intuit everything." If you do, you're going to be right about half of the time. So what can you do to understand how to better use the subconscious, intuition, or the collective unconscious?

You can begin to use this as a system. When I talk about *systems around me support continued success,* I have in mind a system that says, "I'm going to give you ideas. I'm going to give you resources. I'm going to give you time. I'm going to give you direction and filters. I know over time the answer is going to appear when it needs to appear." Not only is it going to appear, but it's also going to appear in the right syntax so I can apply the wisdom gained.

This has been very effective for me over the past few years. I need to do more writing on it to show mechanically how it actually works. Perhaps it works because I'm a dominant intuitive according to the (Jungian functions) Myers-Briggs Type Indicator. But I think it will work for everybody, not just dominant extroverted intuitives, because everyone has a subconscious, and the subconscious mind works in much the same way. Pop psychology and motivational gurus tell us about the subconscious, but not really how to use it. *You can get into big trouble* if you do not understand how to use your subconscious mind and you start acting willy-nilly on everything that it produces!

Most people don't understand that your subconscious mind doesn't necessarily work in the same framework as a goal-driven system. Is there a goal-driven set of properties to your subconscious mind? Absolutely. But it's not going to work efficiently if you hammer it with goals unless you're achievement motivated. That's only 30 percent of us. What about the other 70 percent? What are you going to do if you don't really respond to goal-driven direction? You're going to fight it. Now, you've just introduced into your subconscious a tremendous amount of resistance. How can you expect it to play when you introduce so much resistance?

We have to find out intuition for the other 70 percent of people instead of the goal-driven, reticular-activated, thalamic type of reticular system that many people are talking about in pop motivation.

> The extended reticular-thalamic activating system (ERTAS) may be the neural mechanism behind the observed brainwave changes. The reticular formation of the brain stimulating the thalamus and cortex (referred to as the ERTAS) governs cortical brainwave patterns. Acetylcholine, provided via cortico-thalamic projections, either inhibits or excites areas of the cortex by neutralizing or enhancing the effects of noradrenaline and serotonin coming to the cortex via "fountains" from the locus coeruleus and the raphe nuclei.
> (*https://www.monroeinstitute.com/content.php?content_id=6*)

For those of you who are achievers, it works very well, while for those of you who are not achievement-driven or wired, it's not going to work very well. Consequently, you'll get disillusioned. The important thing is to understand when you're getting good information and when you're not. That's the challenge. A lot of times we get bad information, though it's not bad until we put it into use. It becomes a system that *does not support our continued success*. It is actually going to get in the way of success.

I believe this is why pop psychology is so ubiquitous in our civilization, just as folk mythology has paved the way for this psychology to be used in a way that doesn't help most people. For one thing, it's done without enough vertical complexity to understand what I've been saying; and second, it's generalized from exemplars who are vertical enough to benefit from these actions without support. Realistically, people in general need lots of support—systems around them that support the use of these more complex adaptive systems. That's my opinion and therefore why I've criticized *The Secret* by Rhonda Byrne so much. Care, real care, has not been taken to encapsulate these secrets and how they can be used. Like giving people penicillin, if you use it when you don't have an infection, it doesn't do anything, except make you get sicker the next time you have a bacterial infection. That's how I view the work done in *The Secret*.

The other part that I would like to put into the statement, but I'm not going to would be:

Systems around me support continued success and happiness. The key thing there is to make sure you have two converging vectors to where success and happiness are two different things. *Success* means requirements in the requirements world. *Happiness* is values-based and is the return you get from your motivation and your means-and-ends activity. They can be separate. You can be extraordinarily happy, but at the same time not successful as defined in the environment that you call "success." Many people are like that today: successful but not happy, or happy but not successful.

Remember, success is always defined by the reality that you define it with. Therefore, you can't say, "Because someone is sitting on the street they're. . . . " It's like the Colombian street sweepers I mentioned earlier who were out real early in the mornings when I'd get up and run. They were really happy. They were whistling. They had their little carts and brooms. You'd think that somebody had just given them the winning lottery ticket.

The street sweepers were successful because they were doing a good job with cleaning the streets, and they were happy. Success is always defined by the scoreboard you choose to function against or with or towards or in concert with. The idea is that once you define success, once you identify what kind of scoreboard that success has, then the systems around you have to be able to support that, or most likely you're going to give up happiness. That's the key thing in resilience.

Many people are talking about resilience today as if it were only success. In my view, you do not have resilience until you have success and happiness. Therefore, in the environment you choose, in the ecology of the requirements that you choose, you are termed successful by the scoreboard that you and those people create. The second piece is that you're also happy and have a lot of free energy to apply, because your values-based happiness is completely aligned with what your means-and-ends activity is. I'm making it sound easy, but this is no easy task. In fact, it's probably the grail that everybody keeps talking about. And we can actually create this mechanically. We do not need to go find it. It's within us already.

It's like what M. Scott Peck said in *The Road Less Traveled* about the work he was doing. The Hebrew Bible, as translated, says, "The Kingdom of God is within you." Peck writes that they made a mistake; the Hebrew word actually means "among" not "within." Therefore, the statement should read, "The Kingdom of God is among you." The systems around you, the collaboration around you, are what are going to create your success. It's not always going to be *within* you. That's the key thing to understand at this particular level.

Using a scale of 1–10 for each, calculate Requirements – (Capability) x Importance = Priority Score

Score each element on a scale of 1–10; 1=low, 10=high	Req	Cap	Imp	PS
Systems around me support continued success.				

"Integrated strategies in all directions yield accomplishment."

This element is tricky, because it involves several complex ideas. The first thing is *integrated strategies*, which means you would already have to be moving in the direction of success and happiness. You would have to understand the *prior* element. This statement means that these systems, these strategies have been put together to *cause* things to take place. The key is that they operate in all directions, in an *array-like* fashion, like the sun's rays shooting out from all directions.

To *yield accomplishment* means that accomplishment can only come from emergence. For instance, if we were to take eggs, milk, and flour and the cake pan and grease it and put in some salt and yeast and all kinds of other good things that our recipe called for, what would emerge from that mix would be a cake. Those of you who are not freehand bakers could go to the store and get a cake mix and follow the directions. I guarantee you, every time you did what that recipe on the box called for, a cake would come out. That's what I'm talking about. Because you have integrated strategies in all directions, the only thing that can possibly come out is accomplishment.

Now you're going to ask, "What is accomplishment?" Well, that's a tricky one. The first thing people think of in terms of accomplishment is the achievement of goals. What's the difference, for instance, between an entrepreneur and accomplished entrepreneur? The person who is accomplished has put together the puzzle, so to speak. They have the ability to continue to make the puzzle work for them. That's what I mean by accomplishment. It's not just achieving goals or being at the top of your field. It means that the things around you daily give you success and happiness. That to me is accomplishment in this particular frame.

In the previous element we were looking at a basically tactical system. The ideas in this one are strategic. What works best with a tactical system are appropriate strategies, and of course, we're saying that the strategies themselves are integrated. In order for someone to discuss this element with me, I'd want them to show me how the different areas of their professional life are integrated. If, for instance, someone says to me, "I'm doing a really great job as a professional, but because I'm never home, I never see my kids. I'm not able to help raise them. They don't know me." To me that's not accomplished, because it's not integrated. Our lives have to be integrated so that we're not completely focused on one, overriding system and creating entropy in another system such that it's not doing well at all, or worse, is in a constant state of chaos, never finding any order.

Human life as being, doing, having, and becoming means we work completely from an equilibrium. *We never work from balance.* This is not about balance. This is about integration. For instance, if you understand your own motivational sensitivity you know that in order for you to get values-based happiness, you yourself will be out of balance. You're not balanced across all of your motivational sensitivities. Some things are going to make you bored and frustrated, while other things are going to create virtue and free energy in your life. You're always going to be out of balance.

What differentiates the systems I've developed and the practices I suggest is that *you do not try to attain balance by working in areas of your life where you have limitations.* It must be some puritan ethic in some people that causes them to want to be balanced, or to develop weaknesses, as if proclaimed virtuous by some higher source. To me, with what we know today, balance is an oxymoron—at best!

The point here is that although you may be out of balance, the integration of the rest of your system does not have to be. My true pet peeve with the integral work as we see it today is the focus on individual balance. To me, there should be a focus on individual integration, not individual balance, because balance means that we would pretend to be motivated in areas that we are not and try balancing those areas. In my view, that's not the key because then you're working on your weaknesses, not on your strengths.

If you're integrated, however, you can't just rely on a strength area to push through your entire life without there being consequences. Attached to every strength is a weakness. Therefore, this integrated strategy in all directions is something you want to look at continually and upgrade, evolve, innovate around, design around to where you can say, "Look, getting up every day is an accomplishment. Just by being here things are happening in the way that they need to happen for me and for my being, doing, having, and becoming in this life." That requires a special kind of resilience that I feel you can only do through integration.

Using a scale of 1–10 for each, calculate Requirements – (Capability) x Importance = Priority Score

Score each element on a scale of 1–10; 1=low, 10=high	Req	Cap	Imp	PS
Integrated strategies in all directions yield accomplishment.				

"Nurture relationships to gain deeper wisdom and insight."

The point I made just above was that you're going to be out of balance. Therefore, if you're not a relationship person, and you're not motivated to things like interdependence or family or social contact, then you have a tendency to keep relationship activity to a minimum.

It that is the case, however, you will suffer. Now, what must you do? You must at least understand that nurturing relationships creates deeper wisdom. What is deeper wisdom? It's the alignment between your own success definitions and happiness. The other part of deeper wisdom is staying generative, in other words, emerging accomplishment, not destruction.

There is an insight that happens to a person here. I'm not so much interested in changing the way I form relationships. But if I don't understand that nurturing relationships is critical and that I continually have to have insights around that to produce a deeper wisdom, I'm not going to be able to be resilient in these areas, because my external reference and reaching out are too low to sustain ongoing wisdom in a complex world.

Recently, the Center for Creative Leadership said that the lack of productive relationships has become a key in leadership failure, replacing the lack of impulse control in earlier years.

In the upping-the-downside system, the actual nurturing does not have to be done by you; it can be done through systems. This is something that I myself am working on innovating around more and more every day. I realize that relationship activity for me is very tiring when it moves out of the realm of abstract ideas, information, knowledge, and the *thing* environment. I do a lot of nurturing of my ideas through the use of my subconscious mind and the mechanical systems I've set up. It doesn't have to do so much with people. When I get into the *people* environment, it's difficult for me to even think about nurturing—it's not on my radar. And as I get older, I find I feel motivated to do it less and less, even though I *know* it has to be done.

If I listened to the pop-culture gurus, they would have me in sensitivity training and relationship-building activities, and all of it would create huge resistance, steal all my free energy, and would not—like teaching a pig to sing—work. It would annoy me, as well, as do pig-singing lessons.

For those of you who are oriented to people, you have to understand that one can nurture relationships with ideas, with things. It's not just about people. I often hear people say, "There's nothing in life but love." Actually, there is. Love is a strategy that you certainly want to integrate, but there can be love of ideas as well as there is love of your fellow man and compassion. There can be compassion for ideas. These are things that you want to understand. This is why I did not key this element to say nurturing relationships *with people*. I wanted you to understand that there are relationships with everything. Those of you on the *thing* side have to understand that nurturing relationships with people is critical. Those of you on the people side have to understand that nurturing relationships with innovation, ideas, learning, and growth is critical.

Understanding these constructs and *knowing that* changes what you say "yes" to and "no" to. At this level, the idea of relationships becomes key to understanding the next ability, to create insights. That's what *nurturing relationships to gain deeper wisdom and insight* means.

Again, I wouldn't expect people to give these statements the same meanings that I do when they're first taking the survey. I'm fine with that. I wouldn't expect them to even be able to hear what's in these statements for the most part. Nor am I saying that I'm any good at this. I'm just saying that these are the things that, over a period of time, I've noticed in people who seem to be resilient.

In working with more than fifteen hundred clients one-on-one and thousands of people around the world people, and with way more than ten thousand hours of coaching logged before I stopped counting, these are the ideas that have surfaced for me that are important for someone to consider if they're talking about resilience at this level. They will create a map for you to begin to understand the professional resilience territory. In fact, a next step would be to create a map of your relationships, so that relationship density could be codified, and next steps designed!

Using a scale of 1–10 for each, calculate Requirements – (Capability) x Importance = Priority Score

Score each element on a scale of 1–10; 1=low, 10=high	Req	Cap	Imp	PS
Nurture relationships to gain deeper wisdom and insight.				

"Differentiating my professional life is a deliberate practice."

This one is a bit paradoxical, but actually it's quite simple. Do I see myself as just a lawyer, a doctor, a plumber, a coach, a facilitator, an executive? Do I see myself only as that, or do I realize that within my professional life, I am many things to many people, and I have many roles? When I say deliberate practice, I'm talking about your daytimer or whatever you use for a planning system. The first thing I do when I go to work with a professional is have them show me their schedule.

Most of the time it's not kept by them, but by an administrative assistant or someone who is close to them. I've even started to see some people using their stakeholders to keep it for them and help them create their day.

The idea here is, do you understand the different roles you have in your professional life? Have you taken the time to differentiate them? Do you realize that you are a mentor to the people you work with and perhaps in some cases the people that you serve? Do you realize that you may even be coaching people? Do you realize that a lot of the time you could be facilitating one, two, three, four, or more groups of people or families? Do you realize that you're sometimes asked to provide advice?

In fact, as a professional you're expected to give advice. Do you realize that's not your only role? My point is, can you see the many different roles you have in your life and have you taken the time to actually make those *deliberately* real? Or, do you just glide through the schedule unconsciously? Do you realize that part of each day has to be developmental for your employees or your stakeholders? Do you take time out to say, "Look, part of my day has to be learning, growth, and innovation for *me*; it has to be developmental for me."

Can a person begin to understand there are many different role activities that they perform? Can they understand themselves as differentiating the parts of their day, rather than silently switching hats, so to speak? Can they do this in a way that allows them to become more efficient, effective, and sustainable in each of these roles over time?

I know a lot of professionals who are great professionals. But they are terrible mentors, coaches, facilitators, leaders, and parents. Do they take the time to begin to look at these different roles for themselves? This is what that I'm asking for in this particular area.

Using a scale of 1–10 for each, calculate Requirements – (Capability) x Importance = Priority Score

Score each element on a scale of 1–10; 1=low, 10=high	Req	Cap	Imp	PS
Differentiating professional life is a deliberate practice.				

"Enlightenment is natural for a sovereign global citizen."

This last element is tricky, because when we look at the classic case of enlightenment, I would suspect that most people have not studied Eastern religion in depth. Yet, there will be a greater percentage of people who take this survey who have an *enlightened view* of professional work. People wanting to work on resilience who read this book will be the kinds of people who are looking into some of these areas and most likely will be curious or have a specific need in this area. What I'm saying here is that as we become a global professional citizen, and when we look at the universal nature of becoming a professional citizen, whether we're in the United States, Europe, Eastern Europe, Russia, Asia, Australia, Canada, Hawaii, or wherever, do we understand that there is an obligation that exists to all other professionals, to all other people on the planet?

I found this out when I began traveling worldwide a few years ago. I realized that there seems to be a bit of sovereignty that one gains when they become a professional, when they are seen as an expert. It's more specific to those people who practice their expertise on the road, away from where they live. Other countries confer the status of professional on you, if you have credentials and expertise at all, to a certain extent, because you are from another place. Therefore, when you begin to understand that there is this whole nature and nurture of global citizenry, what in the world does that mean?

I think that's where the enlightenment comes in. Rather than just focusing on spiritual enlightenment, which many people do, my idea is the enlightened street sweeper. Can street sweepers be enlightened? Of course they can. They can be in touch with this idea of sovereignty, this idea that they are no longer who they thought they were, but they are part of something much bigger than they ever thought they could be a part of. What I'm talking about is experiencing a oneness with all that is.

I'm also trying to get people to look at that statement and ask some questions of themselves. What does *sovereign* mean? When you're a sovereign global citizen, you don't belong to the United States. You don't belong to Europe. You're not an Arab per se or an Asian. You're a person who is a global citizen. What are the aspects of creating a global citizenry?

While we can't go into them in depth here, my sense is that you would look at your own life and begin to understand your life in terms of the planet and its life.

For instance, if you're doing things in your professional practice that fly in the face of what's good for everyone, then perhaps you want to give some consideration to that. When people look at this level of resilience and begin to think of themselves as a planetary professional, not just a professional in their town, city, state, country, or ethnic or cultural group, that's when you begin to open up a Pandora's box. You realize that there is no such thing as right action, because in every right action I can find a wrong action, which can emerge, even though it may be dislocated and delayed by complexity.

Fifty to seventy-five years ago in Australia, they found an amazing Artesian basin. They decided to irrigate farms and create agriculture and well-being. They ended up sucking the artesian resources dry, and the area became a desert. Even though they created a lot of good, and it was the right action to use the water in such a wonderful way to help people have better lives, they ended up creating a bigger problem down the road.

I think there is no way out of that; we are going to make mistakes— even when we are *most* certain what we are doing is right. Is there, however, a way to minimize these effects? I think there might be, as one begins to imagine their way through orders of consequences. This is what I'm asking you to do as a sovereign global citizen: to think through an order of consequences as a benefit chain.

For instance, if we do something, if we start a business, then what's likely to occur?

If that occurs, then what is going to happen when that happens?

If that occurs, then what's going to happen?

If that occurs, then what's going to happen?

It's just like me. I was sitting there on a plane, flying back from Dallas eating those honey-roasted peanuts that I really enjoy. I was thinking to myself, every time I eat a single-portion pack of these peanuts, I'm actually polluting and creating high energy use, because to package something in an individual container uses more energy than if they brought the whole can down the aisle and let everybody take a handful. Then you think, "Wait a minute. Most people wouldn't want my hands in their food." Now we're safe from one another, but now we have this problem to where we're utilizing more energy, and we're throwing all that packaging away.

How do we get around it? I guarantee you that plastic-lined foil probably has the half-life of plutonium. I don't think it will ever degrade. These are the things we need to begin to understand and consider over time.

On one hand, we have created this wonderful, safe, healthy, timely, convenient, and very much appreciated package of honey-roasted peanuts. On the other hand, we're actually contributing to what's taking place in terms of environmental impacts. Part of the reason I introduce this particular concept at the tail end is that this opens up a whole new area of thinking. When we think about what kinds of things can we do to get safe peanuts for all of us and not cause so much waste, the first thing somebody might say is, "We could recycle the packaging. It could be made out of recyclable material." That would be a question we could ask.

Again, to innovate at this level is really enlightenment to me.

The key thing is to know what insights we need to have. The second thing is to understand what the innovation really means. That's part of the process that works at this level of resilience. To be more resilient as a planet, we're going to have to consider the impact of our actions once they are beyond our sight or out of our awareness. So much of what we're doing today, as soon as it's beyond our awareness is gone. It's like the Bucky Fuller quote I mentioned earlier: "When you flush a toilet it goes somewhere." Where is the somewhere? That's part of thinking through and understanding the things we do every day.

I must admit, one of the things developmental research has taught us is that people who function at these broader levels are not as happy as people who have the ability to compartmentalize their life and not see their actions in the whole. I don't think the population is quite ready yet for these more complex levels of awareness and resilience. The amount of unrest and the apathy and paradoxical lack of ambition that you have because you realize if you take an action it's always going to be wrong will get you into some kind of trouble cognitively. This may seem to some a negative. But essentially, it's important to be realistic and to note that if you feel that it's negative, then having a discussion about it with a coach or consultant could help you discover that your focus may be on moving up, instead of building resilience where you are.

Using a scale of 1–10 for each, calculate Requirements – (Capability) x Importance = Priority Score

Score each element on a scale of 1–10; 1=low, 10=high	Req	Cap	Imp	PS
Enlightenment is natural for a sovereign global citizen.				

Now you can tally all your integroism scores:

Integroism				
Survival of my professional life is paramount, but unnecessary.				
Deepening connections to my professional roots allows wisdom.				
Consciously engaging others when necessary is easy.				
Systems around me support continued success.				
Integrated strategies in all directions yield accomplishment.				
Nurture relationships to gain deeper wisdom and insight.				
Differentiating professional life is a deliberate practice.				
Enlightenment is natural for a sovereign global citizen.				
Total				

Remember, if you need help, we offer monthly tele-development training in this system, as well as qualified coaches to support your resilience journey in upping the downside. Register or log in at *www.upping-the-downside.com* for more information.

Epilogue
by Mike Jay

There is an old Baha'i saying: "Everything works out in the end. . . . If things haven't worked out, you are not to the end." That pretty much fits this situation. In the end is the beginning, one of my favorite axioms. My hope is that you can find some ideas here that will help you in this PR age.

In 2002, the BBC made a documentary called *Century of the Self*. It's worth purchasing and watching. Or, as long as it stays on *youtube.com*, the links for this documentary are at *mikejay.com/self*. Please enjoy it and learn from the tenets, which are that people today have figured out how to get right past our conscious filters and right into our pocketbooks.

What does resilience have to do with pocketbooks?

As long as you have resources, access to resources, or friends with resources, you'll never for a moment doubt the future. It seems funny to say this, and sad, that so many people don't have resilience because their resources are so limited. What I did in this model was to give you the best of my learnings from working with my own faults and frailties, as well as thousands of clients around the world. In the end is the beginning.

Start your emergency fund now. As soon as you do, build a go-to-hell fund right on top of it, and then enjoy your life contributing to others. Now, what I'm saying is not easy, I know that. Mine is still in progress. But the closer I get to the one thing I recommend you do right now—to having these kinds of funds in place, the bad debt gone—the better I feel about myself and the future.

Let's face it, neither I nor anyone else can predict the future. Yet I can tell you what you want to be, have, do, or become when you get there. If you follow this model of professional resilience, and perhaps learn to raise your personal resilience as well, your life will not, like our friend Shakespeare said, "be taken at the flood." The rising tide—your rising tide—will float all the boats around you, and that is what it means to be generative.

I hope you enjoy the essays brought to you by my Resilience Club and use them to your benefit. Feel free to contact any one of the authors or me if you want or need help with anything, and I hope to meet you on the trail as I reach my own resilient peak in 2010.

Until then, as we say out here on the Oregon Trail:

> *May the trail rise up to meet you,*
> *May the wind be always at your back,*
> *May the sun shine warm upon your face,*
> *The snow fall soft on the hills around you,*
> *Until we meet again.*

The Author

Mike Jay has been a professional business coach, consultant, and entrepreneur for more than forty years. An award-winning U.S. Marine and collegiate athlete, he initially parlayed his leadership experience into agribusiness innovation and, subsequently, management success in medicine, hospitality, and business services. In 1999, he founded a premiere business and executive coach training system. Through more than 10,000 hours of coaching sessions, Mike has served business leaders in more than twenty-seven countries in such companies as Aditya Birla Group, Avery Dennison, Banswara Fabrics, Bharat Petroleum, Blow Plast, Cadence Design Systems, Carat, Central Bank of Indonesia, Coca-Cola, DLine, Duraline, EDS, Eureka Forbes, Exxon, Ford, General Dynamics, Glenmark Pharmaceuticals, Godfrey Philips, Godrej, Grey India, GroupM, GSK Consumer Healthcare, Hewlett Packard, Hindalco, Hi Tech Carbon, ICICI Prudential, Ispat Group, JK Tyres, Lupin, Marico Industries, Mediaedge, Novartis, Pantaloon, Pepsi, Rediffusion DY&R, Reserve Bank of India, Telekom Malaysia, Vodaphone, UGS.

References

Anderson, Chris. *The Long Tail: Why the Future of Business is Selling Less of More.* New York: Hyperion, 2006.

Argyris, Chris, and Donald A. Shön. *Theory in Practice: Increasing Professional Effectiveness.* San Francisco: Jossey-Bass, 1974.

Beck, Don Edward, and Christopher C. Cowen. *Spiral Dynamics.* Oxford: Blackwell Publishing, 1996.

Brafman, Ori, and Rod Beckstrom. *The Starfish and the Spider: The Unstoppable Power of Leaderless Organizations.* New York: Portfolio Hardcover, 2006.

Buber, Martin. *I And Thou.* Glencoe, IL: The Free Press, 1971.

Buckingham, Marcus. *Go Put Your Strengths to Work: 6 Powerful Steps to Achieve Outstanding Performance.* Glencoe, IL: The Free Press, 2007

Byrne, Rhonda. *The Secret.* New York: Atria Books, 2006.

Covey, Stephen R. *The 7 Habits of Highly Effective People.* Glencoe, IL: The Free Press, 1989.

Covey, Stephen R. *Principle-Centered Leadership.* New York: Fireside, 1999.

Cowan, Christopher C., and Natasha Todorovic, eds. *The Never Ending Quest: Dr. Clare W. Graves Explores Human Nature.* Santa Barbara, CA: ECLET, 2005.

Durant, Will, Ariel Durant, and Grover Gardner. *The Lessons of History: The Most Important Insights from the Story of Civilization.* Riverside, NJ: Simon & Schuster, 1968.

Gladwell, Malcolm. *Blink: The Power of Thinking Without Thinking.* New York: Little, Brown and Company, 2005.

Hill, Napoleon. *Think and Grow Rich.* San Diego, CA: Aventine Press, 2004.

Jay, Mike R. COACH2 *The Bottom Line*. Victoria, BC, Canada: Trafford Publishing, 1999.

Jay, Mike R., ed. *The 101 Things to Do to Avoid a Recession*. Digital ebook, 2000.

Jay, Mike R. CPR *for the Soul: Creating Personal Resilience By Design*. Mumbai: Leadership University Press, 2006.

Jay, Mike R. *Dynamic Inquiry*. http://www.dynamicinquiry.com, 2005.

Jay, Mike R. *Right Action—Right Results* (originally titled *Now What*). Digital ebook, 2000.

Kaplan, Robert, and David Norton. *The Balanced Scorecard: Translating Strategy into Action*. (Cambridge, MA: Harvard Business School Press, 1996).

Kiyosaki, Robert T., with Sharon L. Lechter. *Cash-Flow Quadrant: Rich Dad's Guide to Financial Freedom*. New York: Warner Books, 2000.

Kiyosaki, Robert T., *Rich Dad, Poor Dad*, Lebanon, IN: Warner Books, 2000.

Mack, Ben. *Think Two Products Ahead: Secrets the Big Advertising Agencies Don't Want You to Know and How to Use Them for Bigger Profits*. Indianapolis, IN: Wiley, 2007.

Myers, David G. *Intuition: Its Powers and Perils*. New Haven, CT: Yale University Press, 2002.

Peck, M. Scott. *The Road Less Traveled, 25th Anniversary Edition: A New Psychology of Love, Tradional Values and Spiritual Growth*. New York: Touchstone, 2003.

Pilzer, Paul Zane. *Unlimited Wealth: The Theory and Practice of Economic Alchemy*. New York: Crown Publishing, 1991.

Rath, Tom. *StrengthsFinder 2.0: A New and Upgraded Edition of the Online Test from Gallup's Now, Discover Your Strengths*. New York: Gallup Press, 2007.

Reivich, Karen, and Andrew Shatte. *The Resilience Factor: 7 Essential Skills for Overcoming Life's Inevitable Obstacles*. New York: Broadway Books/Random House, 2002.

Ridley, Matt. *Nature Via Nurture: Genes, Experience, and What Makes Us Human.* New York: HarperCollins Publishers, 2003.

Stanley, Thomas J., and William D. Danko, *The Millionaire Next Door: The Surprising Secrets of America's Wealthy.* New York: Pocket Books/Simon & Schuster, 1996.

MIKE JAY has been an active Business and Executive Coach since 1988. As a business leader for the past 25 years, he has experienced first-hand what it means to make a payroll and deal with difficult management issues in complex environments.

An award-winning U.S. Marine and Texas Aggie quarterback, Mike's experience in leadership has led to success with clients around the world.

After coaching managers in business and corporate environments or over 15 years, Mike founded B\Coach Systems, LLC, a virtual coaching network in 1999; and Leadership University, a global leadership develop-ment forum in 2003.

He has been featured internation-ally for his innovations with clients and has received the Highest Achievement Award from the Dale Carnegie Speaking Program. Mike currently speaks and writes on business, leader-ship and coaching systems that generate personal and organizational effec-tiveness.

Email: coach@leadwise.com
For info: www.mikejay.com
Telephone: 877.901.COACH

Upping the Downside is a personal and professional resilience sys-tem that creates enhanced resilience through design. If you're interested in knowing more about the system, or havng Mike or the co-authors speak about the system, visit: www.uppingthedownside.com or email coach@ leadwise.com.